Best
Wishes
09
from
the

Love, from Dicky
& Olga

FRONT PAGE CHALLENGE

history of a television legend

Alex Barris

MACMILLAN CANADA
TORONTO

Canadian Cataloguing in Publication Data

Barris, Alex, 1922–
  Front page challenge

Includes index.
ISBN 0-7715-7662-5

1. Front page challenge (Television program). I. Title.
PN1992.77F76B37 1999   791.45'72   C99-930953-6

Cover & interior design: Kyle Gell art and design
Front cover photograph: National Archives of Canada
Front cover & interior television graphic: Images® copyright 1999
  PhotoDisc Inc.

1 2 3 4 5   FP   03 02 01 00 99

This book is available at special discounts for bulk purchases by your group or organization for sales promotions, premiums, fundraising and seminars. For details, contact: CDG Books Canada, Special Sales Department, 99 Yorkville Avenue, Suite 400, Toronto, ON M5R 3K5. Tel: 416-963-8830.

We acknowledge the financial support of the Government of Canada through the Book Publishing Industry Development Program for our publishing activities.

Macmillan Canada
CDG Books Canada
Toronto, Ontario, Canada

Printed in Canada

acknowledgements

Most of the photographs in this book were taken for the Canadian Broadcasting Corporation's television series, "Front Page Challenge," by various photographers, among them Page Toles, Fred Phipps, Norm Chamberlain, Harold White, Roy Martin, Herb Nott, Albert Crookshank, Eric Trussler, Paul Smith and Robert C. Ragsdale. Robert Ragsdale also took the cover photograph.

The author is indebted to all the above, as well as to Peter Robertson and Dan Somers at the National Archives of Canada for their considerable help in tracking the photos down.

A word of thanks, also, to Jill Lambert, who worked so diligently at editing the text of this book, and the others at Macmillan Canada who helped put it together.

Finally, a word of thanks to my wife, Kay, whose patience and support defy description.

contents

My father, while not a man of great wealth, had a fever on him that required he purchase every new gadget produced. This collection grew over the years to include a "liquifier," now called a blender, in which he tried to liquefy an egg, shell included. He owned a vast number of cameras and trick lenses, likely many more than he needed even though he was a photographer. He might have been a little late in replacing the icebox with a fridge but he had to have a television set even though there was nothing on. Not like now when we say there is nothing on…in 1951 there was NOTHING on. Two years of test pattern and the odd snowy image from Seattle and Bellingham soon were forgotten when CBC went on the air with film of the coronation of Queen Elizabeth II, which had to be flown in from London. However, the most fun of all was the advent of "Front Page Challenge" in 1957. I was eleven and I loved it. We all did. No one I knew would miss it. FPC kept you up to date and you got to see the son of Winston Churchill look as if he might fall out of his chair. What better education could you possible imagine?

To be honest the main reason my eleven-year-old self was so inclined to watch "Front Page Challenge" was that my father's very best friend in the world was on it. You can imagine what cachet that provided me at school in Vancouver. I knew someone who was on the television every Monday night, on a show that came from Toronto.

Pierre Berton had red hair then, but of my friends, only I knew that, due to my CONNECTIONS. He was tall too, I was quick to point out. Everyone thought he must be a short guy because he sat behind that little desk. I was a bragging fool but he was my greatest claim to fame. Still is.

Thirty years later, well after my father had died and I had managed to secure a good job as an interviewer with CBC-Radio, I was invited to appear as a guest panelist with FPC. The show travelled frequently and Vancouver was a regular port of call. I accepted and then the panic began.

Apart from the fear of not being completely up to date on all the front-page stories, which was a given, I had nothing to wear. However superficial that may seem I was going to sit beside the best-dressed woman on Canadian TV. Betty Kennedy, a charming and clever woman, was always perfectly turned out and frankly, I was not always perfectly turned out. That's radio for you. My mother helped me find a once very expensive Italian skirt and an equally expensive Italian shirt at a shop that features stuff from the last decade. Apart from looking as if I was from the last decade, I did not look half-bad.

Before the show the panelists assembled in a small green room to discuss the possible guests and stories. I had met Betty, Fred and Foth on several occasions and I knew Pierre as if he were a relative. I was somewhat intimidated by their journalistic shop talk…in other words I was scared to death of making a fool of myself on television and embarrassing Pierre. Breathing became a problem.

One of the most intriguing bits about "Front Page Challenge" was that the guests were unseen by the panelists, as was the case with the first guest. The questioning began with Alan, to which he received a series of answers, yes and no. Then Betty advanced the story but still did not get it.... Then it was Pierre's turn to question the hidden woman. He was on the wrong track and I knew it. I had already recognized her voice and hoped against hope that the other three wouldn't get it. But they couldn't and it was my turn.

Sports and competitiveness were never my strong points but there was, at that moment, a rush of power that came over me when I knew I had it. In fact I had not only the story but I knew the woman's name and the name of her book. My heart was trying to escape my chest as I calmly revealed her story. Was she an author?

Had she been an undercover agent during WWII? Had she managed to escape the wrath of the Nazis? Yes, yes, yes.

They even invited me back a few more times, but it was never quite the same. I guess that is what they all say.

—Vicki Gabereau

chapter 1

SUMMER
OF '57

To any reader under the age of fifty, it would be difficult, if not utterly impossible, to comprehend how
vastly different television was in the 1950s from what it is today, as we
approach the end of this—dare I say it?—millennium.

The 1950s, after all, happened before they were born, and thus would
be banished by the young to the dreary category of ancient history. It is
an all-too-human failing when we are young: we believe, somehow, that
history began only when we were born.

That distant era was, of course, long before today's age of the information highway, high-technology TV, of superstations or multichannel
availability, giant backyard disks, remote-controlled sound muters, instant channel switchers, the inescapable Internet and the now-ubiquitous
VCR, on which the young can watch old flicks. Even what constitutes "old"
is debatable. To the young, a classic is a hit of perhaps seven years ago.

With regard to television, we are talking here in terms of the dramatic
difference between, say, the horse-drawn wagons that bumped warily across
the prairies and the supersonic jet planes that whiz smoothly across the
oceans. Perhaps the only real perceivable similarity between television in
that Stone Age of the medium and television of today is the cornucopia of

commercials that permeates both ancient and contemporary television history. Today's media moguls even have the temerity to call some of their longer spiels infomercials.

In the late 1940s and early 1950s, many of those people in Toronto or Windsor or Vancouver who could afford them bought television sets, perhaps because of their novelty, but mostly to watch shows they could pick up from nearby American border cities. A year before Canadian television came into existence, there were some 50,000 regular Canadian viewers of WBEN in Buffalo, and the same degree of curiosity was evident in other border cities.

Television began in Canada in September 1952, first in Montreal, on September 6, and two days later, in Toronto.

Pioneer CBC viewers in the Toronto area may recall a minor accident that launched CBLT, the Canadian Broadcasting Corporation's Toronto outlet, on September 8. That happened also to be the day that a noted criminal, Edwin Alonzo Boyd, and two of his gang, escaped from the city's grubby Don Jail. The TV station, determined to be *au courant* with a breaking story, began its broadcast history by flashing a photo of Boyd onto our screens—upside down!

In hailing the new broadcast medium, the *Montreal Gazette* featured an editorial headlined "Revolutions in Everyday Life," and while one can applaud that awareness of the winds of change, it seems unlikely that even the editors of that august journal had the remotest idea how revolutionary this new living room gadget would eventually become.

In 1948, there were perhaps 10,000 television sets in Canada, all of them, of course, tuned to U.S. stations. By 1951—a year before the birth of Canadian TV—WBEN Buffalo was even carrying at least one American program sponsored by a Canadian company. By the fall of 1953, when Canadian TV was a year old, there were 300,000 television sets in use across our land.

In those early days, of course, it was monochrome, black-and-white television. The "revolution in everyday life" was just starting to crawl, never mind walk. But walk it would, and stride boldly, too, right into our everyday living. Today there is barely a room in any Canadian household whose furnishings do not include a television set. We may well be the only country in the so-called civilized world that has more TV sets than people.

There were, naturally, clergy, teachers, sociologists and other sages who viewed the new medium with alarm. Television, a good many of them predicted, would turn us into a slack-jawed society of non-talkers, mesmerized into obedient silence by the idiot box. Instead, the opposite turned out to be the case: people got into the habit of talking, conversing, during television programs, in the comfort and privacy of their own homes. Later, many of them transported this annoying habit with them to their local movie theatres.

It was, inevitably, a shaky start for the CBC. A year or so later, however, there were Canadian television stations not only in Montreal and Toronto but in Hamilton, Windsor, Sudbury, Kitchener and London, all in Ontario, and also in Halifax and Sydney, Saint John, Regina, Edmonton, Calgary and Vancouver, among other Canadian cities.

In what many older Canadians like to think of as the Golden Age of Television—from the fall of 1952 to the late 1960s—the customary practice at the Canadian Broadcasting Corporation (at the time the only Canadian television network in existence) was to broadcast its most popular programs for thirty-nine consecutive weeks (or three-quarters of the year) and then give such programs, as well as performers and CBC planners, a thirteen-week breather. As had long been the practice on American television networks, where television had begun to blossom within a year after the end of the Second World War, the CBC wisely used this thirteen-week summer hiatus to try out new programs. It was a mildly risky, but reasonably logical, approach.

The summer TV-viewing rate, it was generally agreed, was considerably lower than in the rest of the year, partly because so many people were away on holiday, loafing at secluded lakeside cottages that had no television sets, or else were out of the country for several weeks at some time between late June and early September. Thus, the summer season was a good and safe time to try out new programs. How much harm, it was argued, could a new, hitherto-untried program do in just thirteen weeks?

Even the dreaded television critics on newspapers didn't, as a rule, pay too much attention to these summer-replacement shows, probably for the same reason: that not too many people were watching television during the dog days.

Inevitably, the budgets on these summer-replacement shows were pretty meagre, even more so than the winter budgets. If the rest of the continent knew that the rate of television viewing was significantly lower during the summer, so did the big companies that advertised soap, cigarettes, beer, cosmetics, shampoos, cars or gasoline via television. Hence, the tight budgets were imposed in hopes of luring the scarce summer advertising dollars from the ad agencies that had them to spend.

Of course, the tightened budgets were almost self-defeating, in that they made it that much more difficult for any network to come up with programs strong or appealing enough to have much chance of attracting many viewers during the slack summer months. If a summer show flopped, the logic went, it could be quickly dropped from the schedule, swept under the carpet of TV history and soon enough forgotten. If it worked out reasonably well, a place in the fall or winter schedule might be found for it, if not immediately then somewhere down the road.

Naturally aping American television, the CBC gave its audiences a broad array of variety shows featuring singers, dancers, instrumentalists, jugglers and other novelty acts, along with the occasional comedy sketch, whatever the season. There seemed to be, at that time, a healthy appetite for this sort of light (as opposed to "serious") programming, and the CBC, like the U.S. networks, saw neither risk nor harm in satisfying that appetite.

Among the numerous Canadian variety series during that Golden Age (starting in the fall of 1952) were such shows as "The Big Revue," with Doug Romaine and Mildred Morey, among others; "Showtime," with Shirley Harmer and Don Gerrard, who was succeeded by Robert Goulet; "Cross Canada Hit Parade," with Wally Koster, Phyllis Marshall and Joyce Hahn; "Music Makers," which featured an orchestra led by Jack Kane; "Don Messer's Jubilee," with Messer plus Charlie Chamberlain and Marg Osborne; "Holiday Ranch," with Cliff McKay, King Gannam and Fran Wright; "The Billy O'Connor Show," following Saturday Night hockey, and its eventual successor, the ebullient "Juliette"; "Jazz With Jackson," with Calvin Jackson; "Country Hoedown," with Gordie Tapp, the Rhythm Pals and Tommy Hunter—and a then-unknown young background singer whose name was Gordon Lightfoot. (There was also the comedy duo Wayne and Shuster—Johnny Wayne and Frank Shuster—who already had a substantial following via radio but cautiously waited a few years before they took the plunge into television in the mid-1950s.)

Other popular Canadian TV-variety performers of the time included Joyce Sullivan, the Leslie Bell Singers, Alan and Blanche Lund, Jack Duffy, Joan Fairfax, Sylvia Murphy, Barbara Hamilton, Jackie Rae and Denny Vaughan.

CBC Television also offered musical programs of a more serious nature: Gilbert and Sullivan operettas, classical ballet and the occasional spotlighting of a concert artist or symphony orchestra, more often than not the CBC Symphony. Almost invariably, these programs were unsponsored, since advertisers had little faith in the drawing power of such highbrow entertainment. But the CBC felt it was a solemn part of its mandate to include such lofty efforts in its programming schedule, even if they did not always command large audiences, not to mention sponsors.

During the Golden Age, drama was represented largely by such series as "GM Presents" and "Ford Startime" (both sponsored), and "Scope," "Folio" and "Festival" (unsponsored), which were more or less anthologies, often with compelling dramatic presentations but with no fixed casts of players.

Thus, fairly or not, variety performers who were seen regularly on TV became better known to the viewing public than equally talented and versatile actors who turned up now and then on this drama or that, but had far less chance to build any substantial loyal following. It was regularity that bred familiarity, and familiarity that bred stardom, to the extent that any stardom was acknowledged in Canada in those days, either by the public or by the CBC. (Remember, too, that the CBC was the only game in town. A second network, CTV, came along a few years later.)

This situation did not change significantly until some years later, with regular dramatic, comedy or action series like "Wojeck," with John Vernon;

"Quentin Durgens, MP," with Gordon Pinsent; "King of Kensington," with Al Waxman; "Seeing Things," with Louis Del Grande; "The Beachcombers," with Bruno Gerussi; and "Danger Bay," with Donnelly Rhodes.

From the beginning, CBC Television carried commendable coverage of the news, as it had long done on radio, from the beginning of the Second World War, in 1939, when CBC News really came of age. And, of course, sports, especially National Hockey League (NHL) games, received extensive coverage on television as well as radio.

There were also some notable public affairs programs on the network, including "Close-Up" and "Graphic," the latter a bald imitation of Edward R. Murrow's highly successful "Person to Person," with Joe McCulley as the host. And, some years later, there was the hard-hitting and sometimes sensational "This Hour Has Seven Days," with Patrick Watson, Laurier LaPierre and Larry Zolf.

The most successful panel show of those early years was "Fighting Words," with the articulate, imperious Nathan Cohen as moderator, and various guest panelists. And there was "Court of Opinions," which started on radio and then was simulcast, for a time, over both radio and television. Neil Leroy was the show's moderator and Kate Aitken and Lister Sinclair were regular panelists.

Children's programming was represented by such popular shows as "Uncle Chichimus," with Percy Saltzman and Larry Mann; "The Friendly Giant," with Bob Homme; and "Razzle Dazzle," featuring Michele Finney. There was also "Howdy Doody," another Canadian copy of an American program, with Buffalo Bob "Canadianized" into Timber Tom.

Among the variety performers who got their first regular exposure by way of the summer-replacement route were Tommy Ambrose, the Rhythm Pals, Allan Blye, Shane Rimmer, Tommy Hunter, Lorraine Foreman, Ruth Walker, the Haymes Sisters, Tommy Common, Jack Kane and Jackie Rae. (Rae's own weekly show began as a summer replacement for a program called "Mr. Show Business," hosted by veteran showman Jack Arthur.)

It was in the quest of a thirteen-week summer replacement for one of those variety series, "The Denny Vaughan Show," that the most popular summer-replacement program in Canada's television history was born.

There is a dispute about how "Front Page Challenge" came into existence. The disagreement centres around the question of who actually "created" the show. This dispute, however, did not come to light until some time after the program was well established and, in fact, did not get much public attention even at that time. There is nothing remarkable about this. Television viewers either enjoy a program or they don't. The question of who created it is usually of little interest to anyone who is not somehow connected with the show. Most television viewers can't tell you who the producer or director of a program is, let alone who "created" it; and the only people who bother to read credits at the end of a program are those who are involved in the television business, and possibly the middle-level brass of a network.

The show's first writer was John Aylesworth, by then something of a TV veteran, despite his youth. He and his partner, Frank Peppiatt, had started working at an advertising agency in Toronto, but their irrepressible flair for humour soon propelled them toward the new medium of television. They wrote, and starred in, one of the CBC's first variety shows, "After Hours," and also became comedy writers for "The Big Revue" and other, later, series, including "The Jackie Rae Show" and "Here's Duffy." By 1957, Aylesworth, then aged 29, was writing "Cross Canada Hit Parade" and Peppiatt was writing, and occasionally appearing on, "The Jackie Rae Show."

Because Aylesworth and Peppiatt usually worked as a team on numerous other shows, it has often been reported that Peppiatt was also involved in the creation of "Front Page Challenge." He was not; on this particular project, Aylesworth worked alone. "I had an idea and it was a game show, it was 'Front Page Challenge,'" Aylesworth recalled many years later. "The title was based on 'The $64,000 Challenge,' which was a popular U.S. show at the time. I figured you couldn't just call it 'Front Page.' That doesn't say what it is. If you call it 'Challenge' that adds the game element."

Aylesworth took his idea to the CBC's Light Entertainment Department and, after some thought, the Corporation decided to try it out. The way Aylesworth remembers it, the CBC first rejected the idea. So he went to Lever Brothers, who loved it and persuaded the CBC to change its mind.

Producer/director Harvey Hart, who had hitherto worked on such prestigious dramatic series as "Folio," was assigned to the program, in part because Hart had earlier produced the CBC's "Fighting Words," a kind of panel/quiz show aimed at an educated audience. Aylesworth was hired to write the summer-replacement series, for the traditional thirteen weeks.

But that's not the way Bob McGall remembered it. McGall was, at the time, supervisor of Light Entertainment for CBC Television. His recollection, expressed some time after the fact, was that "Front Page Challenge" was based on a British Broadcasting Corporation (BBC) program called "What Happened Last Week"; he claims that he assigned Hart and Aylesworth to "develop" the idea and the result was "Front Page Challenge."

(Only a year later, Bernard Slade, then a busy television writer in Toronto, went to McGall with an idea for a new panel show called "One of a Kind." According to Slade, McGall told him he would think it over. The next time they talked, McGall told Slade he had "looked in the files" and found an "almost identical" program idea there. So, Slade was offered the job of writing "One of a Kind," but the question of its ownership remained in limbo for the one-year period the program lasted. Then the CBC cancelled "One of a Kind" and replaced it with a similar show, "Live a Borrowed Life," which the CBC clearly owned, and which lasted for several years.

The dispute about the origin of "Front Page Challenge" might never have come to light but for Mike Wallace, who was by then an increasingly hot name in American television. He had already started his hard-hitting interview show in New York in 1956 and the following year it was expanded to the full ABC television network.

While Aylesworth was still writing "Front Page Challenge," Mike Wallace was invited to be a guest panelist on the Canadian show. Impressed by the program, Wallace talked to John Aylesworth about the possibility of doing an American version of it. Aylesworth went to New York and met with ABC network executives. He gave up on the idea of selling the show there partly because ABC seemed determined to change everything about the program that Aylesworth felt was important and worthwhile. Among other things, Wallace and ABC wanted to dispense with a panel of skilled journalists and substitute glamorous Hollywood names. Aylesworth shuddered and beat a hasty retreat to Toronto.

It was during the course of these proceedings that Aylesworth's dispute with the CBC erupted. When Aylesworth mentioned the overtures from ABC, the Corporation told him that he didn't have the right to negotiate for "Front Page Challenge" in the United States because the program was the property of the CBC. This news stunned the young writer who, for some time, had been living under the delusion that he had invented the show.

Aylesworth further maintained that after protracted negotiations with the CBC and attempts at a compromise, he and his lawyer (Royce Frith, later a senator) met with two Corporation representatives (but not McGall) who candidly acknowledged the legitimacy of Aylesworth's claim, but argued that if he pressed the matter further they would simply take "Front Page Challenge" off the air. Loath to see the program killed, Aylesworth backed off, unwilling to be responsible for denting the careers of those people making a living via "Front Page Challenge," most notably the panel and the moderator.

McGall later said he "believed" that the CBC eventually paid Aylesworth a sum of money—he didn't remember how much—to settle the claim. Aylesworth insisted that he received nothing beyond his salary as the show's writer, except the theoretical right to sell the show outside Canada, but with the daunting knowledge that if he did the program would be cancelled in Canada.

Whatever residue of bitterness Aylesworth may have felt toward the Corporation was soon forgotten. It's certain he never made more than a few hundred dollars a week for writing "Front Page Challenge" during the first couple of years of its existence. Soon after that, he and Peppiatt moved to the United States, where they had long and fruitful careers as television writers and producers, working with Perry Como and Jonathan Winters, among others. Later, they created, wrote and produced the remarkably successful CBS series "Hee Haw." (They conceived it and sold it to the network as a country-western version of the immensely popular series "Laugh-In.") Several years later, when CBS decided to drop the show,

Peppiatt and Aylesworth bought back the rights to it, continued to produce and market it via syndication (market by market) and eventually
sold all their rights to the program for a reported $11 million. That's U.S.
dollars, of course.

And what of "Front Page Challenge," the little summer-replacement
show that Aylesworth was positive he had invented?

It went on to become the longest-running game/panel show in the history of television, on either side of the border, and indeed, one of the
longest-running shows of any type in the history of television anywhere.
It was on the air for thirty-eight years.

With all due respect to both John Aylesworth and the CBC brass, the
program's remarkable longevity is attributable more properly to the producers and writers who worked on the show and, certainly most of all, to
the people who appeared on-camera—the often famous, frequently fascinating "challengers," the smooth, unflappable moderator and the sharp,
unpredictable, irrepressible, irreverent regular panelists.

And how that came to be is surely worth examining, even now, long
after the dust has settled and the controversy has cooled down.

chapter 2

UP FROM THE BASEMENT

With whatever misgivings, "Front Page Challenge" went on the air that June 24, 1957—unsteady, perhaps, but live. Buzzers buzzed, glitter lights glittered; decorative models daintily escorted uneasy challengers to the interview chair; everybody fumbled a bit, unsure of who should speak or when.

When it was over, the panel had identified, and viewers had met, Alfred Scadding, a survivor of the Moose River mine disaster; Madame Alex Legros, a midwife present at the birth of the Dionne Quintuplets; and Montreal's Mayor Jean Drapeau.

But getting to that first night on the air entailed a good deal of preparation, and more than a little sweat.

If it can be said that any television program has an identifiable, physical birthplace—apart from the brain of John Aylesworth—"Front Page Challenge's" birthplace was the basement recreation room of Harvey Hart's house on Betty Ann Drive in Willowdale, in the north end of Toronto. That was where numerous potential panelists were auditioned during the spring of 1957, at a series of informal evening get-togethers, where fruit was served and the game was played over and over again, with different people serving as potential panelists.

Gordon Sinclair, one of the first to audition, estimated that a total of eighty prospective panelists were tried out over four nights in Hart's basement. "I remember he served us watermelon," Sinclair said, then added, "Funny I should remember that."

"They ran auditions for every son of a bitch in the country except me," Pierre Berton recalled years later. "I was never auditioned. I went on the show. I had to drive down from Haliburton. And I did the show. I think there were three guests, and I got them all. I got two, anyway. That was the big thing then."

Berton was not on the very first show (Scott Young was the guest panelist) but he soon became a regular. "I used to go home at night," he remembered, "and Janet (Mrs. Berton) would say, 'Who was on tonight?' and it was out of my mind already, and I could not remember. I was on to something else."

Hart and Aylesworth began by laying out some basic guidelines for themselves as to what sort of panel and moderator would work best. But it was a long and tortuous trip from Harvey Hart's basement up to the CBC's Studio 4, at 1140 Yonge Street, where, after still more run-throughs, the show would be brought to life that summer.

The game itself was quite simple. There was a challenger (sometimes hidden behind the panel if the person's identity might be too large a clue) representing a front page headline from the past. Ideally, the challenger would have a fairly direct connection with the headlined story. Members of the panel would take turns asking questions in an attempt to track down the headline, or, at any rate, the story. When necessary, the host (or moderator) would answer for the challenger, ostensibly to keep the panel on the right track.

Once the game portion was completed, the guest challenger moved to another chair to face the panel and was then interviewed by the panel. The interview might be directly related to the story, or, if the challenger was a celebrity, might wander to other areas of interest to the public—or, at least, to the panel.

But getting any new television series ready to go on the air—especially in that era of live television—is always an incredibly hectic job. Every game or panel show goes through many changes during seemingly endless run-throughs. No way around this has ever been found, because it is only by playing and replaying the game that the flaws in the program's structure, or its personnel, can be discovered and corrected.

There's much more to mounting a successful television show than deciding on the panelists and moderator. Rules have to be worked out and constantly revised, to cover every possible situation. A studio set has to be sketched out, designed, constructed, put up, tested and then often adjusted again. Judgments have to be made: Is the game too easy? Is it too hard? Will music be helpful to emphasize dramatic stories? Should the panelists work independently or be allowed to consult? (At first huddles were allowed, but this practice was soon dropped.) Should the audience be let in on the answer or would the program be more successful if the audience had to play along with the panelists?

On this last point, Hart and Aylesworth made a lucky and, as it turned out, wise decision. That was to let the audience, both in the studio and at home, know what the story was and who the challenger was—without that information being given to the panel, of course.

The reason this was a good decision has to do with the viewer's own ego. Quickly forgetting that he or she has been given information denied to the panel, the viewer soon feels superior to the panelists, who are desperately groping through questions in an attempt to identify the story and/or the challenger within a specified amount of time.

"How can they be so stupid?" the viewer asks. "It's easy." The viewer therefore feels smarter than the panel, which makes the viewer feel good and he or she tends to enjoy the show that much more. The viewer is, of course, not aware of this emotional factor at the time, but this kind of smug self-satisfaction makes for a happier audience.

A second element that helped "Front Page Challenge" succeed was its ability to focus on human beings—world leaders, movie stars, industrialists, authors, athletes, plus hitherto-unknown ordinary people who had a legitimate connection to a compelling front page news story from the past, be it a mine disaster, the birth of quintuplets, an invention or discovery, an earthquake or flood, a bank robbery, an election or an eyebrow-raising political scandal.

The third ingredient that virtually assured the success of the program was the emerging personality of the panel, both individually and as a team. Over a period of time, viewers felt they *knew* those people who came into their homes every Monday night—knew what kind of questions they would ask during the game. And after the game, during which the audience's sympathy tended to be with the challenger, the viewer's focus shifted subtly to the panel once the interview started. A few minutes earlier they might have been rooting for the challenger (to stump the panel), but now they loved it when Gordon Sinclair asked a stuffy entrepreneur how much money he made, or when Pierre Berton went relentlessly after some shifty-eyed, evasive politician.

"We started the run-throughs in Harvey's basement," Aylesworth recalled. "Harvey and I decided that the kind of panel we needed included 'The Curmudgeon,' and who could be better than Gordon Sinclair...and a pretty lady like Arlene Francis, of 'What's My Line?' We tried a number of people, but Toby Robins was head and shoulders above everyone else."

Aylesworth also remembered that from the beginning he wanted Win Barron as the moderator. "Initially, when I first pitched the show," he said, "I had Win Barron in mind as the host."

Barron had been working for Paramount Pictures since 1942, when that company's newsreel division began doing a separate Canadian version of its weekly Paramount newsreel. Barron spent the next fifteen years taking a train to New York each weekend to record the narration for the Canadian newsreel, returning to his Toronto home on Tuesdays. Paramount, perhaps because of its affiliation with Famous Players Theatres, had a greater Canadian presence than most American film companies of the time. By now, his voice and, to a lesser extent, his face, was known to countless thousands of moviegoers across Canada.

John Aylesworth talked about the choice of Barron for "Front Page Challenge": "I didn't know whether we could get him, but who better than the voice of Canadian Paramount News? And I had met him and he was a charming guy and seemed knowledgeable and everything. So, Win came to a lot of the run-throughs. He was quite pleased and he got an OK from Paramount to do the show." Actually, it was at about this time that

Paramount decided to discontinue its newsreel—another victim of the growing competition that television represented to the movie-theatre business—so the timing was perfect for Win Barron and for "Front Page Challenge."

At first, Gordon Sinclair told me, he was ambivalent about doing the program. When Harvey Hart first called him to ask if he would audition as a panelist, Sinclair balked. "No," he told Hart, "I'm too old and bald and wrinkled. What's more, I'm impolite. They'd kill me."

Hart's recollection, however, was somewhat different:

"I remember a funny incident with Gordon. He had said something in the paper (in his column in the *Toronto Star*) about not being interested in ever doing one of those silly game shows. And I called him up and said, 'Gordon, I read where you say you weren't interested in doing one of these silly game shows.' And he said, 'That's right.' So, I said, 'Would you like to try out for one?' And he said, 'When?' That was how I got him over to the house, and the rest is history."

Other prominent journalists and broadcasters who went down the stairs to Harvey Hart's basement to try out for the as-yet-unborn show included Claire Wallace, Jack Dennett, Ralph Allen and Frank Tumpane, all known names in Canada and most of whom would subsequently serve as guest panelists on the program from time to time.

Sinclair had his own theory about why he was chosen: "I had an edge because they were looking for one person who could remember things back to, say, 1910, or something like that (Sinclair was fifty-seven when he joined the show), and I think they had me in mind for that."

Whatever the reasons, Sinclair was an absolute natural for such a program. He had become famous simply by being outspoken, often outrageous. And he knew this. He learned as a young man that the secret to journalistic popularity was being noticed—not necessarily being liked, not even being accurate. He parlayed that knowledge into a singularly enduring career. Pierre Berton remembered the first time he met Sinclair:

"He was wearing a mustard-coloured check jacket, green pants, a purple shirt, a bow tie made of calfskin and a jolly little hat. Somebody said,

'Gordon, none of this goes together.' Gordon replied, 'That's my costume. I'm in show business.' That was Gordon, above all, a showman." It was said of Gordon Sinclair that his idea of travelling incognito was wearing a jacket and trousers of the same colour.

Sinclair didn't merely cover news—he made it. Long before "Front Page Challenge" came into being, Gordon knew how to attract attention.

Fred Davis recalled the first time he saw Gordon Sinclair: "Back in the 1930s when I was in high school, Sinclair would come back from his tours of India and Africa and turn up in my school auditorium for a speech wearing his pith helmet, brandishing the spears given to him by natives, wearing short pants, his tropical khaki jacket. It was a wonderful show."

And I can still remember my own first meeting with Sinclair. It was around 1951, not long after I had begun covering entertainment for the *Globe and Mail*. I was at a press cocktail party and noticed Sinclair talking to a man I knew, so I moved over to that spot. The man I knew greeted me, then introduced me to the famous man. Sinclair nodded vaguely in my direction, then mused aloud: "Alex Barris, Alex Barris. I've heard that name somewhere."

Having always been deficient in reverence, I replied: "Gordon Sinclair, Gordon Sinclair. I've heard that name somewhere."

Sinclair took it in stride. He laughed and then we shook hands. After that, we ran into each other occasionally at press conferences or cocktail parties, and always got along well.

Once, in the early 1950s, Sinclair walked into a downtown Toronto car dealership, asked the price of the Rolls-Royce on display in the window, said he would take it and then bowled over the salesman by taking a wad of bills out of his pocket and forking over the full price of the car— $16,000—in cash. A few years later, he posed for photographers with his car outside the CBC's Studio 4, where "Front Page Challenge" was produced.

One doubt that lurked in Hart's mind was whether the program would be able to attract suitable challengers who could be persuaded to travel to Toronto to appear on a brand-new, untested game show. Other than shameless publicity seekers, would busy, important people go to that trouble, perhaps at the risk of being made to look ridiculous, all for the dubious glory of appearing on a program nobody had even heard of?

"It's one thing to play it in your own home," said Hart, "and another to see whether people would actually come on as challengers. And to try to describe to them (over the phone) what it was."

John Aylesworth found it amusing, years later, to recollect what the program looked like when it first aired. "On the first couple of shows, we thought, well, we've gotta be like a big-time American show, and we had these two beautiful models escorting the challengers from the hidden spot down to the interview chair. We had glitter lights and all that; of course, that was cut out after two or three weeks."

"The first set," according to Hart, "was monstrous, an unwieldy set. I'm wondering why people didn't break their legs. It was worse than appearing on the Academy Awards. And we had two models escorting people down to the interview spot for a very good reason: because we never thought they'd make it on their own without tripping."

In the beginning, pace was considered of paramount importance. "When Harvey and I started the show," Aylesworth remembered, "the whole idea was to keep that pace going, to really make it an entertaining show, with information. We always had three challengers and one more waiting in the green room, and we always made sure three people got on. So that made it move like crazy. Four minutes of questioning, then a thirty-second film recap of the story and maybe a minute and a half of interview, and let's move on to the next one."

Another indication of how the program changed over the years was the amount of time allocated to the "game" portion, as opposed to the interview. When "Front Page Challenge" first went on the air, up to four minutes were allowed the panel to track down the story and/or the challenger. In time, this was cut back to three minutes and, eventually, to two minutes.

It took some time for the emphasis to change with the gradual realization that the headline was simply a device to lure interesting, sometimes celebrated people to the program as challengers. What the home viewer really wanted was more time for the interview. It was the interview, rather than the story or the game, that was the real meat of the program, along with, of course, the panelists' growing ability to make the interview not only entertaining but stimulating and frequently controversial.

A quarter of a century later, Aylesworth still had vivid memories of working on that first season. "There was so much energy and activity," he told me. "The whole place felt like a newspaper office, tracking down stories and guests."

In that same talk, Aylesworth said: "When we first discussed the program, one of the chief objections was that we'd run out of big news events before our thirteen weeks were up. But now, we find we have enough material to last us for years."

When the summer season began, on June 24, 1957, the regular panelists were Gordon Sinclair, Toby Robins and myself. As mentioned earlier, the guest panelist on the first show was Scott Young. (Other guest panelists in the early days included Pierre Berton, Frank Tumpane, Lister Sinclair, June Callwood and Charles Templeton.)

Gordon Sinclair got the knack of the show from the beginning. "Gordon went after people," Hart explained. "This was one reason for the show's early success. He would go after someone and he wouldn't let go. He was the one who enjoyed the interview period. He was slightly abrasive, but very frank. He found his personality quite early in the series."

Also, by the third or fourth week, Sinclair had hit upon the knack of making the questions often as colourful as the answers. It was then that he began using an omnibus question that would serve him well for the next twenty-seven years: "Does this story have anything to do with love, money, conquest or disaster?"

The Hart/Aylesworth choice of a moderator met with less success. "Little did we realize," Aylesworth later recalled, "that Win Barron, charming guy that he was, a wonderful-looking man and with his background with Paramount News, would just be a terrible host. He couldn't handle the mechanics, he was terribly ill at ease, and he froze and just didn't know what to do."

In the early weeks, the production team tried and tried to improve Barron's performance, but nothing seemed to help. Barron felt uncomfortable on-camera, and it showed. What Hart and Aylesworth had failed to consider was that Barron's reputation had been based largely on his voice; he read the narration for Canadian Paramount News, but he did this in a recording studio, not on-camera, where he would be in full view of audiences both at home and in the studio.

Aylesworth remembered that Barron kept promising "to get better." They had extra rehearsals, additional run-throughs, to no avail. Within a few weeks, Hart and Aylesworth were seriously considering the possibility of replacing him, if the show was to continue beyond its original thirteen-week mandate.

By the sixth or seventh week, two important decisions were made: the CBC decided that the show was successful enough to continue into the fall, and Hart and Aylesworth agreed, however reluctantly, that Barron had to go when the show began its fall season.

Also at that time, Harvey Hart took me aside and told me he didn't think I was working out too well as a panelist. Too flippant, not tenacious enough in playing the game, he explained.

(I have to plead guilty to the charge of being flippant. Irreverence was always one of my vices; making quips was another. On one of the early shows, a challenger was Grey Owl, the pseudo-Indian icon. I rashly referred to him as White Owl—the brand name of a cigar—and thus managed to offend some viewers. Incidentally, it was Pierre Berton, a frequent guest panelist during that first summer, who succeeded me as a regular panelist.)

In that talk with Harvey Hart, I was also told the show was going to replace Win Barron. This was supposed to be confidential, but by the end of August much of the press was speculating about who might be Barron's successor. Among those mentioned in the newspapers were Austin Willis, Paul Kligman, Barry Morse, Frank Tumpane and Byng Whitteker.

What really happened was this: Harvey Hart asked if I was interested in trying out for the role of host, since I would be off the panel. I agreed to give it a shot. I didn't know it until later, but the same offer was made to Fred Davis, at about the same time. Fred recalled:

"There were a number of people being considered for host, but you and I ended up auditioning on air. Terribly risky. I got a call and I went in and did the show, and I thought, 'Gee, I hope I did all right.' Next week, I thought, 'Well, I guess Barris got it,' because you were on. The third week, I got another call, and I thought, 'Gee, I'm back in the running.' And I did the third week. You did the fourth week. I thought, 'What is this, co-host time?' And neither of us knew what was going to happen. Strange way to do it, but I suppose it's one way to see how you do under fire. I don't know of any other show that did it that way."

After the fourth week, Davis got the nod. (By way of consolation, I had a scoop on every other newspaperman in town: the appointment of Fred Davis as the permanent host of FPC.) In all honesty, not even I can possibly question the wisdom of that decision—Fred's reign lasted as long as "Front Page Challenge" stayed on the air: thirty-eight years.

Fred Davis's broadcasting background was impeccable. As a young man, he had been a musician, his instrument the trumpet. During the Second World War he was with Captain Robert Farnon's excellent orchestra in England, which was heard almost daily over the Armed Forces Network by Britons, Canadians and Americans. Fred was also a member of a smaller jazz-oriented band that played various club dates and dances. On one such concert party, Davis got his first taste of performing—without his trumpet:

"We had a scriptwriter with us. A guy who later did walk-ons on the old 'Red Skelton Show' was our sergeant; he was British, had a very plummy accent, which I used to imitate behind his back. He caught me one day and wrote me into a comedy script as a Colonel Blimp character. I'd never been in front of a microphone before, other than with a trumpet in my hand. I didn't mind doing the accent, but I was playing in front of a British audience, that's what worried me. But I got through it and that may have been where the microphone bug was born, the fact that I was able to talk to an audience."

After the war, he went to Lorne Greene's Academy of Radio Arts, in Toronto, and, after graduation, was offered a job as an announcer in

Ottawa. By 1953, he was hosting a National Film Board television series called "On the Spot." Three years later, he co-hosted, with Anna Cameron, a CBC afternoon show titled "Open House."

The week after Barron was dropped as host and moderator of the program, "Front Page Challenge" decided to do a story on one of the most famous disaster stories of the twentieth century: the explosion of the *Hindenburg* at Lakehurst, New Jersey, in 1937. The challenger was legitimate enough: a film cameraman who had been assigned to cover the German dirigible's arrival and was therefore on hand and poised with camera when the spectacular explosion occurred. He recalled the story vividly, but he did not have, nor did he own, the sensational film of the disaster.

"The only available film," Aylesworth recalled, "belonged to Paramount News—Win Barron's employers. So the only way we could get the film was to call up Win and ask if he could get the film for us, as a favour. He was very nice about it and agreed. And he just made it. Just as the show was going on the air (live) he came rushing into the control booth with the film of the *Hindenburg*. And we thanked him, but it was kind of embarrassing, because he stood in the booth throughout the show."

Such minor embarrassing moments aside, "Front Page Challenge" soon showed some promise of advancing from the awkward steps of a foal to the winning stride of a champion.

chapter 3

GORDON, TOBY, PIERRE AND FRED

The choice of Toby Robins for a spot on the panel was obviously something of a risk. That she was both beautiful and talented as an actress is indisputable. But she had absolutely no journalistic background.

Aylesworth later revealed that Toby Robins's name was picked from a list of ACTRA (the Alliance of Canadian Television and Radio Artists) television actresses. "We had located plenty of newspapermen without difficulty," he said, "but women reporters were so rare we realized we would have to give a few actresses a trial. Toby was one of seven or so who had no connection with newspapers."

When "Front Page Challenge" was about to begin its twenty-fifth season on the air, I talked with Toby Robins, who was by then living in London, England. She remembered many of the details:

"I remember auditioning at Harvey Hart's house, and it was a rather peculiar thing, because I didn't read the papers much. I guess they were just looking for a pretty face. And, funnily enough, there was one particular (news) event that I guessed and I'm sure that's how I got the show. It was a fire in Boston, in a nightclub, and it so happened there was a lady pianist who had survived that fire, and her sister was living in our home—my mother's home—and I was only a child, but I could remember her phoning desperately to Boston, the tears on the telephone. So, I remembered the event and I think they (Hart and Aylesworth) were so astonished, and I was astonished, needless to say."

(The fire Toby remembered hearing about in her childhood occurred on November 28, 1942, at the Cocoanut Grove in Boston, with a terrible death toll of 487. Among the casualties was the veteran movie cowboy star, Buck Jones, who happened to be in Boston on a U.S. war bond–selling tour. Incidentally, the Cocoanut Grove fire story was never actually used on "Front Page Challenge." Perhaps the producers were afraid that it would be too easy for Toby Robins because she had guessed it in one of the early run-throughs.)

The almost immediate success of Toby as a panelist surprised some people (including Hart and Aylesworth) but that was because they hadn't realized what a tenacious pro the gorgeous actress was. In a magazine piece written after the show had become a hit, journalist June Callwood said of Toby:

"She had never read an entire newspaper front page in her life and rarely even noted the headlines. Her practice with the daily newspaper was to turn to the drama pages, devour every item about the theatre, scan lightly the women's page and any pictures that intervened, then return to her study of the new script she had to learn." Callwood described "the remarkable conversion of Toby Robins the expert ornament into Toby Robins the ornamental expert."

Robins spent hot summer afternoons in libraries, leafing through brittle newspapers printed before she was born. "Some things rang a bell," Toby told June. "Names like Dieppe and Dunkirk. I had a fuzzy recollection of them. But almost everything else was brand new to me."

The homework paid off, despite a few errors early in the summer series. On one show, the challenger was Canadian runner Richard Ferguson, who had finished third behind Roger Bannister and John Landy in the Miracle Mile run at the British Empire Games in Vancouver.

During the interview, a slightly flustered Toby asked Ferguson, "Who do you think was the better runner, Roger or Bannister?" But the viewing audience was quite willing to forgive these minor gaffes, at least in part because Toby Robins was so likeable.

For its first thirteen weeks of life, "Front Page Challenge" had the shaky Win Barron as moderator and a regular panel consisting of Sinclair, Robins and Barris, plus various guest panelists. Then, when that first fall season began, two major changes were visible: Fred Davis replaced Win Barron; and after a few weeks of testing other panelists (Ralph Allen, Charles Templeton, Ralph Foster), Pierre Berton took over the third regular panelist's chair—and kept it for thirty-eight years.

Gordon and Toby were the two holdovers from the summer season. Having worked side by side during the summer, they had already formed a good relationship. Despite his age, Sinclair was not immune to the charms of a beautiful and gracious woman like Robins.

And Toby obviously enjoyed being on the program: "The show was fun to do. First of all, they're darling and second of all they're unusual. I mean, Gordon Sinclair is one in a million. He's such a unique individual."

Pierre Berton soon became a Robins fan, too.

Said Berton: "There is a kind of glow about Toby that is her special asset. It comes in part from a bubbling enthusiasm which is really a very professional attitude toward her work...If the worries of the world rest heavily on Toby's shoulders, she doesn't show it."

When Berton became the third regular panelist on the program, things really began to fall into place.

The chemistry between the panel members didn't kick in overnight. Those things take time. Over the months, however, the three regular panelists became a team, playing the game like seasoned pros, then going on enthusiastically to the interview, delighting the audience, and either charming or confounding the often celebrated challengers.

They had a common goal: to guess the headline and the identity of the challenger. It didn't matter which one of them succeeded, so long as one of them did. There really was a team spirit. They truly felt challenged, as if their reputations as newshawks were on the line.

In the interview section of the show, their individual styles and personalities took over—Toby light and bubbly, Pierre hard-nosed, Gordon as freewheeling and blunt as everyone expected him to be.

Toby Robins was the surprise hit of the show—to virtually everybody. Viewers and critics who had been prepared to dismiss her as merely a vacuous beauty soon had to change their opinions as the plucky actress proved her worth on the panel. Everyone connected with the program expressed great admiration for Toby's valiant effort to make up for her lack of a news background. "She certainly did her homework," Harvey Hart reflected.

Toby admitted, much later, that she had to do just that. "I mean, you're very aware how vulnerable you are, you feel terribly stupid without having some news background."

Before long, she was the subject of magazine pieces by June Callwood and others.

Fred Davis later commented: "Toby sitting beside Gordon was manna from heaven—the vivacious, beautiful woman who did a lot of homework. I always respected Toby."

Barbara Frum, who was later to become a frequent guest panelist, remembered Toby from the early days of "Front Page Challenge":

"I think that Toby Robins is an incredible factor in explaining the success of the program. Because the whole country was in love with her. Because of her charm and the kind of liveliness she brought. She was never stuffy."

In 1981, long after she had departed from "Front Page Challenge," Toby recalled its beginnings: "When I started out to do the show, I was pregnant and I thought, oh, well, it's a nice sitting-down job until I have the baby. And then it went on."

Late in 1957, viewers could hardly fail to notice that Toby was very pregnant, but she kept turning up for each show and she even boasted that she was going to have her baby without missing a program. Toby (Mrs. Billy Freedman in private life) did indeed have her baby without missing a program, but that was just sheer luck. A Liberal Party convention preempted the program for one week, which gave Toby enough time to have her child and return to the FPC studio in two weeks.

Barbara Frum also commented, some years later, on the incident involving Toby's pregnancy:

"I remember when she was pregnant and stayed (on the program) right through to her ninth month—it was long before maternity leave and long before women's lib... To even be pregnant in public, at that time, was a disgrace. People used to hide in their houses (during pregnancy). They wouldn't go out in a gown and on television in their ninth month. It was unheard of. I think Toby was a formative figure, and I don't think she did it deliberately. It was just one of those unconscious, natural things she did that was so charming that everyone accepted it."

As for Toby, she shrugged off the whole incident:

"But I enjoyed doing the program very much," she told me. "When I look back it was an amazing period for me, and it stood me in good stead for the rest of my life, because I was a little green kid in Toronto with no newspaper background and you're awed by the world out there.

"And when these people came in, very eminent people who had achieved great things in their various fields, and you were given a chance to talk to them, and you found out they were frightened and they were unsure and they were all the things that you were. So I learned, rather early on, a lesson that might have taken me another twenty years to learn. And I was very grateful."

Larry Mann, who did the audience warm-ups in the program's early years, had this to say of her: "Toby had an inner beauty as well. She outgraced Grace Kelly."

Gordon Sinclair was something of a media star—certainly a well-established personality—via his newspaper and radio work, long before the birth of "Front Page Challenge." During all his years on radio (CFRB) he had a sizable, if ambivalent, audience. Some were often shocked by things he said, but they listened anyway. Some were simply fascinated to hear what outrageous cause he would adopt, or denounce, this time. (A good indication of how times have changed since those days is the case of the studiedly coarse American radio talk-show host, Howard Stern. By comparison, Stern makes Gordon Sinclair seem like Little Lord Fauntleroy.)

It was the same once "Front Page Challenge" began: there were viewers who professed to hate Sinclair ("You never know what the son of a bitch is going to say next!"), but they also hated to miss him. They were like boxing fans who cover their eyes when the fight gets brutal, then peek between their fingers so they won't miss anything.

I had known Sinclair for a number of years before "Front Page Challenge" first aired. On a number of occasions, he asked me to fill in for him on his daily "Show Business" broadcasts on CFRB when he was on vacation and later complimented me on my work. Years later, when he was considering giving up some of his busy radio schedule, he told me he had recommended me to replace him on "Show Business," but CFRB had other plans.

"I don't enjoy vacation time," he once told me. "I hate it and that's my difficulty, that's my major difficulty in my whole life. There's some of us like that. You get bored stiff. And then if you reach for the bottle it's worse. That's absolutely no solution."

He went on further on the subject of drinking:

"If I get very tired it takes me a long time to bounce back, and certain types of liquor absolutely throw me off. I can't touch gin. Just makes me a madman. If I ever murder anybody, Alex, you'll know I've been drinking gin. I can't touch gin, and I like it. I don't like rum, so I don't drink it, and I don't care much for rye, so I don't drink it. But I do drink Scotch with a certain amount of regularity."

Of all the panel, Sinclair cared most about winning the game—not necessarily that he must figure it out, but that the panel must. He talked freely about this and other aspects of "Front Page Challenge":

"The success of 'Front Page Challenge'? I think that part's easy. First of all, it's the unexpected. We don't know what to expect and the audience doesn't know what to expect because we don't know what's coming up. Secondly, we don't act towards each other as rivals or competitors. We are a team."

Sometimes, he admitted, facing the program's deadlines got a bit tiresome:

"I think any actor, any performer, must come to this. A fellow who's doing a long-run Broadway play that's been running for months and months, or years, he must get nights when he wished he didn't have to do it. Well, I've had that.

"But that's about my only complaint. I've also come away from a few shows feeling that I've made a fool of myself and I probably have. But I can't really remember those things. It's a pleasant thing about the memory, you know, that I've come away thinking, well, what a bloody fool I've made of myself tonight. But that feeling is gone by the next day.

"Sometimes I have checked myself. I have held back. And I kinda have regretted it. You know, you are what you are, Alex, and when you get to be my age you're not going to change your personality. Yes, I'm a little sorry that I stayed away from some (controversial) questions."

Sinclair also had a remarkable knack for sensing when to shift gears in an interview. This is illustrated in a story recalled by Alfie Scopp, who wrote the show for several years:

"We had a mercenary on once (in 1962), a young, almost illiterate English kid who had been a mercenary in Africa. This was just after a horrendous massacre in which a lot of news people were involved.

"I think June Callwood was the guest panelist. And the three panelists went after this kid, in the interview, about the morality of taking money to kill. He didn't know what the hell they were talking about. And then it got to Gordon, and the others were so incensed, and the kid wondered 'What have I done? These people are mad at me.'

"And Sinclair saved it. He said, 'How much does a mercenary make these days?' It just lifted the whole show, and he did it instinctively. And you'd think Gordon would have gone after him, too, but he's too much of a show business animal; he can reach in from left field, with nothing that the writers had thought of, when it's sagging, and drop his bomb and we're away again."

When Sinclair died in 1984, at the age of 84, Pierre Berton observed that his late colleague had achieved "the status of lovable old coot, an eccentric uncle who's indulged by his family... 'Front Page Challenge' was never quite the same without him."

Like Sinclair, Pierre Berton was certainly a known commodity before "Front Page Challenge." Born in the Yukon and educated in Vancouver, he became a special writer for the *Vancouver Sun* and the youngest man ever to be city editor of the *News Herald*.

He had already sold a few pieces to *Maclean's* when, in 1947, he got a message that a Mr. Scott Young, of that magazine, was at the Hotel Vancouver and would like Berton to drop by. Years later, in his autobiographical book *Starting Out*, he recalled that first meeting with Young.

"You've got a magnificent city here," said Young.

"You bet we have," replied Berton.

"You're lucky to live here."

"I'd be crazy to live anywhere else," Berton agreed. "Only a fool would want to leave Vancouver."

"Gee, that's too bad," said Young, "because I was about to offer you a job on *Maclean's*."

Without missing a beat, Berton said: "I'll take it."

Berton moved to Toronto and by the time he was thirty-one, he was appointed editor of *Maclean's*.

When he joined the panel of "Front Page Challenge," he was also being heard regularly on CBC-Radio's "Court of Opinions" and had made appearances on "Close-Up" and other television shows. Not long after joining FPC, he got into a dispute with *Maclean's*, so he quit, and immediately started writing a daily, and instantly popular, column for the *Toronto Star*. He later had his own long-running interview show on television and, not incidentally, wrote dozens of best-selling books.

Not everyone saw Berton the same way. Jack Webster said Pierre was "an entertainer more than a journalist." Producer Ray McConnell agreed, to an extent: "Pierre is a performer first."

Larry Mann, a longtime friend of Berton's, said: "To the unwary onlooker, Pierre appears to be everything he isn't."

And Vicki Gabereau said: "To me, he's an absolute hero. I think he's completely underrated by a generation of people. They take him for granted."

Berton and Gabereau's father were old friends. She recalled Pierre's visits to Vancouver:

"He would come in like a colossus. It was fantastic. They were just terrors. They used to do close-order drill in the living room. They stayed up all night. They screamed. They yelled. They sang. They jumped on the furniture. My girlfriend came over and she said, 'I can't believe it's Pierre Berton.'"

It wasn't too long after he joined the FPC panel that Berton became a sort of unofficial team captain. It's in his nature to take charge rather than sit back and wait for someone else to lead. He quickly earned the respect of his colleagues on the show. In later years, he pretty well took over the matter of negotiating with the CBC whenever contract-renewal time came around, and the others were content to let him carry the ball.

Berton candidly admitted he was the unofficial "shop steward" for the entire panel—plus Fred Davis, who was paid the same as the panelists.

He recalled the earlier days, when they were being paid a few hundred dollars per show and were pretty much taken for granted:

"I'd go into the parking lot (at the studio) and, of course, everybody is parking there except the panel—electricians, everybody's got a parking spot except us. I'd have to walk through mud for two blocks carrying my suit, and I thought, 'What's going on here? If this was Hollywood, I'd have a star on my door and somebody to come out and drive me here.' So I said, this has got to stop.

"So, then, Gordon and I sat down. Gordon got the ratings; Gordon found out what they charged for commercials. And we worked out what the show cost. We knew the budget of the show and what they were getting (for commercials), they were making wonderful sums, they were making big money. So I went to, I've forgotten, maybe Ray (McConnell) and I said, 'This is no good. The CBC is making huge sums out of exploiting us.' We were getting three or four hundred a show then. We went up to a thousand then. I said, 'Well, we want our own parking spaces with our names on, and we don't want to sit in that tiny little room you put us in, we want to sit in the big room, put the guests in the small room. Which they did. I said, 'Christ, we're the stars of the fucking show and you're treating us like nobodies.' Which is typical CBC."

In the program's last few years, the panelists and Davis were being paid $2,500 a show.

Lorraine Thomson, who worked for twenty years on "Front Page Challenge," said this about Berton:

"Pierre is one of those introverted extroverts. He's a shy egomaniac. He stands off to one side at most parties, seemingly reluctant to take part in conversation. A lot of people take this shyness as arrogance."

Author and broadcaster Lister Sinclair said of Berton: "Pierre is essentially a poor guy who happens eventually to have a lot of money. In attitude and sympathies, Pierre is always on the side of the victims."

Berton has admitted to this shyness in social circles, but also claimed that he's not shy "professionally."

"I'm a ham," he told journalist and broadcaster Knowlton Nash. "There's no use pretending that you're not a ham if you're in show business."

On a related subject, Berton has said:

"Anybody who says they don't like being a celebrity is a hypocrite, because you don't have to be a celebrity. Nobody *has* to be a celebrity, there's all sorts of things you can do. Some people say, Oh, it's awful being a celebrity, and people bug you…you hear that B.S. Everybody who is a celebrity really likes it. I like it. I like going to St. John's and people walk down the street and ask for my autograph. Why wouldn't I? It's nice to be known."

There's a pragmatic side to Berton. Reluctant at first to go on TV, he quickly realized its advantages. After one of his first television experiences, he recalled: "The next morning, some cab driver said, 'Oh, I know you. I saw you on television last night.' And I thought, 'Oh, boy. That's powerful. I'd better revise my feelings. TV sells books.' And that's why I really went into television. It sells books."

On an earlier occasion, he told me:

"The question I get asked most when I go across the country on these (book) promotion tours, the question that really baffles me is, 'Why do you do "Front Page Challenge?" Why do you keep on with that?'

"Christ, I say, why wouldn't I? It's easy money. And it doesn't take any work. I mean, do you think I sit at that studio for twenty-four hours a day? For Christ's sake, I go down there every other Monday for three hours and I get a lot of dough. And I'm a nationally known figure, so when I'm promoting a book, you'll ask me all these questions. I mean, it's an unbelievably dumb, naive question."

Like the others on the panel, Berton always had a high regard for Gordon Sinclair:

"We learned a lot from Gordon, listening to the way he asked a question, and I learned it's not just the question, it's how you frame a question. Of course, it can be framed in a dull fashion or a blunt fashion, or you can give it a little spin, which he does. I remember, they had all our wives on one Christmas. Together, behind us. And Gordon guessed it, I don't know how he figured it out. And his question was marvellous. He said, 'Have I slept with any of you?'"

And, like Sinclair, Berton has always been aware of the importance of teamwork on the program:

"All of the panel members like and respect each other. I don't think the show would work if this weren't so. You know, Gordon's a kook and I disagree with him a lot, but I love the guy, I think he's a great guy and I admire him. And Betty (Kennedy) and Gordon work well together, and Fred and Betty and I are old friends, too. I think that if there was a tension between the panelists that would show up instantly to the viewer."

Bernard "Bunny" Cowan was the "Front Page Challenge" announcer through most of its lifetime, the man whose voice accompanied the film footage re-creating the events surrounding the headline. Cowan said of Berton:

"Pierre is a very successful socialist in a capitalist environment, who is incorporated. And the irony is that he's incorporated and Gordon isn't, and refuses to be. Yet, Pierre Berton espouses certain socialist causes with a passion and with an articulateness that you don't find on other programs because he has his image to project and he knows what his image is. He's secure with his image and he applies his image to every story that comes up."

Ray McConnell, the show's producer for nineteen years, offered another insight into Berton's personality:

"Pierre Berton doesn't take himself half so seriously as everybody thinks he does. From the control room I can see him when he's not on-camera. Pierre doodles. He does clever caricatures of guests, the panel, himself. I have some of these cartoons on my office walls."

When Berton first joined the program, Fred Davis had difficulty getting close to him. He thought Berton a "cold fish." Fred added, "He inhibits me. I can't get next to him." He once asked a friend and colleague about this. "He's inordinately shy," Barbara Moon told him. "He's not a slap-you-on-the-back type."

Davis added: "He is still shy, but he covers it up with bravado and all his success."

Pierre didn't often bother to defend himself, but he did tell Knowlton Nash:

"Over the years, I've developed a skin as thick as an elephant. You have to in our business. I don't care what they say. I was attacked viciously for asking tough questions on 'Front Page Challenge.' I was the villain. Gordon was never the villain."

Berton's reputation for arrogance was noticed by others on the program. Steve Hyde, for many years the show's studio director, commented on Pierre's apparent arrogance: "Pierre was probably the most unpopular with the crews because they found him very snobby, very aloof. He was all for the working man but he didn't want to rub shoulders with them."

(Hyde was never known for his tact. When Indira Gandhi was a guest challenger, she was slow in getting seated, so Hyde hurried her up with: "Put your little ass over here right now, dearie." Another challenger Hyde "welcomed" was Isaac Stern, the world-famous, pudgy violinist. "Sit here, Tubs," said Steve.)

In a way, the most enigmatic figure on "Front Page Challenge" was "Mr. Smooth"—the moderator, Fred Davis.

He, too, was an experienced performer well before "Front Page Challenge" came along. In his youth, in Ottawa, he studied trumpet and was determined to become a full-time jazz musician.

"I loved and still do love music. It was very gratifying being a musician, but I think I made the right decision. I hope I'm a better moderator than I am a trumpet player."

That he became a consummate television moderator, particularly on "Front Page Challenge," is beyond dispute. Anyone who ever watched the show was aware of his coolness, his cordiality with guests, his warm rapport with both panelists and challengers and his remarkable ability to remain calm at all times, even in the face of awkward exchanges between a panelist and a challenger or, on occasion, a distinguished guest whose feathers were ruffled after a grilling by Berton or Sinclair.

Throughout his long and distinguished career in television, Davis earned and kept the respect and admiration of virtually everyone he ever worked with.

Berton: "Fred was a genius at what he did in that he made it look so casual and so easy."

Betty Kennedy: "If you could think of anything that could go wrong, Fred would think of it. Of all of us, he was the biggest worrier. And yet he always came off as though he didn't have a care in the world, as though everything was smooth as silk."

Jack Webster: "Fred was the man with an iron grip inside his suede glove. I never had a cross word with him in all the years I worked with him."

His success on "Front Page Challenge" led to many other offers of work, some of which he turned down. He had a long, happy association with Du Maurier, doing cigarette commercials and then hosting the company's various new talent showcases. But he turned down a lucrative offer from General Motors.

His agent in New York wanted him to move there because he would find plenty of good work in television in the United States, but he promptly rejected it:

"I really didn't want to make the move," he told me. "The business was good to me here and I think the longevity factor if you're making it in Canada is a little better than in the United States. You can be a hero one year (in the U.S.) and a bum the next. Also I'm a nationalist; I wanted my kids to grow up here."

Not many people, least of all the viewers, had any idea what Fred was like on the inside, how much of an effort it was for him to convey convincingly that calm, cool, always-in-command image.

As Pierre Berton told Knowlton Nash:

"I think you might have cast Fred on the enigma side. Fred was not a man who revealed himself in public. One of the things that really didn't come across was that he was very, very funny. He had a crackling wit."

In an interview with me, Berton said: "I happen to know that each show night Fred's stomach turns flip-flops as he enters the studio and sets his stopwatch. I doubt he would be successful if he felt any other way. He is a man who knows better than to take his work for granted."

Davis himself acknowledged that the public image of him as cool and calm was off the mark: "I was supposed to be 'Mr. Relaxed,'" he told me, "yet all the ulcer juices were going inside. That was the toughest thing."

The Davis temper was almost always kept in check, but it *was* there, as some of his colleagues were to learn.

"When he let go, and he very seldom did," said Allan Fotheringham, "but when Fred let go offstage…it was ballistic. It didn't last long, but he could dish it out."

FPC producer Ray McConnell: "Fred had a volcano boiling inside him. But you wouldn't see any bursts of anger in public. You might have seen things slammed down sometimes."

Once, in an airport coffee shop, waiting to board a plane for the trip back to Toronto from Yellowknife, Davis's mood was decidedly grouchy. "He had a face that said life is not worth living," McConnell recalled. Then Jack Webster came along and set down his old tartan suitcase. Fred looked at the bag, muttered "Jesus Christ!" and kicked the big suitcase halfway across the coffee shop.

"I only saw him get mad twice in fifteen years," reported studio director Steve Hyde. "Fred had to be perfect and always wanted to know which camera he was working to well ahead of air time. Once, they were busy in the control room and didn't tell him. He got mad, threw down his pencil and said, 'I won't do a fucking thing until someone tells me what my camera is.' Fred was Mr. Cool outside and Mr. Uptight inside."

Davis himself admitted to his failing in an interview with Knowlton Nash:

"Yes, I've been known to blow my cool on occasion off-camera. I try to keep that part of my nature hidden because you never accomplish anything if you flare up at somebody. The older I get, I think I get a little more crotchety. I want things to go smoothly. Also, I don't want to sit at the back of the bus. I want to go first-class. I figure I've earned it. I want to be rested and prepared if I'm going to do a job, and if there are arrangements that won't work, I might give vent to my feelings. You can't be Mr. Nice Guy all the time."

These people—Gordon, Toby, Pierre and Fred—were the chief strength of "Front Page Challenge" during those first four years when it rose from obscurity to national prominence.

There were other important personalities too, of course, and their contributions to the ongoing popularity of the show must also be acknowledged.

chapter 4

MERCHANTS
OF GLOOM

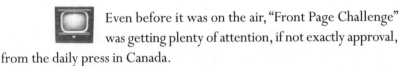 Even before it was on the air, "Front Page Challenge" was getting plenty of attention, if not exactly approval, from the daily press in Canada.

My own column, in the *Toronto Telegram*, may not have carried the first announcement of the projected summer-replacement program, but it wasn't too far behind.

On May 16, 1957, this item appeared in my column:

"Look for a panel show based on news stories...Tentative title is Front Page Challenge, the idea being that a panel (perhaps of newspapermen) will meet people who have had some connection with a big story and will then try to identify the story."

A month later, Scott Young told his readers (in the *Globe and Mail*) about the experience of auditioning for FPC. He described Harvey Hart (the show's first producer) as "a nice chap, dark and jovial and diplomatic," and wrote about the gatherings in Hart's basement, where "we played the game, enjoyed it, laughed a great deal, changed the rules, ate vastly of grapes, melons, pineapple, oranges, cakes, drank coffee and went home about midnight."

A week or so later, Scott was one of a group of eight finalists called back for another run-through, this time in a CBC studio. "We had Win Barron as moderator, we toiled from nine to midnight, and we were paid."

When he got home that night, Scott related, his wife asked how he had made out. He said he'd had a good time.

"Think you made it?" she inquired.

"No."

"Who do you think did?"

"Toby Robins, Gordon Sinclair and Alex Barris."

He added, in his column: "There is no use being falsely modest about how I arrived at those three. I have a logical mind. Toby Robins is prettier than I am, Gordon Sinclair is older and Alex Barris is thinner."

In the end this may have been one of the more accurate predictions made in the press about "Front Page Challenge." The panelists he predicted would win did, and Scott Young himself was the guest panelist on the very first show, and made a number of other subsequent appearances.

Many years later, Young told me that shortly after that tongue-in-cheek column was published he ran into Toby Robins at the CBC and learned that she was very upset by what he had written. She felt it was "nasty," especially to Sinclair and me. Young was taken aback by her reaction, and a little hurt at the realization that she hadn't understood he was kidding.

"Front Page Challenge" hit the airwaves on Monday night, June 24, 1957, and the press was generally unimpressed. Indeed, much of the press's coverage was on the snide side.

William Drylie, a columnist for the *Toronto Star*, was away in New York the night the program had its debut, but that didn't stop him from reviewing it:

"Spies accuse me of sneaking off to New York to escape Front Page Challenge," he wrote a few days later. "They also assure us the thing died, although the corpse will be kept around for weeks yet, perhaps for autopsy purposes."

A week later, having actually seen the second program in the series, Drylie told his readers: "After a long hard look at Front Page

Challenge some of us think disaster is not far off. We're convinced thirty minutes can be a long, long time."

(At the risk of appearing to be paranoid, I feel it should be pointed out that the fierce rivalry between the *Toronto Star* and the *Telegram* in those days might have been a factor in Drylie's relentless carping about the show. Many years later, when somebody else in the *Star* was writing a retrospective article about the long-running series, the argument was made that the CBC had not kept to its announced intention of using newspaper people on the original panel, dismissing me as "a CBC regular." The fact is, when the program began I had been a Toronto newspaperman for a decade.)

The *Telegram's* TV critic, Ron Poulton, was marginally more tolerant, perhaps out of a sense of loyalty to a colleague: "Comparisons between the debut of Front Page Challenge, June 24, and its second CBC-TV show Monday night are inevitable. The pace had been increased—but only to the point where the first looked like a tortoise in full flight and the second moved like a small boy bound for school."

Later in the summer, Poulton aimed another dart at "Front Page Challenge": "This week's first contestant was a lady who stopped the Royal procession of 1951 on Bloor Street when she was being rushed to a hospital to give birth to a daughter. When she was asked by one panelist if she had been 'involved' in the incident (the moderator) answered: 'Partly.' Leading me to wonder how involved one can get."

What Poulton neglected to mention in his column was that the pregnant lady was representing the story of the Royal Tour, not the birth of her baby.

A review in the *Ottawa Citizen* voiced a different complaint: "Some of moderator Win Barron's answers to the panel's questions are so misleading that he might be expected to show up with his nose in a cast some week, but so far the panel has been slow to anger. Personally, I'd rather see some good lively cheating than so much dull sincerity."

The press in western Canada tended to ignore the new panel show from Toronto, no doubt on the traditional theory that anything from that far east couldn't be of much interest to westerners. Papers in Vancouver,

Calgary and Winnipeg deigned to list the new network series during the first few weeks, but that was about it.

Indeed, the *Vancouver Sun* erroneously listed "The Denny Vaughan Show" for Monday, June 24, even though the debut of "Front Page Challenge" had been announced to the press by the CBC several weeks earlier. The first longer mention of the new program to be found in the *Vancouver Sun* was in that paper's TV supplement of August 13—seven weeks later. Under "Monday Highlights," it informed its readers: "Former *Vancouver Sun* writer Pierre Berton is guest star on Front Page Challenge..."

But by mid-July, Ron Poulton had written in the *Telegram*: "Now that the panel has found more to talk and smile about, it (FPC) might even attract enough of a following to warrant its continuance as a regular, instead of just a summer show."

However, the *Star's* Bill Drylie wasn't letting up. One week he went to the studio to watch the show from the control booth: "Front Page Challenge seemed better Monday, but shows always look better from the studio. Other viewers say it hasn't improved."

At least one viewer liked the show enough to write to the *Toronto Star* asking that it "please stop panning Front Page Challenge. I know people around Toronto compare these quiz shows with those on American networks, which is okay for those where there are many channels available. Here, however, in North Bay, with only one channel available, please leave our one and only network quiz alone..."

In September, Drylie tossed another brick: "Just incidentally, of course, but FPC's live audience Monday was way down, with more empty seats in the bleachers than you'd see at a Balmy Beach game in driving snow."

Nevertheless, by August the CBC had decided to keep "Front Page Challenge" on the air beyond the summer, as a regular replacement for Denny Vaughan's musical variety series. Some critics who had not been notably supportive of Denny Vaughan's show during its three years on the air began shedding copious public tears over its cancellation. The *Vancouver Sun*, which had failed to publish any serious appraisal of "Front Page Challenge" during its first ten weeks on the air, carried a story expressing outrage over the CBC's dropping the Vaughan show from the fall schedule. (Vaughan

The first program. Gordon Sinclair, Toby Robins, Alex
Barris and Scott Young were the panelists.

Beautiful Toby and hairdresser Jimmy Keeler.

The first 'important' international guest the program landed was Mrs. Eleanor Roosevelt.

Fred Davis and early guest panelist Mike Wallace, who wanted to do the program in the U.S.

Ottawa's Mayor Charlotte Whitton proved an outspoken challenger.

'America's Sweetheart,' Mary Pickford, was born in Toronto as Gladys Smith.

Challenger Errol Flynn had fun mystifying Sinclair, Robins and Young.

A young Alex Trebek was an early guest panelist on the program.

Betty Kennedy and guest panelist Peter Worthington.
His father was a challenger on that show.

In 1972, the spouses of the program's regulars were mystery challengers. (Gladys Sinclair, Gerhard Kennedy, Janet Burton and Jo Davis.) The guest panelist is Bill Walker.

Prime Minister Trudeau being quizzed by Pierre Berton.

Sinclair, Kennedy, guest panelist Mavor Moore and Berton had trouble identifying Groucho Marx.

Newspaper tycoon
Roy Thomson
proved a feisty
challenger.

Randolph Churchill,
son of Winston,
looked soberer
than he was.

TV interviewer David Frost was accompanied to the studio by Diahann Carroll.
She drew more attention than he did.

Guest panelist
Marilyn MacDonald
and Berton try to
identify Ed Sullivan.

Music director Lucio Agostini and his small but effective
Front Page Challenge orchestra.

moved to Montreal and later returned to television, appearing on various CBC radio and TV shows, among them "The Wayne and Shuster Hour.")

Most critics were stunned into uncharacteristic silence. Not much press notice was taken of the summer program's evident survival and its renewal for the fall/winter season.

Even those connected with the program were a little surprised at its success in surviving the thirteen-week summer tryout. Not every summer-replacement show was that resilient.

John Aylesworth recalled that at about this time Gordon Sinclair called him and producer Harvey Hart aside for a serious chat.

"I want to caution you on this," Aylesworth remembered Sinclair saying. "I'm fifty-seven years old. If this show is a hit and goes on a long time, shouldn't you get a younger man?"

"And we all laughed," Aylesworth added. "And Gordon said, 'What the hell, suppose it goes for ten years?'"

Hart and Axlesworth laughed some more at Sinclair's overactive imagination and assured him he was worrying over nothing.

By the following year, "Front Page Challenge" had begun to build a substantial and loyal audience, but it still failed to charm some newspaper critics. One of the more controversial programs of 1958 dealt with fluoridation of water—a subject on which Gordon Sinclair was almost fanatic in his opposition. He invariably referred to it as "rat poison." The challenger was Dr. Wesley Dunn and the headline was: "Vancouver Approves Fluoridation."

Writing in the *Ottawa Citizen*, journalist Bob Blackburn said:

"I thought Sinclair rather made an ass of himself by repeatedly yelling about people dumping rat poison in his water supply, while the others were trying to argue reasonably..."

The chorus of damnation (or, at least, scornful dismissal) from the news media simply would not let up. Not for years.

In December 1962, Gerry Barker wrote in the *Toronto Star*:

"There is good reason to believe that Front Page Challenge will have its last front page at the conclusion of the season."

And ten days later, the same paper's Bill Drylie had picked up the scent:

"How right can I be? I said Front Page Challenge wouldn't last. Now, after six years on TV, it's going to fold."

The following month, Drylie was on the warpath again:

"When Front Page Challenge dies at the end of this season, CBC viewers may be in for a bonus. Flashback may die with it. Logic seems to dictate killing off the cheap imitation if the original and genuine article must go."

("Flashback," a panel show that started in 1959, lasted for five years. FPC managed to keep going for a mere thirty-eight years.)

When "Front Page Challenge" began its ninth season, in the fall of 1965, a familiar cry was heard from the *Toronto Star*:

"Front Page Challenge has had its day, served its purpose and should be withdrawn from the schedule next year for a new program—any program, regardless of format, content or personalities."

In 1966, Gordon Sinclair missed a few programs due to a mild illness. The night he returned to the panel, one of the challengers was the Rev. Kenneth Greet, who had been involved in preparing a pamphlet called *Sex and Morality* for the British Council of Churches.

On the program, the Methodist pastor said that one of the problems his council faced was the matter of how to discuss sexual intercourse with an older generation that was still shocked by four-letter words.

"What about three-letter words?" asked Gordon. "What's wrong with a word like 'lay'?"

In the next day's *Toronto Star*, Roy Shields wrote slyly: "You don't have to be a doctor to realize that Sinclair is healthy again."

Now and then, the program got some unexpected support from the press. In 1970, for example, the *Toronto Star* carried a story in which Fred Davis was hailed as "the very model of a model moderator—congenial, sincere, self-assured, and so infuriatingly perfect in everything he does that one might think he's been cleverly programmed against every contingency that might arise, like a superbly constructed robot."

The same article said of the panel: "One would have to go a long way to find a better quartet of personalities for a television panel show and it's no wonder it has lasted as long as it has, nor that its future looks so secure."

But that kind of press was a rare exception to the rule.

Even in 1971, the program's fourteenth year on the air, it was still subjected to the occasional slings and arrows of outrageous critics.

In January of that year, Bob Blackburn (by then writing for the *Toronto Telegram*) took the program to task because the microphone of a challenger didn't work and because a studio monitor had been facing the panel, thereby making it easy for the panelists to see the mystery guest.

"C'mon guys," beefed Blackburn, "how many seasons does it take before you get it right?"

A few weeks later, on March 2, Blackburn wrote:

"Front Page Challenge turned up Miss Nude World as one of the challengers. Fully clothed, she was. Where's the fun in that? She was chosen by a panel of judges which included Gordon Sinclair. That should have been fun, too, but nothing happened. People just kept asking her what she was going to do for an encore. Ho hum. The other guest was some baseball player whom we were all supposed to know, evidently."

The name of the presumably obscure baseball player "we were all supposed to know" was an obscure New York Yankee slugger named Mickey Mantle. Mr. Blackburn evidently never got around to perusing the sports pages.

During the 1976–77 season, "Front Page Challenge" visited Vancouver (not for the first time) to do some shows there. One critic, Michael Bennett, of the *Province*, commenting on one of the shows, said it was "about as exciting as the annual wallpaper festival for art deco apprentices."

Perhaps understandably, during the program's lengthy life, the press paid most attention to "Front Page Challenge" when something startling or controversial occurred on the air. Curiously, the appearance of almost any unusual challenger rarely raised eyebrows in the press—not hawkish Vietnam generals nor long-haired sixties hippies nor fringe-party politicians nor even the madam of a Nevada brothel. But if any panelist was perceived as being rude to a challenger, the item was reported—and the mail flowed in.

One such occasion was the appearance, in 1980, of Prince Edward Island's premier, Angus MacLean. The headline dealt with the thorny issue of the constitution, over which Prime Minister Trudeau and eight of the provincial premiers were bitterly divided.

Mr. MacLean described himself as "a Prince Edward Islander, a Maritimer and a Canadian—and in that order."

The panel, all rather ardent nationalists, pulled no punches in interviewing Mr. MacLean and he gave not an inch of ground. It was a lively interview, though it settled nothing, of course.

The press, however, had a field day, and some of the public reacted. According to Carroll Hicks, then a production assistant on the program, the show received a lot of mail, much of it from Prince Edward Island, but also from western Canada. Fred Davis was criticized for not interrupting the interview and for not telling Berton he was being rude. And Betty Kennedy received a copy of an editorial damning her for saying something she insisted she never said.

Another way the press showed interest in "Front Page Challenge" was when there were rumours (however unlikely) that the CBC was throwing away public money on this or any other program. There was one such incident in the show's second year on the air.

Lady Nora Docker, a wealthy and colourful eccentric, appeared on the program in relation to a story about her being kicked out of Monaco. Her husband, Lord Bernard Docker, accompanied her to Toronto from England, as did their son.

Press reports included one to the effect that the Dockers and their son were brought to Canada by the program for two weeks with all expenses paid. Totally wrong.

In fact, the Dockers were paid just over $2,000, but that went mostly for return fare for the three of them (by sea, because Lord Docker didn't like flying), so they didn't exactly get rich on Canadian tax dollars.

A quarter of a century later, when CBC Enterprises, the publishing arm of the corporation, issued a video of highlights from "Front Page Challenge" during its thirty years on the air, a *Toronto Star* columnist did a big "exposé" article about Canadian taxpayers footing the bill for this and other CBC videos then being issued. His argument was that since these videos were not to be found in many stores and had to be ordered through CBC

Enterprises, Canadians had to pay sales tax and also postage and handling on all such videos. At no point in his article did he mention whether or not the videos were any good.

No story in the program's thirty-eight-year history attracted as much press (and public) outrage as the one that aired on the Monday, January 20, 1969 show. (You will have noticed, perhaps, that after a dozen years on the air, the program still retained its Monday-night time slot.) That was the night when Elaine Tanner, the young Canadian swimmer who had won a collection of seven medals in the 1967 Pan-American Games, held in Winnipeg, was a challenger on the show.

During the interview, Sinclair said that when he was young it was taken for granted that girls did not swim during their menstrual period. "Now," he added, "they swim no matter what. Is there any explanation?"

"Well, no," said the young swimmer.

"You just go right ahead and swim."

"Yes."

"Thank you."

That was the full extent of the exchange between Sinclair and the swimmer. If Elaine was embarrassed, she covered it well. The show proceeded. Jack Hutchinson, the program's writer at the time, recalled: "She handled it really well. She was not upset. She took it in her stride."

A couple of days later, however, the *Vancouver Sun* columnist Les Wedman voiced his outrage:

"No, Gordon Sinclair doesn't bother me because I just don't watch Front Page Challenge, but I'm more than willing to launch a Get Gordon week, month, year or any length of time it may take to get this boorish bore off the air. And there's only one legitimate way to do it and that is for all viewers of the same mind to write to Front Page Challenge producer Don Brown... Don't scold, threaten, plead or admonish. Merely let him know that his show won't be welcome in your home unless and until Gordon Sinclair is retired. There have been complaints about this crude, rude panelist but they're all mild compared to his latest insensitive insult when he stunned and embarrassed guest Elaine Tanner by demanding to know if she swam during her menstrual cycle."

(One could be forgiven for wondering how Wedman was so well informed as to the show's content when he began his tirade by claiming he
didn't watch it. Possibly Wedman was a graduate of the Bill Drylie School
of Absentee Journalism.)

Wedman was not alone in his outrage. Some 3,169 angry viewers wrote
to the CBC to complain about Sinclair. This was reported in the *Toronto Star*
by critic Patrick Scott, who added that the program's sponsors were concerned. Then, gazing searchingly into his crystal ball, Scott predicted that
Sinclair would be "the only survivor of Front Page Challenge's present
panel."

And a British Columbia M.P. (Ray Perrault) told the House of Commons
broadcast committee that he had received "an unprecedented number of
protests" in his mail about "the improper line of questioning" pursued by
Sinclair in this exchange.

Producer Don Brown recalled that he was taken to lunch by "the brass,"
who wanted to know what he was going to do about Sinclair. "I'm not
going to do anything about him," Brown told them. He pointed out that
the program had received as much mail praising Sinclair's outspoken-
ness as it got letters damning him. The brass, he added, said "fine."

Sinclair himself magnanimously offered to resign from the program,
an offer that was promptly rejected by Brown, who evidently was aware
of the value to the program of publicity—even negative publicity.

In April 1973, the *Toronto Star* carried a story from Ottawa about a
Newfoundland member of Parliament, Walter Carter, who told the House
of Commons broadcasting committee that the CBC was "over-loaded with
Toronto-oriented hacks," and he mentioned Gordon Sinclair and Pierre
Berton. Mr. Carter told the *Star* that Sinclair was "egotistical and over-
rated," Davis was "a powder puff" and Berton was a "know-it-all."

Three years later, on the program's twentieth anniversary program,
Elaine Tanner was back as a challenger. After the program, she was photographed kissing Gordon Sinclair on the cheek—evidence that she had
long since forgiven him his shocking transgression.

The day after the hour-long twentieth anniversary program aired, in
1976, Jack Miller wrote in the *Toronto Star* that it was a dull show by "Front

Page Challenge" standards, "more evidence of the almost mystical staying power of the quiz that in its spectacular span has paraded the principals of the world's biggest stories for a generation before the Canadian audience."

In 1982, at the start of the twenty-fifth year of "Front Page Challenge," the president of the CBC, A. W. "Al" Johnson, sent a glowing telegram of congratulations to the program's regular panelists—Gordon Sinclair, Betty Kennedy and Pierre Berton, and also to moderator Fred Davis. It was the first (and last) time they were to be thus honoured by any CBC president. Predictably, Canada's press barely took notice of this event.

Five years later, there was an equally big "Front Page Challenge Special," marking the start of the program's thirtieth year on the air. Although some of Canada's press yawned, there was at least one notable exception.

The *Toronto Star* paid tribute to "Front Page Challenge" as "one of the great consistencies of TV since its humble beginnings as a summer fill-in show in 1957. Its formula never changes, its regular panelists are rarely switched and its ratings have always been around a million or more—close to two million in the early days."

It's interesting that for the most part Fred Davis was not attacked by the press, as were some of the panelists, especially Sinclair and Berton, and the program itself. Indeed, Fred was the recipient of a rather glowing appraisal by Frank Moritsugu, in the *Toronto Star*:

"Fred Davis is so good at what he does on Front Page Challenge that one rarely notices it. Confronted by an adroit panel whose job is to ask unexpected and provocative questions, and a series of varied guest challengers some of whom have never appeared on camera before, Davis smoothly keeps the weekly show moving with a quip here and a subtle lead there. He is rarely tricked by a tricky point during the guessing parts of the program. And his wind-up of guest appearances are the most graceful goodbye thank-yous done under the TV clock's unrelenting pressures."

Davis felt, in 1981, that the press had mellowed toward "Front Page Challenge": "There were the sour-grapes people early on who resented Pierre's or Gordon's success, but we've outlasted them. If the show has established a kind of institution-like quality, they're not going to get anywhere by knocking it. We're not going to be dumped because of what they

say, so they've given up on that. Also, there are more enlightened press
people now, who are not going to carp at (the show) for the wrong reasons. Criticize it if it deserves to be criticized, but don't give me this small-
time 'It's-been-on-too-long-so-dump-it."

The same year, Pierre Berton told me: "The demise of Front Page
Challenge had been regularly predicted. As you remember, Bill Drylie (in
the *Toronto Star*) made a lifetime work of predicting it would be off the
next year. Everybody said what a terrible program it was and everything—
dull. But there's something about television shows that go on long enough...
people get so used to them that they become like intimates."

Berton was also aware of how much the program had changed over the
years:

"Ray McConnell (the producer) made an interesting point about me. I
used to be known as the villain on the show, and I'm not now, and
McConnell said, 'You're still asking the same questions, you haven't changed
a bit, but the perceptions and the times have changed so you no longer
look villainous asking those questions."

Whatever Canada's press felt, or wrote, about "Front Page Challenge,"
its popularity over the years continued. By the early 1980s, the program
was being viewed by anywhere from 1,500,000 to 3,000,000 Canadians.
In evaluating the importance of these numbers, however, it is important
to bear in mind another factor about television that is relevant to any mea-
surement of FPC's popularity.

The nature of the program made it virtually impossible for the CBC to
do normal publicity to help increase its viewership. This placed the show
at a disadvantage against other types of programs. For example, if Carol
Burnett announced on her program that Bing Crosby or Mary Martin was
to be a guest on the show the following week, she could be fairly sure of
some Crosby or Martin fans as additional viewers. Or, if Ed Sullivan mentioned that the Beatles were scheduled to appear on an upcoming show,
it was a fair bet his ratings for that particular week would shoot up. Even
drama programs could promote the upcoming appearance of a big-name
Hollywood or Broadway star (a Henry Fonda, say, or a Julie Harris) to en-
sure a shot in the arm to the program's ratings.

However, any show that dealt in surprises—"Front Page Challenge" or American game/panel shows like "What's My Line?" or "I've Got A Secret" couldn't do that, for obvious reasons. Therefore, it says something about the loyalty of the viewers of such programs that they watched without knowing in advance what stars might turn up. Incidentally, it's significant that "Front Page Challenge" outlived not only all other Canadian game shows, but both the popular American panel shows mentioned above.

Ironically, the biggest play the program ever got in Canada's newspapers was in April 1995, at the conclusion of its thirty-eighth year on the air, when it was suddenly and unceremoniously cancelled. Some of the country's major newspapers considered the demise of "Front Page Challenge" important enough to rate front page space. Some of the press coverage of the television program's sudden cancellation even managed to hint at a note of regret, but only barely. Jim Bawden, the television critic for the *Toronto Star*, quoted Ray McConnell, the CBC producer who had helmed the program for nineteen years, as saying: "Sad, that's how I feel..."

During its record-smashing run, "Front Page Challenge" played host to leading political figures and statesmen, renowned scientists, stage and screen stars, bizarre daredevils, astronauts and ambassadors, unsung heroes, spies and former spies, champions and charlatans. Everybody loved winners, so the program had numerous Oscar, Grammy and Juno winners; Olympic medalists; hockey, baseball and boxing stars; and no less than five Nobel Prize winners—Martin Luther King, Lester B. Pearson, Dr. Linus Pauling, Dr. Charles Best and Dr. Gerhard Herzberg, three of them Canadians.

Dr. King was a challenger on the program in 1959. Nine years later, when Malcolm X was on the show, guest panelist Charles Templeton asked if it was true that the challenger had once called King an "Uncle Tom."

Said Malcolm X: "I never called him an Uncle Tom. I would say that Uncle Martin is my friend."

The poised, articulate Black Muslim leader went on to comment that he didn't think Dr. King's approach to achieving desegregation was doomed to failure. (A few months later, Malcolm X was assassinated.)

Over the years, "Front Page Challenge" explored many serious issues, often from divergent points of view, over a period of time.

To cite but one example, the program tackled the then still-thorny issue of McCarthyism, the witch-hunting phenomenon of the 1950s that drew its name from the controversial tactics of Wisconsin Senator Joe McCarthy, who accused virtually everyone who disagreed with him of entertaining Communist sympathies.

In 1957, its first year of existence, "Front Page Challenge" featured Joseph Welsh, the erudite lawyer whose masterful handling of the televised Army–McCarthy hearings helped to deflate the McCarthy balloon.

Two years later, Herbert Philbrick, a former Communist turned FBI informant, was a challenger on the show.

In 1965, John Henry Faulk, a New York radio personality whose career was destroyed by the McCarthy era blacklisting, appeared on the show.

In 1968, Roy Cohn, McCarthy's chief aide and most loyal defender, was a mystery guest on "Front Page Challenge."

And in 1975, Ben Barzman, one of the numerous Hollywood writers victimized by the blacklist, was a challenger. (He was not one of the famous "Hollywood ten," but escaped prosecution by leaving the country.)

The late Barbara Frum, a frequent and effective guest panelist on "Front Page Challenge," summed up the program's achievements in 1982:

"Front Page Challenge has done more good raw journalism for the past twenty-five years than a lot of pretentious, expensive public affairs programs."

Sometimes even the challengers, particularly Canadian ones, voiced their feelings about the value of being on the program. In 1976, when singer Burton Cummings was a challenger on the program, he said: "At last, my mother will think of me as a star."

chapter 5

"TONIGHT'S GUEST PANELIST..."

The very nature of "Front Page Challenge" imposed a number of serious burdens on the show's producers, most notably in the matter of getting publicity for the program. Because it was vital that the panelists not know in advance the identity of the challengers on any given show, stringent precautions were taken to avoid any mishaps that could spoil the fundamental spontaneous aspect of the show.

(Perhaps inevitably, there were always a few cynics around who convinced themselves that "Front Page Challenge" was "fixed"—especially following the TV quiz-show scandals in the United States in the late 1950s. These detractors were wrong, of course, if for no other reason than that there was no big money involved in FPC, no fat jackpots to be won, no $64,000 prizes to be awarded. Besides, even if anyone involved in the production had entertained such a notion, people like Berton, Davis, et al., would have taken no part in such perfidy.)

Strict precautions notwithstanding, on a few occasions there were mishaps—a panelist inadvertently running into a visiting friend and learning the friend was slated to be on the program that night, for example. When that happened, the panelist would invariably disqualify him- or herself from that round.

For the most part, the panelists were sincere in wanting the game to be on the up and up, seeking no special edge or inside information that would enable them to show off their prowess by guessing a story to which they had somehow been tipped off. There were occasional, if rare, exceptions.

One show night Gordon Sinclair "happened" to walk into the Ports of Call, a restaurant near the studio where that night's challengers were having dinner. The panelists knew this was where the challengers went for dinner and had been warned to stay away from the restaurant. Roger McKean, in charge of arranging the dinners and making sure the security was maintained, spotted Sinclair at the bar, walked over to him and asked him to leave. I remember telling him later that his walk out of the forbidden restaurant reminded me of a hockey player skating to the penalty box.

McKean proved to be a valuable addition to the "Front Page Challenge" team. A former public relations man, McKean bought his uncle's jewellery store in Galt, Ontario, but each week, on show day, he journeyed to Toronto and devoted his time to the care and feeding of VIPs visiting Toronto to appear on the panel show.

"The dinners are the most fascinating part of the job," McKean told an interviewer. "You get a chance to know what these people are like. On the whole, I find that in private ninety percent of them are very genuine people—interested in what's going on in the world, interested in you, very good company."

Producer Jim Guthro commented on McKean: "It takes a special kind of person to handle the job. You need someone very flexible, unobtrusive, a man who can sublimate his own feelings."

McKean was all of that: a tall, distinguished-looking man, he was soft-spoken and civil, gentle in his handling of celebrities, but tough enough to lay down the law to Sinclair on that occasion when he "wandered" into the restaurant where the guests were dining. He stayed with the show for several years.

For its own promotional purposes, the program usually informed the local press, in advance of a program, of the impending arrival of some famous person. The papers were given the opportunity to interview the celebrity, provided that the interview be published only after the program had aired.

Usually, the paper would go along with this procedure. And who could blame them? Within months after its birth, "Front Page Challenge" was attracting a wide range of appealing, sometimes compelling, guest challengers. Here were interesting, otherwise unavailable names that the papers could splash across their pages, provided only that they respect the release time and not try to scoop the television program.

And yet, on a few occasions, one or another of the Toronto papers revealed the arrival in town of some distinguished person to appear on "Front Page Challenge," which tended to ruin that night's show, at least from the standpoint of the panel's guessing the identity of the challenger.

(Some press people were still tipped off about incoming guests, but on a selective basis; that is, editors or columnists who could be trusted to respect the ground rules were notified. During the four years that I wrote the show, I often managed to get brief interviews with visiting celebrities, but I made sure they were never printed until after the program had aired.)

It soon became apparent that the best, or, at any rate, the safest, way to get publicity for the program was by announcing who the guest panelist on any given night was going to be. This practice was especially productive in the early days, when the announced appearance of some noted person as a guest panelist was considered newsworthy. Famous American guest panelists included Bennett Cerf, Drew Pearson, Mike Wallace, David Brinkley, Marguerite Higgins, Bob Considine, Morley Safer and Walter Cronkite, all of whom were guest panelists during those days. (It was on "Front Page Challenge" in 1962, incidentally, that Cronkite first informed North American television viewers that he would soon be taking over the CBS evening news program, which was soon to bring him a level of fame and respect unequalled by any news anchor, anywhere.)

Over the years there were also numerous Canadian guest panelists whose names were impressive on the "Front Page Challenge" celebrity list, such as Gordon Pinsent, Barbara Hamilton, Scott Young, Barbara Frum, Peter Gzowski, June Callwood, Mavor Moore, Max Ferguson, Judy

LaMarsh, Lloyd Robertson, Adrienne Clarkson, Charles Templeton, Gary Lautens and Lister Sinclair.

Being a guest panelist on the program, however, was anything but an easy chore. Most guest panelists, especially on their first appearance, felt intimidated and ill at ease, certain the regular panelists had an advantage over them. This was not because they were any less qualified or intelligent or poised, but because they were not as familiar with the routine of the show, and the specific demands the program made on panelists, as the regulars were.

Betty Kennedy recognized that guest panelists often fought an uphill battle:

"It's much tougher on the guest panelists, because they don't have the rhythm of the team. And I think also it's harder on the guest (panelist) because he's so nervous he can't listen, and if you can't listen you probably ask something that's already been asked."

Pierre Berton also once commented on this:

"Guest panelists have a terrible time on that show, anyway. My own feeling is that we should have a panel of about ten guest panelists and use them and make them part of the family, because I don't think that the guest panelists who are brought in from left field—I don't think it's fair to them."

At times, Berton could be sympathetic to guest panelists:

"I sometimes hand the guest panelist, if I think they're nervous, a list of areas to cover, so they'll have something to say. It doesn't matter if we get the story or not, but it's bad when they ask just a single question and pass to me in a state of absolute abject terror. So I'm the guy who sits next to them, so my job is to try to help them."

Unless, that is, he doesn't like a particular guest panelist:

"If I don't like them, to hell with them. The only one I wouldn't help was Charlotte Gobeil. She's a good-looking blonde French Canadian interviewer. She's a snob. She was on once before and she called Gordon a name which I didn't like, so…"

Never mind guest panelists brought in from left field. A number of guest panelists who would qualify as mainstream also felt intimidated on "Front Page Challenge." A few examples will illustrate the point.

After one of his appearances as a guest panelist, an experience in which he referred to himself as "a goldfish among the piranhas," Peter Gzowski wrote about the experience for the *Toronto Star*:

"I was chatting—or trying to chat—with Pierre Berton during the rehearsal of Front Page Challenge...when a thunderbolt of understanding cracked into my mind: These people are serious. After twenty-two years of doing what a more pretentious journalist I used to know called 'playing a parlor game for money,' they *care*. To Gordon Sinclair, Betty Kennedy and Berton, Front Page is a blood sport."

Berton still recalls an incident, during the program's first year on the air, when a famous guest panelist ended up feeling distinctly uncomfortable. The panelist was Drew Pearson, the widely read American columnist. "I don't know anything about Canada," the apprehensive Pearson told Berton.

"I told him it was an international show, with international stories and he'd have no problems," says Berton.

But one of the stories that night was about the 1950 discovery of the Chubb Crater, in the remote Ungava region of Quebec. "He didn't know anything about it," recalls Berton. "He gave me a look for that. I don't blame him."

One person who is probably uniquely qualified to assess the pitfalls of guest panelism is Lorraine Thomson, who had been in that role many times before an FPC producer hired her to work on staff.

"The regulars, Pierre, Betty and Gordon, talk in shorthand," she told me. "The guest panelist doesn't know who was on last week or the week before. The panel have been there so long they've got a routine."

George Bain, for many years a distinguished journalist with the *Globe and Mail* and later head of the School of Journalism at King's College in Halifax, was a guest panelist several times during his newspaper days. He always found it "a little intimidating" because the regular panelists knew all the rules by heart. "I recall not knowing how they performed this arcane art. They had devised methods of asking questions."

Once when Bain was on the program the mystery challenger was Bryce Mackasey, then a Liberal cabinet minister. Bain recognized Mackasey's "whisky Irish voice" but he didn't know whether or not to announce the fact. "I knew the voice," he recalled, "but I didn't know what to do—hang back or show off? . . . I hung back for a minute. I didn't know what the hell I was supposed to do. I finally blurted it out."

June Callwood had been a guest panelist so often on "Front Page Challenge" that she was regarded as a semi-regular. It was on a trip to New York that she learned a valuable lesson about that status.

She was invited to appear on a television talk show hosted by Virginia Graham. When she arrived at the studio, she was shunted aside by the regulars at the studio, virtually ignored by all.

"What I was struck by was that I was an outsider. Everybody knew one another, they all adored the makeup man, they all adored the hairdresser, the producer stuck his head in, they all adored him, too. They all adored one another and no one spoke to me at all."

The next time she did "Front Page Challenge," she viewed the experience through new eyes:

"I saw what we did. Hello, how are you, darling, there's Pierre, and oh, here comes Gordon, and here is Margaret doing makeup and here is Jimmy Keeler doing the hair, and oh, isn't this fun, we're all together.

"But I knew what the outsiders felt like. What we did—I'm calling myself one of the insiders here—habitually, was exactly what I'd been exposed to in New York. And it was awful. So I made it my business to find the guest (the guest panelist for the evening's other show) to take them around and introduce them and make up for everything that had ever been done to all the guests who had suffered as I had in New York. I never stopped being conscious of what it was like to walk into a dressing room where everybody was darling but you."

Juliette, the TV singing star, was an occasional guest panelist, but never felt comfortable with the regular panelists:

"They scared me. In the green room they're going over headlines and ideas and I'm sitting there wondering, 'Oh, God, what am I doing here?' They took it so damn seriously. And on the air you had to jump in because they didn't let go of their questioning. They were not generous at all— so very competitive. You were strictly on your own."

On the other hand, Bill Walker, a guest panelist on several occasions, said he never felt intimidated or like an outsider. In 1967, when Walker was a guest panelist, one of the challengers was Dr. Benjamin Spock, the world-famous baby doctor who had by then become an outspoken foe of the Vietnam War. At one point, Dr. Spock referred to the conflict as an immoral war.

Bill Walker's rejoinder stopped the good doctor cold: "Would you mind defining a moral war?"

Barbara Frum, who became one of the most popular semi-regular guest panelists on FPC, talked about her own experiences and feelings about the show:

"It's a clean game. It's also a hard game. It's hard to do, and I don't know if people quite realize that. Especially for the guest (panelist). I mean, the regulars even know all the continents that begin with 'A.' I haven't done that since grade seven, so that was kind of hard.

"You're dying to turn around (to see who the challenger is). It is such decency on the part of the guest panelist not to turn around. Those other people are disciplined. One could always forgive a guest panelist, I always felt, for doing just a little twist. Sometimes I have to consciously say to myself, 'Don't turn around and look.'"

So, given all these problems and all this intimidation, why did journalists, broadcasters and other reasonably mature, bright people subject themselves to the fear and torture, the intimidation, the paranoia, the stage fright, the risk of humiliation, the ordeal of sitting between two regular panelists and trying to figure out who the hell was standing behind the panel and disguising his or her voice?

It couldn't have been just the money. When "Front Page Challenge" started, in 1957, guest panelists were paid $150 for an appearance. By 1980, the twenty-third year of the series, the fee for guest panelists skyrocketed—all the way up to a lavish $200.

So why did they do it? Authors were glad to appear as guest panelists so they could flog their latest book. Actors or performers could always use the exposure, plus a chance to plug a new movie. Politicians could rarely resist the temptation to lure, and possibly charm, a few potential voters.

Probably the chief reason it was not difficult to find guest panelists, particularly after the first year or so, was that this was "Front Page Challenge," not some lightweight game show or flighty interview-and-chat show sandwiched in between an old afternoon movie and the early evening news. This was the flagship show of the CBC's Light Entertainment Department, in prime time, and destined to become Canada's most popular panel show and, with the exception of NHL hockey, the longest-running series in the Corporation's history.

"Front Page Challenge" was on its way to becoming a Canadian institution. To be thought worthy enough to be asked to participate was not exactly unflattering. To be seen on the show, lumped in among those towering Canadian superstars, not to mention the world figures who so often turned up as challengers, was worth all the pitfalls and risks.

Perhaps the late Barbara Frum explained it best when I talked to her in 1981:

"My father-in-law was the ultimate "Front Page Challenge" viewer. It didn't matter how many things I did on 'As It Happens' that were superb. It didn't matter if I got to talk to Mr. Solzhenitsyn, it didn't matter if I got to talk to the original King Kong, the prime minister of South Africa or the prime minister of Canada.

"The great thrill, and I used to relish those moments when I could call him up and say, 'Guess what? I'm going to be on "Front Page Challenge."' That was his yardstick, that I had made it. He had no daughter, he only had my husband, his only child, but his thrill in life, towards the end of it, was me, and the ultimate thing I could do was be on 'Front Page Challenge.'

"As a matter of fact, I referred to it once on the show. Fred said, 'You're here, Barbara, because you've just written a book, and congratulations.' And I said, 'No, excuse me, Fred, I'm not here because I wrote a book. I'm here because it's the only thing that makes my father-in-law respect me."

For most guest panelists, occasional appearances on "Front Page Challenge" were regarded mostly as prestigious boosts to their standing in their other professional work: authors, performers, politicians, journalists, lawyers, sages. Few of them regarded these periodic guest appearances as anything more important than that, however pleasant they might be.

There were, however, a few exceptions. For instance, Lorraine Thomson, who started out in television as a dancer and later became an adroit interviewer, was one of the more reliable guest panelists on "Front Page Challenge," making dozens of appearances in that role. In 1970, producer Don Brown hired her to work on the program's staff, mostly to book guests. She lasted in that post for some twenty years and leaving it was her own decision, based, as was Toby Robins's decision, on personal priorities.

During that time, besides her work with the program, Thomson found time to do other television work. By then, she had become a recognized TV personality herself, and for several years she hosted a CBC television program called "V.I.P." It was a kind of spin-off of "Front Page Challenge."

The initials stood for Very Interesting People, and Thomson lured lots of them to the show, including a good many of the celebrities on "Front Page Challenge," who would finish their appearances on that show, then walk across the hall to another studio to be interviewed (on tape) by Lorraine, in a cozy, relaxed atmosphere, and for a longer period of time than was possible on "Front Page Challenge."

Two other frequent guest panelists on "Front Page Challenge" who made good use of their periodic appearances were Allan Fotheringham and Jack Webster, both of whom were destined to become regular members of the panel.

One of Fred Davis's fondest memories of "Front Page Challenge" was one night when Walter Cronkite was a guest panelist:

"A marvellous man. And I took a chance. You know, you think with these big-timers, they're so busy, or they want to be alone. And sometimes they end up in their hotel room with nothing to do. And I said, after the show, 'You wouldn't like to come home and have a cup of coffee or a drink, would you?' And he said, 'I'd love it.' And three of the most valuable hours I've ever had followed. Jo (then Mrs. Davis) and I and Walter Cronkite, sitting there."

chapter 6

SEARCHING
FOR STORIES

Once the show was on the air, it was up to the skilled panelists to track down the story and the challenger. Over the years they became phenomenally good at this, and even better at the interview that followed.

Long before any of this could happen, it was up to the show's producers, writers and researchers to come up with the stories and the challengers—not always as easy as it might seem.

From the outset, producers of "Front Page Challenge" were daring enough to try long shots in their quest for important guest challengers. This what-have-I-got-to-lose attitude took root in the very first season.

Harvey Hart, the program's first producer, even tried to lure former U.S. president Harry Truman, then aged 73:

"I remember somehow I got Harry Truman's phone number in Independence, Missouri, and I called, just for the hell of it. I expected to hear 'The Missouri Waltz' in the background. And, lo and behold, who answers the phone? Harry Truman. So I spoke to him and I described it (the program) to him, but I think at the time it was getting a little dicey about travelling, for him. But he sounded interested and was very civil. It was a series of incidents like that that made me feel, yes, people might be interested."

Not every idea worked out, not every challenger was eager and willing to appear on the program, and not every challenger was worth the bother it sometimes entailed.

John Aylesworth, creator and first writer of the series, once got it into his head to go to New York to find a witness to a notorious gangland murder—the slaying of Albert Anastasia in the barbershop of a Manhattan hotel. After striking out with several tight-lipped barbers, obviously savvy enough to deny having witnessed a gangland slaying, he went into the flower shop next door, which was separated from the barbershop only by a glass partition. There, he spoke to an employee who readily admitted he had actually witnessed the execution—through the glass partition. Aylesworth gleefully booked the man to come to Toronto as a challenger. But, the following week, when the man turned up on the program, quite possibly alerted to the dangers of such candor by the more cautious barbers on the other side of the glass partition, he left his memory behind: he now (on the air) said he had heard some shots but had seen nothing. The interview was a total dud.

Another time during the first summer of the series, Aylesworth tried to get John T. Scopes as a challenger. Scopes was the Dayton, Tennessee, schoolteacher who had been tried, in July 1925, and convicted of teaching Darwinism, thus arousing the ire of Christian fundamentalists in the Bible belt. He was convicted and fined a token $100. The Scopes Trial was a landmark case (Clarence Darrow defended Scopes and William Jennings Bryan was his equally famous and flamboyant foe) that attracted international press attention and was the basis for the play (and later, movie) *Inherit the Wind*.

Aylesworth reached Scopes, then 56 years old, but the man flatly refused to journey to Toronto to appear on the program. Eight years later, when I was writing the program, I went through the same chore of trying to entice Scopes to do the show. This time, the invitation was finally accepted, but it turned out to be a bad idea. Scopes was inarticulate, uncommunicative and dull, and his appearance on the program was a resounding flop.

Every one of the producers of "Front Page Challenge," from the beginning to the end, has a story or two about some of the attempts they made—sometimes having to resort to devious means—to lure appropriate challengers to the show; and not every attempt worked.

Sometimes, in a desperate attempt to "cover" a given story, an inappropriate challenger was selected. A good example of this was a story covered in 1959, when Jim Guthro was producing the program and Aylesworth was still writing it.

"After the Hungarian Revolution of 1956," Guthro recalled, "a lot of Hungarians were coming to this country and we wanted to do a story on the Hungarian Revolution, and I was looking for an important Hungarian living here. Somebody talked me into taking Herman Geiger-Torel. He was the head of the Canadian Opera Company and a lot of these Hungarian immigrants were violinists and singers.

"And I can remember to this day, Herman Geiger-Torel is up there and the interview comes on and Pierre Berton says to him, 'Well, Mr. Geiger-Torel, you were involved in this story. What did you have to do with this revolution?' And he said, 'Nothing.'"

That was when Guthro coined the phrase "Geiger-Torelism," meaning the booking of inappropriate guests to represent stories with which they had no connection. It became an unwritten law that "Geiger-Torelism" was to be avoided at all costs.

There were other occasions when the lure of "names" resulted in the booking of inappropriate, sometimes totally useless, challengers whose connection with a given story was tenuous at best.

One such incident occurred in 1974, with the booking of Tony Bennett in connection with a civil rights demonstration in Boston. The story was about entertainers boycotting cities where school busing to achieve racial integration had been opposed.

According to Betty Kennedy, Bennett "hardly knew where Boston was, let alone anything about the political ramifications of the busing story."

And Fred Davis agreed:

"Tony sings great, but a civil rights activist he is not. We're getting into this racial thing with Tony, and that was painful. And Gordon saved that one. He could feel it falling apart; he knew we weren't going to get anywhere with that line of questioning, so he asked Tony, 'What was your first million-dollar record?'"

On an earlier occasion, FPC did a story about the Conservative Party in England winning an election over Labour. This was a perfectly legitimate story, to be sure, but the challenger chosen to represent the story was Jayne Mansfield, the well-endowed blonde movie star. And just what was her connection with the story? She happened to be filming in England at the time of that election.

As it happened, I was a guest panelist on that show and while Miss Mansfield was pleasant enough to gape at, I cannot honestly claim that my comprehension of the British electoral system was much enhanced as a result of being exposed to her expertise on the subject.

Guthro, who produced the program from the fall of 1957 through the end of the 1960–61 season, got an early feather in his cap by luring Eleanor Roosevelt to the program. She was, up to that point, by far the most prestigious figure to appear on the show, and one result was that other internationally respected persons then consented to appear. Mrs. Roosevelt had tacitly put her stamp of approval on the program.

As Fred Davis recalled it:

"Then, we were able to say, when we'd phone Hollywood or someplace, if they asked, 'Well, who do you have on this Front Page Whatever-it-is?' We could say, 'Oh, people like Eleanor Roosevelt,' and toss it off like we had them on all the time. She was the first big name to come on…and then we started getting others." (Two of the Roosevelt sons, James and Franklin, Jr., subsequently appeared on "Front Page Challenge," quite likely on their mother's recommendation.)

The panelists were awed by Mrs. Roosevelt, if only because of her international stature. Toby Robins recalled feeling relieved when she realized that even Mrs. Roosevelt could display such a human emotion as nervousness. Gordon Sinclair, not noted for timidity, later acknowledged that when the widow of FDR was on the program, the panelists, himself included, became so tongue-tied that Mrs. Roosevelt had to save the show by virtually interviewing herself. (She further endeared herself to the people on "Front Page Challenge," by saying: "Whatever the fee is, I want you to donate it to the March of Dimes," the charity founded by her late husband.)

Kurt von Schuschnigg had been chancellor of Austria in 1938, when Hitler took over his country. Von Schuschnigg had spent the entire war as a Nazi prisoner. Jim Guthro wanted to get von Schuschnigg as a challenger on "Front Page Challenge" (in 1958) but didn't know how to locate him. One of Guthro's researchers tracked von Schuschnigg down in St. Louis, Missouri, where he had been living and teaching for some years.

"I didn't even know there was a St. Louis University at the time," Guthro recalled. "But there was and that's where I reached von Schuschnigg by phone."

The expatriate Austrian leader agreed to appear on the program. The guest panelist that night was the noted American TV journalist, Mike Wallace, who was amazed to find out that von Schuschnigg had been living in the United States for many years.

Guthro and writer John Aylesworth would strive to come up with challengers who had a legitimate but unusual connection with a well-known story.

"We were looking around for a Canadian story and this perennial one turned up—the Regina Cyclone of 1912... It turned out that a troupe of British actors had been stranded in Regina that day."

One of the actors was named William Henry Pratt, but he later changed his name to Boris Karloff and became a world-famous movie star, initially as Dr. Frankenstein's scary monster.

Guthro recalls:

"He (Karloff) told the story from his point of view, how he was pressed into working—the relief fund came in and they paid these actors, I don't know, 25 cents an hour, something very small, and they worked around the city helping people, setting up soup stands, putting up tents, because the whole city was pretty well levelled."

The appearance of Boris Karloff became another kind of benchmark—the exact opposite of "Geiger-Torelism," in that it presented a famous name who had a legitimate connection to a big story and could relate it believably.

Alfie Scopp, who wrote the program for several seasons, first under producer Jim Guthro, then Bob Jarvis, was a great believer in inviting celebrated people by letter rather than on the phone, on the theory that somebody too busy to take a phone call from some person would usually be civil enough to answer a written invitation.

"I found that was the most useful thing I did for the booking of the guests," he said later. "They would always write back. I had letters from Golda Meir, Indira Gandhi, all these people."

One of the celebrated people Scopp wrote to was Sir Edmund Hillary, the world-famous conqueror of Mount Everest. He wrote to Hillary in New Zealand, describing the program and asking Sir Edmund to call him the next time he was in North America. Sure enough, in time he got a call from Sir Edmund from Detroit, saying he'd be available the following week.

Then Scopp thought of a way to parlay this into a spectacular program. He reached a man named Jacques Picard, in France, who had taken a diving vessel 35,800 feet to the bottom of the Pacific Ocean. Scopp figured it would be interesting to have the man who had reached the highest point in the world and the man who had gone to the lowest point on the same program. Picard agreed to make the trip to Toronto.

Bob Jarvis, who produced that program, recalled a close call on the day of the show:

"A (CBC) publicity department photographer was assigned to take photos of the two celebrated explorers during the afternoon. Somebody got a piece of art card, about two feet by three feet, and an easel to set it on, and they drew a kind of graph showing the high point of 29,000 feet and a dip down to a low point of 35,000 feet. Now, the pictures were taken, the guests rehearsed, the guests were then sent out to dinner and the panel came in for makeup and then to relax in the Green room.

"To my horror, I walked into the green room and there's this damn graph there, still sitting on the easel—with the line and the numbers on it, 29,000 feet and 35,000 feet. It sat there for half an hour or so, with the panel there, and nobody even looked at it."

On December 6, 1961—one day short of the twentieth anniversary of the attack on Pearl Harbor, the first "Front Page Challenge" headline was:

"Japs Bomb Pearl Harbor." As a challenger, there was Captain Mitsui Fuchida, who had flown one of the Japanese airplanes in that attack.

The second story on that same show was headlined: "U.S. Pacific Fleet Destroyed at Pearl Harbor." The challenger was Tony Todaro, an American seaman who had been serving aboard one of the battleships that was sunk.

This was quite innovative—two separate headlines based on the same event, but each seen from a different viewpoint. After both men had been interviewed, there was a third, totally unrelated story, and then there was an extra touch that Bob Jarvis remembered:

"We saved a little time and we brought them both back, and it was very hard to reconcile these two very courtly men, as they had now become, sitting there casually discussing the holocaust we had just seen film of... I found that a very fascinating show."

It was a regular practice for the producer, the writer and the moderator to have dinner with the program's challengers. Scopp enjoyed the preshow dinners. "I enjoyed that," he told me. "It was a fantastic experience. In planning the shows, I would think, 'Let's see, who would I like to have dinner with?'"

One of the dinners that he remembered involved several distinguished guests in various fields, plus hockey superstar Gordie Howe.

"Now, here we are at dinner," said Scopp, "and there are a couple of authors, and I think one guest was a high military or government official. And Gordie Howe. And all through dinner, people would be coming by and getting Gordie's autograph. And he was getting more and more embarrassed.

"All through dinner there was very interesting conversation. And all through it, Gordie would whisper to me, 'Well, I don't agree with that. I think so and so.' And once he had a very good point, and I said, 'Tell them.' And he said, 'I can't do that.' He just refused to, he felt these people were too important, too intellectual. But he was the one the public was interested in."

Scopp also recalled the night in 1962 when baseball star Roger Maris was a challenger on the program. (This was the year after Maris broke Babe Ruth's home-run record.) After the program, Scopp took Maris to the Celebrity Club, then across Jarvis Street from the CBC studios.

"We went downstairs and played darts with Jimmie Shields, one of the owners, and some others, and Maris is playing darts and he can't get the hang of it. And at the end of the night—and we'd been drinking a bit—he said, 'Hell, this is the way to throw them,' and he winds up and throws it just like a pitcher does. The dart hit the wire and bounced back and just ticked his eye. Now, can you imagine if it had hit his eye? I can just picture New York. 'A dart game?'"

Like his predecessors and his successors, producer Bob Jarvis had the attitude that nothing was impossible. Once, he actually tried to call Fidel Castro in Havana, in hopes of persuading him to appear on FPC—this, at a time when Castro was regarded as a prime villain in much of the western hemisphere. (Even though he would technically have been welcome in Canada, Castro never did appear on the show.)

Another time, Jarvis decided he wanted to get Gregory Peck on the program as a challenger. (Peck had just won a Best Actor Oscar for *To Kill a Mockingbird*.) Jarvis found out that Peck was then in La Jolla, California, so he tried to track the actor down by phone. He reached the information operator for that suburb of San Diego and asked for a number for Gregory Peck at La Jolla. Not being conversant with Spanish, he pronounced the town's name phonetically—"La Jolla."

The officious operator couldn't resist correcting him. "You mean *La Hoya*," she said, giving it the Spanish pronunciation.

Jarvis took the rebuff manfully. Then the operator wanted to know who was calling. Jarvis rolled with the punch.

"Oh," he said, "my name is Bob *Harvis*."

Like Jarvis, Alfie Scopp also worked the phones. Once, he managed to get E. P. Taylor on the telephone to invite him as a challenger on the program. Taylor had heretofore rejected countless invitations to appear on TV or in any way seek personal publicity. But this was shortly after Taylor's horse, Northern Dancer, had won the Kentucky Derby—the first Canadian horse to do so. Scopp used that as a lever: since Northern Dancer had brought glory to Canadian horse breeders, Taylor owed it to the public to appear on television and talk about his wonder horse. Taylor accepted the invitation.

While Drew Crossan was producing the program (1962–64), he was able to get Roy Thomson—not yet Lord Thomson, but an internationally known financier and tycoon—on the program. Crossan knew that Mr. Thomson was planning to spend some time with his family in Canada just before Christmas, so he called Ken Thomson, who was then already running the Canadian end of his father's publishing empire, and extended an invitation to the Fleet Street tycoon to appear on the program as a challenger.

Ken Thomson agreed to look into it. He called Crossan back two days later and said his father would be glad to appear on the program—if "Front Page Challenge" would pay his air fare from England and back. Evidently, Lord Thomson knew not only how to become a millionaire but how to remain one.

On the day of the show, Crossan decided to accompany the guests to the preshow dinner. On the way to the restaurant, Thomson asked: "By the way, Drew, who's your guest panelist tonight?"

"It's Jack Webster," said Crossan.

"Oh, Christ. I fired him two years ago." (Webster had recently returned from Scotland, where he'd worked for Thomson.)

"No."

"Yeah… Should be an interesting program."

It was. Roy Thomson and Jack Webster got off a few snarky remarks aimed at one another, but it never got out of hand.

Webster later recalled having worked for Thomson:

"I went over to Scotland and when I was there Roy Thomson's man says, 'I want you to work for me.' I says, 'How much?' Twenty pounds. I said, 'Make it twenty guineas.' He said okay. I worked for him for six months, this was television. And I did the six o'clock news until people in Scotland complained about my Canadian accent."

And, of course, on that program with the press baron, Gordon Sinclair asked Thomson how much money he made last year.

"Four and a half million," said the publishing tycoon.

"Before or after taxes?"

"I'm not going to tell you."

One of Crossan's more complicated coups during his stewardship of the program involved Bennett Cerf and Dorothy Kilgallen, both of whom were then fellow panelists on the popular American TV show "What's My Line?" Cerf had been a guest panelist on "Front Page Challenge" several times and Crossan had urged him to try to convince Kilgallen to come up for a show. Cerf kept trying, but Kilgallen seemed unable to find the time.

Then, the next time Cerf was on FPC as a guest panelist he was in for a big surprise: one of the challengers—hidden, of course—was his friend, Dorothy Kilgallen.

Yet another Crossan coup (and one of which he was justifiably proud) was getting the famous Mary Pickford to appear on the program. Toronto-born Pickford (née Gladys Smith) had become "America's Sweetheart" during the heyday of silent movies and was still revered by older movie buffs on both sides of the border.

Crossan got a letter from a Toronto man who said Pickford was an old friend of his whom he had taken fishing on previous visits. The producer wrote to her at Pickfair, her famed Los Angeles estate, and got an answer that acknowledged that she did know the fishing friend in Toronto, but she didn't do television appearances.

Crossan persisted. He learned that Pickford and her husband, onetime actor Buddy Rogers, were going to be in New York. He called them at the Plaza Hotel and Miss Pickford suggested he visit New York to explain his program. She finally agreed to do the show, making only one stipulation: her fee was to go to the Hospital for Sick Children, "because...I was born on the corner (of University Avenue and Gerrard Street) where the hospital stands."

Don Brown succeeded Drew Crossan as producer of the series (1964–73). Like any producer taking over an existing show, he tried to strike a balance between retaining what was good and introducing new elements that would make it "different," possibly better.

"Not to change in this business is to stagnate," Brown said. He felt that "Front Page Challenge" was regarded as a "quiz show" and he didn't agree with that:

"It had three guests and a three-minute game at that time. Far too much emphasis on the game. I wanted people on the program as guests who were big enough that we only had to have two of them. And I wanted more interview time, so I cut the game to two minutes and the guest list to two per show, and went for bigger guests and more important stories."

In 1967, Canada's centennial year, Brown was able to get Prime Minister Lester Pearson to appear on the program, although this involved some trickery. The program was done from Toronto, while Mr. Pearson was in an Ottawa studio. Rather than a hidden challenger located behind the panel, there was a TV monitor with the image of Mr. Pearson, who could hear the panel's questions and answer them, even though they didn't realize, until the game segment of the program ended, that Pearson wasn't standing behind them.

Also during 1967, when the program emanated from Montreal, Brown got former prime minister Louis St. Laurent to appear on the program.

Another of Don Brown's proudest moments during his decade as the program's producer was the time he persuaded John Diefenbaker to appear as a challenger. The venerable Tory had been asked many times before, of course, but had always declined. Finally, in 1970, he agreed to appear. The occasion was his seventy-fifth birthday; he had retired from politics a few years earlier.

One of the main reasons for his reluctance to appear, it developed, was that FPC was a commercial (read sponsored) program and Diefenbaker felt it would seem undignified for him to be part of it. As a concession, Brown bent the rules a little. He suggested that the program, for that occasion, would have commercials only at the opening and closing. There would be no interruptions for crass advertising purposes. And Mr. Diefenbaker would be the only challenger; the entire program would be devoted to him.

Lorraine Thomson recalled that Diefenbaker was somewhat "apprehensive about Pierre Berton more than anything. He was concerned that Berton might try to corner him because they had such differing views of Canada."

Betty Kennedy remembered Diefenbaker's appearance:

"He was a good raconteur and he knew what made a good story, and he had some humour. He was very good. I guess he'd been on a platform so much of his life he knew what would go."

Of Canada's prime ministers, incumbent or otherwise, only Brian Mulroney eluded "Front Page Challenge." "The number of times I thought I had Mulroney!" Thomson recalled. "But he'd always bow out at the last minute. Finally, I suggested he come on with Mila (Mulroney's wife) but even that didn't do the trick."

Panelist Allan Fotheringham voiced his own theory as to why Mulroney kept declining invitations to appear on the show: "He didn't want to be carved up by Berton and (Jack) Webster."

While Don Brown was the program's producer, I wrote the show for four years. In 1967, he assigned me to attend the Progressive Conservative Party's leadership convention, at Maple Leaf Gardens, in Toronto, on the night when a new leader (Robert Stanfield) was to be chosen. Dalton Camp had been handling Mr. Stanfield's campaign to unseat John Diefenbaker, and I stayed pretty close to Camp, in hopes of getting the new Tory leader as a challenger on the next night's "Front Page Challenge." I didn't succeed, but Brown was content to settle for Dalton Camp as the challenger, representing the story. (Mr. Stanfield appeared on the program a couple of years later.)

Another, arguably less distinguished, challenger Don Brown recalled was Zsa Zsa Gabor. She had been booked twice before but had cancelled and Brown was apprehensive about the Hungarian-born actress's impending appearance. He needn't have worried.

"She 'darlinged' me to death," he recalled. "She couldn't have been more charming. She was absolutely the perfect guest. And the panel took to her, too."

Zsa Zsa's "headline" had to do with an incident when her diamonds accidentally fell down a sink in her hotel suite, some time before. During the interview, the panel seemed skeptical about the legitimacy of her story.

"It was no hoax, darling," said Zsa Zsa. "I was cleaning them with a toothbrush. Everyone cleans their diamonds with a toothbrush."

This happened to be the last show of the season, and there was a small party afterwards, to which all the guests on the two shows done that night (one live, the other taped) were invited. One of the guests on the other show was "Ma" Murray, the feisty and elderly British Columbia newspaper publisher. Brown recalls that the only time during the party when Zsa Zsa's smile froze was when "Ma" Murray addressed her as "Zasu," evidently confusing her with veteran movie actress Zasu Pitts.

The producer who succeeded Brown was Ray McConnell, who did the show longer than anyone else in the program's history—nineteen years. (During that time, FPC's writers included Chuck Weir, Gary Lautens— for his second tour of duty—and Ross McLean. Of all the writers Chuck Weir stayed with the program the longest, seven years)

Luring prominent statesmen to the program was always a top priority. Since Don Brown had succeeded in getting Messrs. Pearson, St. Laurent and Diefenbaker to appear, McConnell felt compelled to continue the tradition. His prey was Pierre Elliott Trudeau, who was then still the country's prime minister. McConnell was up to the challenge, and Trudeau agreed to appear on the show.

This was 1974, by which time using prominent figures as target practice had become an American, if not a North American habit. In the previous decade, John F. Kennedy, Martin Luther King and Robert Kennedy had been assassinated and Governor George Wallace of Alabama had been crippled by a would-be assassin. Thus, even though this was in Canada, security became a factor on "Front Page Challenge." The RCMP checked the studio out very carefully. Says McConnell: "They had men up in the grids, with the lighting crews, just to make sure there was nobody up there." Happily, the show went on the air without any untoward incident.

As had been the case with Mr. Diefenbaker, Prime Minister Trudeau was the only challenger on that program, and the only commercials were at the opening and closing of the show.

Margaret Trudeau accompanied her (then) husband, along with Sacha, their infant son.

Ray McConnell remembered their car arriving at the studio:

"He (Trudeau) got out the side opposite from me…(and) he came around, and the other door opened and Margaret came out with one of the babies, and she happened to be holding the baby in her right arm as she got out of the car and the Prime Minister introduced her to me and she almost dropped the baby transferring the baby from her right arm to her left, to handshake. I didn't know whether to shake her hand or try to grab the baby."

There was a small room backstage, with a television monitor, so that Mrs. Trudeau could watch both her child and the program in progress.

Lorraine Thomson remembered:

"Afterwards, Margaret gave her appraisal of his performance and the prime minister changed the baby. He was good at it, too. He'd had a little practice—this was the second baby."

Even all these years later, Ray McConnell has no hesitation in recalling his "favourite" challenger during his long stewardship of "Front Page Challenge." It was Martha Mitchell, the wife of John Mitchell, who had been Richard Nixon's attorney general and one of those apparently involved in the Watergate coverup. Mitchell, among others, had by then been indicted and subsequently acquitted.

Mrs. Mitchell, who left her husband soon after the Watergate scandal erupted, struck producer McConnell as a genuinely frightened woman, even though this was 1975, when the Watergate scandal was receding into history. (Richard Nixon had already resigned and the new president, Gerald Ford, soon granted Nixon a full pardon.)

Lorraine Thomson recalled:

"I had dinner with her and afterwards she asked me to come up to her hotel room so I could help her search under the bed, in the closets, and outside the window. She wouldn't stay in a room by a fire escape for fear somebody would get at her. She told me the FBI had injected her with something and had her confined to a hospital for being a drunk, for fear of her giving away secrets about Watergate. Eventually, the things she told us turned out to be true."

On the program, Mrs. Mitchell maintained that she had been manhandled by U.S. government bodyguards and was forcibly given an injection.

Writer Chuck Weir said about Mitchell:

"She had the studio audience absolutely dead silent when she, in effect, said that Richard Nixon engineered and knew about the Watergate affair from day one…"

McConnell remembered that he, his wife, his mother and Lorraine Thomson took Martha Mitchell out after the program. They went to the Sutton Place Hotel. Her behaviour could reasonably be described as erratic.

"There was a bunch of American businessmen over at another table," McConnell related. "They didn't recognize Martha, but they suddenly decided that I had far too many ladies at my table and they would invite some of them for a dance. I was the only male there.

"So a couple of them had dances with Martha, and she didn't say much. As we were leaving, she said to me: 'Do me a favour, go over and tell them who they were dancing with.' So I did. I walked over to the table and I said, "Gentlemen, do you have any idea who the lady was you were dancing with?' And one of them said, 'Oh, no, no. She wouldn't give us her name.' And I said, 'Does the name Martha Mitchell ring a bell?'

"And they just about went under the table. I don't know whether they wanted to run out of there or what, but it was really fun. And she was at the cash register at this point, watching what was going on, just chuckling over it. I still don't know whether those five businessmen were CIA men. Who would know?"

By way of variety, the same season that brought Martha Mitchell to "Front Page Challenge" also offered the famous ventriloquist Edgar Bergen. The panel responded so warmly to Bergen during the interview that he suddenly produced the voice of Charlie McCarthy to exchange some dialogue with Pierre Berton.

Writer Chuck Weir remembered:

"It was fascinating, you know, Charlie really 'appeared.' I mean, it was just like closing your eyes and being back in front of the radio when you were a kid."

Ray McConnell cited female impersonator Craig Russell as "the most outrageous" challenger on the show during his years as producer. Russell willingly did ad lib imitations of Marilyn Monroe, Bette Davis, Judy Garland and Joan Crawford, to the delight of both panel and viewers.

McConnell also remembers U.S. general William Westmoreland as "the most frightening" challenger in his experience. "He was the scariest person I ever met. He exuded power. Like, 'I've controlled a million men, so don't mess with me.'"

The American general had commanded troops in Vietnam for four years and made an indelible impression on the entire FPC production staff.

"Oh, boy, was he a general," production assistant Carroll (Hicks) Hyde remembered. "He was right out of a machine for generals. The square jaw and the way he sat there…"

During the interview, Pierre Berton made a reference to the missiles in use that could kill millions of people. According to Steve Hyde, the program's studio director: "Westmoreland drew himself up to his full height, in the chair, and said, 'I'll have you know that we didn't use any missiles in Vietnam that could kill more than a hundred people.'"

Planning Christmas shows was an annual challenge. Sometimes the result was successful, but not always.

"We're always trying to get interesting shows for Christmas," McConnell told me, "and for a number of reasons we normally don't go for the usual type of Christmas story, simply because it's 'Front Page Challenge.'"

For Christmas in 1978, the program had a story that was both unusual and effective. It was the initial TV appearance on this continent of Louise Brown, mother of the world's first test-tube baby born that year in England.

"We were sitting in the office," McConnell recalled, "Lorraine and I, and I said, 'Why don't you phone the baby's parents and see if they'll come on the show.' Jokingly. And she said, 'Well, okay.' Jokingly. She picked up the phone and dialed through to England and Louise Brown was delighted to come on the show, with her baby. She thought it would be a marvellous holiday. And this was before they had signed any big deals with any publishing company, so it was a real scoop for 'Front Page Challenge.'"

Chuck Weir could still recall the astonishment on the face of Pierre Berton when the baby appeared on the show. "I mean, Louise Brown was behind them, behind Pierre, with her mother and father. The panel guessed the story and they turned around and Pierre said, 'Oh, my God, it's her.' Pierre was as delighted as a kid who found a ten-dollar bill on the sidewalk, he was so excited. And I still have the pacifier. For some reason, the pacifier got left behind in my car. I have the world's first test-tube baby's pacifier pinned to my wall at home."

Two years later, the program's annual attempt to come up with a suitable Christmas story led to a panic situation, although the audience never realized this.

The story sounded perfect: two Italian-Canadian men living in Toronto had a mother still in Italy during an earthquake there late that year. When attempts to reach her by phone failed, they flew to Italy, found her safe and sound and brought her back to Canada with them. The idea of the family reunion seemed an ideal story for a Christmas show and McConnell and Thomson tracked down the men, who agreed to appear on the program, and bring their mother with them.

However, they didn't arrive at the studio for rehearsal on show day and the panic signals went up. The two brothers were phoned at their respective homes, but both were out working and their wives knew nothing about the scheduled TV show. All efforts to reach the brothers failed and the day's schedule had to be hastily rearranged.

Steve Hyde later filled in the rest of the story: "We finally did get hold of them about fifteen minutes before we went on the air. Turned out they had taken a job (that day, which was also "Front Page Challenge's" taping day) knocking down a house. They figured out there was more money for knocking down this house than for doing the show, so they just took off. They didn't phone us or anything."

To cope with the problem, Ray McConnell moved hockey broadcaster Foster Hewitt, who was supposed to be the second challenger on that show, up to the number-one spot. Only half a show was taped, at which point Fred, acting on instructions from the control booth, announced: "Now, here is a look at some of the stories we covered during the past years."

And Steve Hyde spent the next night going through tapes of the year's shows and assembling a montage of highlights to flesh out the incomplete program.

One of Ray McConnell's fondest memories of FPC was the thirtieth anniversary program, done live from Ottawa's National Arts Centre. Ross McLean was then writing "Front Page Challenge," but he begged off writing the thirtieth anniversary show because he was busy finishing a book, and Ray McConnell hired me to write that particular program.

It was an hour-long program, in view of the special event, and it was loaded with names. Among the guest panelists were Peter Mansbridge and Jeanne Sauvé, then Governor General of Canada. Challengers included Lorne Green, Rich Little, Martin Luther King III, son of the famed civil rights leader, former British prime minister Edward Heath, Wayne and Shuster and several medal-winning Canadian athletes, including Ben Johnson.

"That was a who's who," McConnell recalled with enthusiasm. "It was probably my favourite show of all, simply because we pulled it off, and it was live. A wonderful moment. That was a tour de force for us all."

Not long after that thirtieth anniversary, the CBC put together a video featuring some highlights of the program's long and rich history. At the end of it, no less a celebrity than Pierre Elliott Trudeau was shown congratulating both the program and its cast on their success and popularity.

chapter 7

OFF-CAMERA

Of necessity, every television program has its unsung or, at least, unseen, heroes. The viewer sees the stars, the set, the glitz, experiences the excitement of the show and has no way of knowing what goes on beyond the borders of the television screen.

Yet, what goes on there is as vital a part of the successful program as are the stars, the stories, the challengers, the set and the excitement. In the case of "Front Page Challenge," apart from the producers, writers, researchers and talent coordinators, there are certain people whose contributions to the program demand recognition.

High on the list of these belongs Lucio Agostini, the music director of the program. How he happened to be there in the first place is one of those little eccentricities that make the CBC so unusual.

"Front Page Challenge" was not the first panel show, either in Canada or on American television. Our neighbours to the south had already pioneered the field with such shows as "Twenty Questions," "I've Got a Secret," "To Tell the Truth" and the most successful of them all, "What's My Line?"

Even in Canada, "Front Page Challenge" was not the first panel show. Preceding it had been "Court of Opinions" (which had started as a radio program, then became a simulcast) and the longer-lived "Fighting Words," with Nathan Cohen as moderator. Both these programs came under the jurisdiction of the Public Affairs Department of the Corporation. "Front Page Challenge," however, was produced by the Light Entertainment (the CBC's euphemism for variety programs) Department. And here was where the wrinkle came in. The CBC had contracts with the musicians' union decreeing that any variety show must have a live orchestra.

"When we started," John Aylesworth remembered with a laugh, "all we had was a recording of a snare drum."

Once it was decided that "Front Page Challenge" would have a life beyond its thirteen-week summer tryout, live music was part of the dressing.

Jim Guthro, who took over as producer in the fall of 1957, hired Lucio Agostini as the program's music director. He composed, and then conducted, opening and closing theme music for the show. There were also musical punctuations, as when a story was introduced, and musical transitions going into and coming out of commercials.

Agostini's biggest job was composing the background music that was used to highlight the film re-creation of the news event. This, naturally, varied widely, depending on not only the content of the story, but the mood. A story about a mine disaster, for example, would require something different from a story about swimming across Lake Ontario. Some of Agostini's short original compositions had to be somber or dramatic; others called for a lighter, more whimsical touch.

"I brought Lucio in," Jim Guthro reminisced. "He agreed that he could underscore the various re-creations and film to make it more dramatic. You see, the problem is that you get little bits of film from different sources, and to tie these things together was almost impossible without a musical line flowing throughout, so the music line was there to disguise the fact that we were using little, disassociated pieces of film. So, he did that quite well."

Agostini provided all those pieces with equal skill and ease. Once the film was assembled and edited (the job of the program's writer), Lucio would view the film and time it, then come up with an appropriate piece of music. Film re-creations could run anywhere from thirty to ninety seconds, depending on the complexity of the story and the availability of appropriate film.

By the time "Front Page Challenge" came along, Agostini had long since proven his value to the CBC. Born in Italy, he began his musical studies there as a child. By the age of sixteen, Agostini was studying, and working, in Montreal. He moved to Toronto in 1944. He became music director for CBC's "Stage," one of this country's most highly regarded dramatic series. He wrote and conducted music for all sorts of productions, from Shakespearean dramas to light musical shows. Just before taking on the "Front Page Challenge" assignment, Agostini had spent a year working in Hollywood, but decided he preferred Canada.

Except for 1970, a year he spent in Spain to work on an opera, Lucio remained with the panel show throughout most of its thirty-eight-year run. ("I didn't like Spain too much," he said later. "I liked it, but not to stay. There's too many parties there, I couldn't do any work. It was good getting back to 'Front Page.'")

In his orchestra, he had some of the finest musicians in Toronto's abundant stable of studio musicians: Peter Appleyard, Moe Koffman, Ron Rully, Gary Gross, Jack Zaza, Bobby Edwards, among others. Most of them stayed with the program for years, to the gratification of Agostini. "No musicians," said Lucio "are as good as Toronto musicians."

Fred Davis provides the following appraisal of Agostini's contribution to the program: "Lucio is so brilliant. He was able to hand-tailor dramatic music for every guest, every story. We went through a period when the panelists would start out by saying, 'Well, that music sounds kinda mournful. Is it a sad story?' But sometimes he'd fool them. It was tailor-made music."

Don Brown, who produced FPC from 1964–73, called Agostini "the most efficient conductor I've ever worked with. I don't know how he stood doing 'Front Page Challenge' as long as he has, because it takes such a little bit of his talent. When you have a crisis, he's right there to help. On the afternoon of the show, if we found that someone couldn't make it and we were going to have to change the whole feeling of the show, you just had to phone him and say, 'This is what happened.' And you didn't get whining. You got, 'Okay, I may be five minutes late for rehearsal.' And the music would be perfect, as usual."

By 1982, at which time Agostini had been with "Front Page Challenge" for twenty-five years, his orchestra had twelve musicians.

When I talked with him that year, he lamented one change in the program's procedure:

"For a few years, we looked at the film in advance, and then it suddenly stopped. All I get now is the subject, and that's it. I don't even see the copy, the narration. When I used to see the film in advance, I'd do the music differently. But now you never know what kind of film you're getting. As a matter of fact, you know the subject, but sometimes it's a comical thing, it can be deceiving. I've been misled a couple of times, and I've had to change it at the last minute."

One striking, though rare, example of this occurred when the program did a story about the 1961 Bay of Pigs invasion, with an eyewitness to that dramatic historical event as the challenger representing the story. The film that was assembled for the re-creation was very graphic—bodies in the water, explosions, and so on. For some reason, however, Agostini didn't get a chance to view it. He had to write the music without seeing the film, after glancing hastily at the script for the narration. In his haste, noticing that the story was datelined Havana, Agostini wrote some light, frothy rhumba music. Fortunately, this occurred during the afternoon rehearsal and he was able to come up with more appropriate music for the show that evening.

Naturally, Lucio Agostini was not seen by anyone at home, except on one occasion: during the program's twentieth anniversary program, in the fall of 1976, there was a brief shot of Lucio conducting the FPC orchestra, standing beside announcer Bunny Cowan, also making his on-camera debut.

Rarely seen on-camera, the warm-up man is a vital part of the production team of television shows that use a studio audience. Yet his role is rarely appreciated by the millions who watch the program at home. He is a preparer, the preface to a book, the overture of a musical play, the coat of primer under the lacquer, the ties under the railway track.

The studio audience for a television show is not just dressing. The audience, properly used, enhances the show. Studio applause and laughter convey enjoyment to the home audience and make that audience enjoy the show more.

A responsive studio audience also helps the performers on the program. The adrenaline flows, they are keyed up for the show. The politician, the movie star, the tycoon, the teacher or preacher, even the panelist, will perform better if the public is present in the studio.

The studio audience, however, comes in cold. For many, going to a television studio is a new experience. They stare at the unfamiliar equipment arrayed before them. They are confused or distracted by the sometimes frenetic activity around them. Some, becoming excited, will talk to their neighbours, pointing out whatever unusual sight has caught their fancy. Others, fearful of misbehaving retreat, into silence, shushing each other, afraid to make any sound whatsoever.

The warm-up man's job is to find a way of relaxing and yet controlling the audience members, making them welcome but not giving them the run of the house, settling them down while livening them up. There are instructions to be relayed, hints to be given, explanations to be offered.

The ways in which these goals are achieved will vary with the particular personality of the warm-up man. Apart from occasional pinch-hitters, in the long history of "Front Page Challenge," only two men have tackled this chore: Larry Mann and Paul Kligman. Starting in the fall of 1957, Larry was the man who warmed up the audience. When he moved to Los Angeles in the mid-1960s, he was succeeded by Kligman, a fine actor and raconteur.

Larry had been a popular disc jockey in Toronto and a stage and radio actor. On television, he had been part of one of the CBC's earliest programs, "Uncle Chichimus," with puppeteer John Conway and weatherman Percy Saltzman. Later, he hosted his own late-night talk show, "The Midnight Zone," and later still, when he moved to Los Angeles, he worked in television and films there, returning occasionally for guest appearances or commercials in Toronto.

"Front Page Challenge" long remembered a night in 1964 when Larry Mann faced a considerable challenge of his own. Normally, there was about a fifteen-minute waiting period in the studio between the first (taped) program and the second (live) program. The warm-up man had to be out there, keeping the audience amused, answering questions, and so on.

On this particular night, the popular entertainer Victor Borge was a guest challenger, but because he was appearing at the O'Keefe Centre and had to leave the studio in time for his curtain, the taping time was moved up from eight to seven-thirty. That taping finished by eight o'clock and the live show was to go on the air at nine-thirty. That meant that Larry Mann had to keep the audience "warm" for an hour and a half. He told stories, answered questions, conducted impromptu competitions, staged a sing-along, gave away gag prizes, interviewed audience members, ad libbed, clowned, stalled and sweated. But he got through his ninety-minute one-man show and won the lasting admiration of his colleagues.

It was not long after this that Larry made the bold move from Toronto to Los Angeles. Before he left, he had this to say:

"You can be a full-time garbage collector in Toronto and you'll be accepted as such. Nobody says, 'If he were any good he'd be collecting garbage in New York.' Or you can be a successful doctor or lawyer or accountant. You're not expected to prove how good you are by moving away to practice medicine or law or accounting in Hollywood or London. Only in show business does this thing exist, where no matter how good you are, none of it counts because you're doing it here."

When Mann departed for Hollywood, Don Brown, the producer of the program, asked Paul Kligman if he would take over the warm-up assignment. Kligman agreed, with the condition that he be permitted to take whatever time off he might need to fulfill other engagements, even if they were out of town.

Kligman had had a varied career, which included numerous appearances with Wayne and Shuster and assorted stage roles. He also wrote a book about his family background (*It All Ends Up in a Paper Bag*), which was subsequently turned into a successful stage play.

The informal arrangement with Brown worked and was the basis for Kligman's long run as "Front Page Challenge's" warm-up man, even longer than Mann's. If he had to go to Calgary or Winnipeg to do a play for a few weeks, he would either fly back to Toronto for "Front Page Challenge" nights, or give the producer sufficient notice so that a pinch-hitter could be hired.

On one occasion during his tenure as warm-up man, he had to miss a taping session because he was appearing in Edmonton, starring in the Shakespearean tragedy *Othello* at the Citadel Theatre. On his opening night, he received a gag telegram from his good friends Wayne and Shuster. It read: "Don't forget to wait for the laughs."

Like the good warm-up man that he was, Kligman knew how to gauge studio audiences. He knew that "Front Page Challenge" studio audiences tended to be on the older side—busloads of senior citizens from Guelph or Burlington were not uncommon. Most audiences, however, also included some young adults.

He'd kid with audience members, sometimes employing tried-and-true bits about the management providing chewing gum for everyone—"under your seat." He'd advise them to stand up and stretch between the two shows, "or you'll become Dead End Kids." He would talk to the audience, find out where they were from, what club or church they belonged to.

During his warm-up, he would also pass along some information and instructions: how to applaud (quickly, because it sounds like more people applauding), and to be careful not to blurt out the name of a challenger when the individual appeared behind the panel because that would spoil the game. If one busload of audience members arrived a little late, he'd assume the attitude of a schoolteacher and scold the late arrivals: "Did you bring a note?"

In all his years of doing that job, one night in particular stood out in Kligman's memory. The challenger was a spokesman for the Nazi Party of Canada and Kligman simply could not get the studio audience to applaud when the challenger was introduced.

"Being of Jewish extraction, I've got the problem anyway," he recalled, "but I can overcome that and say, 'Look, you're an actor and you do your job.' But I couldn't... I danced in front of them, I did everything but they just didn't want to applaud him."

Starting in the mid-1960s, "Front Page Challenge" began going on the road, first to Vancouver and Ottawa, later to cities all across the country, from St. John's to Victoria and Yellowknife. For these trips, the budget dictated that it did not make sense to take along a warm-up man. Instead, Pierre Berton was asked to do that chore. He accepted the extra responsibility willingly.

According to veteran studio director Steve Hyde, Berton was the right man for the job:

"Pierre will go out in between the two shows and just answer questions. That's the man they want, they want Pierre. And you could leave him out there for an hour. He's very good at doing it. He changes his clothes after the first program and then he'll take the microphone and that's it. Until the next show, they just throw questions at him, and he's terrific at that, really."

The one man whose off-camera association with "Front Page Challenge" was the longest was Bunny Cowan. He was the announcer on the very first program in June 1957, and except for a six-week absence in 1970 due to illness, he did not miss another program until close to the end of his life, in 1991. The program itself was to last only another four years. (The other "original" member of the FPC cast was Gordon Sinclair, who died in 1984.)

Cowan's biggest chore on "Front Page Challenge" was to read the off-camera narration that accompanied the filmed re-creations of the stories, which were shown after the challenger had been identified (or not) by the panel, immediately preceding the interview portion.

Cowan was a professional announcer for half a century. But he wasn't your run-of-the-mouth announcer; there was a brain that went with the voice. He was interested in things. He knew about the news and the news behind the news. And he could talk about them with a command of the English language that too many broadcasting "personalities" don't even have the wit to aspire to.

He was a man of many interests. He had been an actor (mostly on radio) in his earlier days. He became active in the performers' union ACTRA, and served that organization well in numerous posts. As an announcer, he was long the corporate voice of Lever Brothers. Later, he filled a similar role for Du Maurier. He was the announcer for Wayne and Shuster for years. Bunny Cowan was, in short, the consummate announcing voice.

It was a fine voice, always in control but with enough range and variety to avoid monotony. The erudite Bunny Cowan was also a stimulating man to talk to, with a wealth of information on a variety of topics and a flair for expressing himself compellingly. He also displayed an impressive grasp of what "Front Page Challenge" was all about and why the program was so successful. In 1981, I spent an hour or so interviewing him, in connection with a book I was doing to commemorate the twenty-fifth anniversary of "Front Page Challenge." Some of the things he had to say during that conversation are worth recalling now:

"It's been almost a way of life, when you consider the program's been on the air for (so many) years. I have three children; my son is twenty-seven, so he was three when the program started. My daughter is twenty-five. She was born the summer of the year before the show started. And my third child was born in 1959, which was two years after the show started on the air. So, I saw my kids grow up, I saw my daughter get married, and I've become a grandfather, all in the span of 'Front Page Challenge'...

"You know, if it had been just another assignment, another announcing chore, then I would have had a different attitude today than the one I have, but when people refer to me as 'the voice of "Front Page Challenge,"' I think back and I was the first sound made on the program...and I've seen all the producers come and go, all of the writers come and go, all of the guest panelists come and go. And if you multiply twenty-four years by approximately thirty-five shows, that's twenty-four times seventy, because we've had an average of two stories per show—you get an astronomical figure of the number of headline stories that have been dealt with by 'Front Page Challenge'.... Of all the programs on the CBC, in fact of all the programs on any network anywhere in the world, this program significantly has touched the twentieth century deeper and with a greater sense of respect and reverence in terms of what the twentieth century has meant to man, than any of the other shows.

"If you mixed up the shows, you could almost do a chronological history of the twentieth century in Canada and beyond with the show. No question about it, because there's never been a limitation placed on the headlines as to point of origin. You will take note that before every game, Fred tells the panel whether it's a national or international story. So everything that's happened on earth and beyond in fifty years or more has been fair game for 'Front Page Challenge,' and that is exciting.

"When you think that every British prime minister and every prime minister has come to this program—from Louis St. Laurent to Pierre Trudeau. And Harold Wilson and Sir Clement Attlee and Sir Alec Douglas-Home...Indira Gandhi...the Maharaja of Baroda... But listen to this: in a short space of time we had Errol Flynn, a few months later he died in Vancouver... Jayne Mansfield, within a very short period of time she died horribly in an automobile accident... Malcolm X, assassinated a month after he was on. Then, we've had Mrs. Eleanor Roosevelt...Mrs. Wendell Wilkie... If you look at some of the resolutions of the United Nations and see the signatures that run down the side of the page, those people were here (on the show), we spoke to them.

"To suggest that it is the panel that has survived and to accord the panel the credit for this longevity is a mistake. I think what one has to say, if one is honest and fair, is that 'Front Page Challenge' represents the most successful marriage that television has been responsible for—a marriage of excellent casting and a great idea.

"So, when I talk of my perception of 'Front Page Challenge,' I'm looking at the twentieth century, the most vital period in the history of man. Vital in the sense that more things happened at a geometric rate than ever before in the history of man, and this program since 1957 has had the very special opportunity of looking at the twentieth century and updating it constantly. The stories of the ascension to the throne of Edward VII, the death of Queen Victoria, the Boer War, the sinking of the *Titanic*, the *Lusitania*, the First World War and all of the special dates of that period, the Treaty of Versailles, the League of Nations and so on, the Hungry Twenties, the Desperate Thirties, et cetera.

"'Front Page Challenge' has been able to focus its attention on all of these stories in the twentieth century, not once but perhaps many times. Each time with a different challenger, with someone who had a different perspective of the particular event, but each giving those three people and their guest (panelist) an opportunity to probe once again into what has made this really the most dynamic century of man's history."

chapter 8

QUOTABLE QUOTES

One of the frequent joys of "Front Page Challenge," as viewers were quick to notice and delighted to witness, was the occasional conversational surprise, not just when Gordon Sinclair said something shocking or Pierre Berton faced down some political Neanderthal, but when a challenger got the better of a panelist, or even when a touch of gentle humour surfaced in an otherwise serious show. The program's thirty-eight-year history is liberally peppered with such moments.

Typical was the appearance, in 1958, of Charlotte Whitton, then the mayor of Ottawa and always an outspoken woman who feared no evil panelist.

It was Pierre Berton who walked blithely into Her Worship's trap by asking: "Why is it that every time I go to Ottawa...the nation's capital...all I hear is complaints about the potholes on the Ottawa roads?"

"Well," smiled the mayor, "we have to leave something as empty as the heads of those who comment on them."

On the same show, Gordon Sinclair asked Mayor Whitton how much money she had. Said the mayor: "Well, I haven't got anything like the amount that allows you to say that you can retire on Earth and to hell with Heaven."

In 1970, one challenger was the Rev. Rolf McPherson, son of the late Aimee Semple McPherson, one of the most dynamic and successful evangelists of her time. Gordon Sinclair had known the famed Bible-thumper during his newspaper days, in the 1930s.

During the interview on "Front Page Challenge," Sinclair asked the Rev. Rolf McPherson if his mother ever drank, and McPherson said, quite emphatically: "No, never."

And then the Sinclair trap snapped shut: "Well, I've got news for you. Over the years, your mum and I split many a jar together."

Just for the record, Gordon Sinclair didn't win every single tussle with a challenger. In 1969, Robert Stanfield, then leader of the Progressive Conservative Party, was a challenger on the program. (Don Brown remembers him as "absolutely charming, the life of the dinner" but as "old stone-face when the camera lights came on.")

The Stanfield visit did, however, yield one notable exchange. Sinclair asked Mr. Stanfield if he didn't think it was unfair for Prime Minister Trudeau not to have chosen one of the new cabinet ministers from Toronto. The Lincolnesque Opposition leader said no, he didn't think cabinet ministers should be chosen on a regional basis but solely on merit.

Then he asked Sinclair: "As a member of the Toronto intellectual set, you would surely agree to that."

If Sinclair thought of a riposte, he suppressed it.

A fairly frequent guest panelist was journalist Peter Worthington. On one of those occasions (in 1964) one of the stories dealt with the signing of the Armistice in 1918, and the hidden challenger was Major General Frederic Worthington—Peter's father.

When his turn in the interview came, Peter Worthington began: "I don't know whether to call you Sir or Daddy."

The panelist then reminded his father that he had been a private in the First World War and a general in the second one. He asked what the general thought of generals when he was an ordinary soldier.

"Well," admitted General Worthington, "I didn't have a very high opinion of them."

An early challenger on the program (in 1957) was Tyrone Guthrie, the famed British stage director who became the first artistic director of Ontario's Stratford Festival. During the interview, he was asked what had prompted him to go to Stratford in the first place.

"I got a wire asking if I'd come to Stratford and give advice, expenses paid," he revealed. "I would go to the North Pole and give advice, expenses paid."

On one of the several occasions that "Ma" Murray, the elderly, outspoken West Coast newspaper publisher, was on the show, she had just written a book about sex. Sinclair questioned her about her expertise in the matter.

"Well, when I was a kid, we didn't even know what the word meant," she said. "We thought sex was the numeral that came after five."

On another Murray appearance, one panelist asked about her low regard for British Columbia premier W. A. C. Bennett.

"Personally, I have nothing against the man," she said. "He's a dictator, he's a gangster, he's sharp…"

When Bennett himself was on the program as a challenger, Pierre Berton tackled him, demanding to know why Bennett, while he had been premier of British Columbia, had declined several invitations to appear on "Front Page Challenge," even when the show was visiting Vancouver. Bennett pleaded that he had been too busy.

This was too much for Berton, who sneered: "A politician too busy to go on television?"

Another famous politician who appeared on "Front Page Challenge"— before, rather than after, becoming premier of his province—was René Lévesque. This was in 1968, not long after he had quit the Liberal Party.

Pierre Berton asked Lévesque what he thought Pierre Trudeau's chances were of becoming leader of the Liberals.

Lévesque was a bit hesitant, then said he was going to be "brutally frank" in answer. His answer referred to a recent trip he had made to western Canada, where, he said, there was "a feeling that a brand-new, modern, sophisticated Negro king has been found for Quebec." This was a metaphor

Lévesque had used before, claiming francophones in Canada were treated the way Negroes were in the United States.

Sinclair tackled nudity when veteran actress Agnes Moorehead was on the program. He mentioned that nudity was by then widespread in films and theatre. Then he asked her if she would ever appear nude on a stage.

She gave him a withering glance and replied: "I would be physically unfit."

George Jessel, the vaudeville star of long ago, was a challenger on the show in 1966. During the interview, Sinclair commented that the last time he had seen Jack Benny the veteran comic seemed to have lost his confidence.

"Lost his confidence?" Jessel came back. "Benny has six and a half million dollars in a bank that I owe 180 bucks to."

After the show, the sixty-seven-year-old Jessel wanted to "see the town," so I accompanied him to the Black Knight Room of the Royal York Hotel, where he overcame his innate shyness and allowed himself to be persuaded to get up and tell a few jokes. Jessel also paid lavish tribute to the voluptuous chanteuse who had just been featured. He tried to make a date with her, but failed. Later, he told me: "I'm at the age where you still chase girls, even if you can't remember what for."

As mentioned earlier, Zsa Zsa Gabor's appearance on the program related to a story about her losing her diamonds. In the interview, Pierre Berton started by saying: "Let's not talk about diamonds."

"Let's not talk about diamonds," echoed Gabor.

"Let's talk about your ex-husband, George Sanders. Are you and he still friends?"

Zsa Zsa smiled coyly and said: "Let's talk about diamonds."

On occasion, the most startling comments came from the most unexpected sources. In 1974, the program headlined a story about the rights of Native people, and the challenger was Native rights activist Jeanette Lavell. She was well prepared and articulate and presented her viewpoint effectively during the interview. Sinclair took it upon himself to compliment her on this. The guest panelist, broadcaster Charlotte Gobeil, felt he was being a male chauvinist and called Sinclair "a condescending bastard."

Often, the panel's bluntness startled challengers (and the public) but sometimes it paid off.

One challenger was astronaut Edwin E. ("Buzz") Aldrin, one of the three men who had walked on the moon in July 1969. Sinclair mentioned that there had been reports of Aldrin's personal problems after his time as an astronaut.

Sinclair: "Do you ever get boozed up? Do you ever use a call girl?"

Without a moment's hesitation, Aldrin replied: "Yes to both."

Another astronaut to appear on the show was Scott Carpenter. Predictably, Gordon Sinclair asked him how much astronauts are paid. Carpenter tried dodging the issue, claiming they were paid "adequately."

Sinclair persisted, and Carpenter finally said he earned "between $12,000 and $15,000 a year."

"Three hundred dollars a week," sneered Gordon, with a combination of pride and disdain. "I could earn $300 in five minutes."

Humorist Art Buchwald proved a delightful guest challenger. Having spent some time working in Paris, he was asked about that.

"When I first went to Paris," said Buchwald, "I discovered the French not only disliked Americans, they disliked each other. Once you discover that, you can get along fine with the French."

Striptease queen Gypsy Rose Lee (once described by showman Mike Todd as "the greatest no-talent star in the history of show business") proved to be a charming challenger. To disguise her voice, Gypsy filled her mouth with marbles just before she began slyly evading the panel's attempts to identify her. At the end of the "game" she took the marbles out, one by one, and commented: "That's how you become an actress. When you lose all your marbles, you're an actress."

Fred Davis remembered:

"We told her to be careful of Gordon Sinclair, the bald guy. And she told Gordon (on the show), 'After my striptease vaudeville days, I'm used to old baldheaded men like you sitting in the front row with their hotel-room numbers etched in lipstick on their foreheads.' Gordon just laughed."

Black comedian and civil rights activist Dick Gregory was a wily guest. He had recently written his autobiography and titled it *Nigger*. Sinclair wanted to know why Gregory would use one of the words most hated by African-Americans as the title of his book.

Said Gregory: "I told my mom, if ever you hear the word 'Nigger' remember they're just advertising my book. If I go to the South and some cop grabs me and says, 'How you doing, Nigger?' I say, 'Nigger doing pretty good—449,000 copies.'"

Political figures were popular on the show, both with the panel and with the public. Sometimes the panel succeeded in tripping them up, sometimes not.

When Stanley Knowles, the revered New Democratic Party member, was on the program (while Lester B. Pearson's Liberals were running the government), Gordon Sinclair began complaining about proposed government cuts to social security benefits, which would have affected him. Knowles listened at length to the complaints of this clearly well-heeled journalist, then commented:

"You sound as if you're hard up." That got a good laugh.

Lord Clement Attlee, the former Labour prime minister of England, was on the program in 1958. Panelist Toby Robins asked him how he could account for Labour's victory over Winston Churchill in 1945.

The British statesman grinned and said: "Stanley Baldwin (an earlier Tory prime minister) once told me, 'They don't put you in because they like you. It's because they're sick of us.'"

Toby mentioned Churchill's description of Attlee as "a sheep in sheep's clothing" and asked him if he had any comment about Churchill. Atlee said that Churchill was "like a chameleon—you put him on blue paper and he turns blue, you put him on yellow paper and he turns yellow."

Another former British prime minister, Edward Heath, was a challenger on the program's thirtieth anniversary program. Heath was also a musician and symphony conductor in his spare time. During the interview following the game, Berton asked Heath to compare the job of conducting a symphony orchestra with that of running Parliament.

"Well," said the urbane British statesman, "with an orchestra, at least one has the feeling that they are all trying to go in the same direction at the same time."

It was Joe Clark, Progressive Conservative leader and briefly prime minister of Canada, who got one of the biggest rounds of applause from the studio audience when he was asked about political polls that showed his party was on the decline.

Clark was rarely perceived as a wit, but his reply on this occasion was a winner: "I think Mr. Diefenbaker was right when he said that dogs had a proper perspective on poles."

In 1967, a guest challenger was former RCMP commissioner Clifford Harvison, who had been called out of retirement to testify in the sensational political scandal involving Gerda Munsinger the year before. During the interview portion of the show, Harvison mentioned that he was writing a book about his experiences, but he wasn't very forthcoming.

The Sinclair patience ran out. "Put some zip in that book," he advised the RCMP commissioner, "or you won't sell nothing."

The FPC panel was rarely at its best with sports stories, although there were exceptions. (Sports stories proved more successful after Allan Fotheringham joined the panel, because he had always been far more interested in them.)

One sports challenger was heavyweight boxer Sonny Liston, who had recently knocked out Floyd Patterson. Sinclair mentioned that some sportswriters claimed Patterson seemed afraid and didn't put up much of a fight. Sinclair persisted: "Did he throw any punches?"

"Well," said Liston, "he throwed a couple of punches, but I wasn't there."

Another heavyweight champion boxer who appeared on the show during its first year was Joe Louis, the famed "Brown Bomber." Although the panel had a tough time identifying him, the ensuing interview proved amiable. At one point, Louis was asked which of his many fights had given him the most difficulty.

Said Louis: "The one I had with the income tax collector."

Ironically, hockey seemed to be a game the panel was generally untutored in. Over the years, Gordie Howe was on the program as a challenger six times. The panel never guessed him. On one occasion, over which the panelists blushed for some time to come, they struggled for four minutes to identify this famous hidden challenger. Even when they had narrowed down the category to sports, they fumbled around, suggesting numerous sports—boxing, baseball, basketball, swimming, wrestling—and not a one of them so much as thought of hockey.

Another famous athlete who appeared on the program (in 1962) was Leroy "Satchel" Paige, the great pitcher who started pitching in the Negro League in the 1920s. It wasn't until he was over forty-two years old—and well past his prime—that he was signed by a Major League team, the Cleveland Indians.

Berton asked Paige if he was bitter about being barred from the Major Leagues for so long because of his colour.

"That's correct," said the soft-spoken former pitcher. "I started in Chattanooga in 1926, and I waited until now... There were other pitchers, too, who could throw great. But you couldn't get into the Major Leagues."

In 1981, on a visit to Vancouver, FPC's producer, Ray McConnell, booked Dave "Tiger" Williams, who had been traded to the Vancouver hockey team and was living in British Columbia. Williams was a last-minute replacement for another challenger who had been injured. The panel was unable to guess either his identity or the headline about his recently being traded.

Betty Kennedy began the ensuing interview with Williams this way: "Don't be offended. We don't even get Gordie Howe."

One challenger that everyone loved was Jesse Owens, the American athlete who had won four gold medals in the Berlin Olympics of 1936. Rather than present the medals to the African-American, Adolf Hitler snubbed Owens by walking out of the stadium.

On "Front Page Challenge," guest panelist Bennett Cerf asked Owens: "Were you aware that Mr. Schickelgruber (Hitler) was cutting you dead?"

"We didn't go there to shake hands with Hitler," said Owens. "We went to run, and run we did." Then, with a smile, he added: "I'm in Canada tonight enjoying myself. Where he is, is no particular concern of mine."

One of the hottest stories of the 1970s was the Watergate break-in in Washington. Producer Ray McConnell tried very hard to get Bob Woodward and/or Carl Bernstein, the two *Washington Post* reporters who had spearheaded the newspaper's investigation of the scandal, to appear on FPC.

He failed to lure either Woodward or Bernstein, so McConnell, determined to cover the story, settled for Alfred Baldwin, a former FBI agent who had served as lookout for the men who broke into the Democratic Party headquarters in the Watergate hotel. He, like those who carried out the attempted break-in, was caught.

Baldwin wasn't an especially effective challenger.

During the interview, Berton said to him: "You weren't much of a lookout, were you?"

As mentioned earlier, in all his years as the program's flawless moderator, Fred Davis never lost his cool. Somehow, he was able to handle the most ticklish situation, whether it be a guest in high dudgeon or a disgruntled panelist.

Only once did he let a little bit of impatience show. This was when Ross McLean, then a CBC producer of public affairs programs, was a guest panelist on FPC. After welcoming him, Davis asked McLean for his assessment of variety shows.

This prompted McLean to unburden himself of a pretty wicked denunciation of variety show personalities as "cardboard people." He took swipes at Wally Koster, Joyce Sullivan, Juliette (saying he'd seen the usually smiling Juliette frown), Jack Kane ("I heard Jack Kane speak three consecutive sentences without stumbling") and other CBC variety performers of the time. Then, he added: "And you...you really aren't Fred Davis."

Davis took all this in his stride. But in wrapping up the program, he thanked the audience and the panel, then saved his last words for the guest panelist. "Ross McLean," he said with an icy half-smile, "it's been mildly pleasant."

Probably one of the most poignant moments in the long history of "Front Page Challenge" came on a show just before Christmas of 1960. The challenger was Lester B. Pearson and the headline had to do with his having won the Nobel Peace Prize three years earlier.

Mr. Pearson had been in London during the Second World War as first secretary to the Canadian High Commission. On this program, Fred Davis asked him if he could recall any particularly memorable Christmas. The Peace Prize winner called up a wartime memory and expressed it with simple dignity:

"Well, apart from my childhood years when Christmases were always memorable," Pearson replied, "perhaps the one I think of as the most dramatic one was in London on Christmas Eve, 1940. It was during the Blitz, during the bombing, and I had gone to bed and was reading when a bomb landed just outside. It was just about midnight, but a bomb landed just outside the window and smashed the glass. It didn't do any damage otherwise, but it was a bit of a shock.

"So I thought this isn't a very nice way to introduce Christmas 1940, so I turned on the radio in order to drown out, if I could, the noise of the anti-aircraft and all the rest of it, the bombs falling.

"And I had the radio tuned to the German short-wave station because I had been listening to (Lord) Haw Haw two or three hours before. And as I turned it on, that station came on and there came flooding into my room the most beautiful carol music that you could have imagined—from that same German source from which the bombs came.

"And I've never forgotten that—the paradox of that beautiful Christian Christmas music and that horrible noise of death and destruction, both of them from the same source.

"I suspect that if we can reconcile the riddle of those two sounds from the same origin, perhaps we will have solved the problem of peace and war."

Unquestionably, the funniest incident that ever occurred on "Front Page Challenge" was in 1963, when the challenger was Bruce Spencer, vice-president of the Society for Indecency to Naked Animals (S.I.N.A.). (Actually, it should have been the Society for *Decency* to Naked Animals.)

Earlier in the year, Spencer and some seventy-five of his supporters had picketed the White House to protest the nakedness of pet animals. They carried pictures and placards, urging everyone to put clothes on their animals. One of the pickets led a horse wearing a diaper.

Betty Kennedy recalled Spencer as "that crazy man who had the league for decency among animals."

After the guessing game, Sinclair turned to her and said: "I don't want to ask him any questions."

"It was obvious," said Betty, "he thought, well, this is some real nut. And then, as the questioning went on, you could see that this man was just having a ball with us."

Inevitably, Sinclair couldn't resist getting into the act eventually.

Here is how the interview went, starting with broadcaster Phil Stone, who was that night's guest panelist:

Stone: Mr. Spencer, the picture showed rhinoceri and lions and tigers. Do you honestly see this spreading to the jungle?

Spencer: No, we're not interested in any large animals in their natural habitat. Our only interest is in domestic animals that stand higher than four inches or longer than six inches. Namely, horses, cows, dogs and cats.

Stone: And do you think a new business is going to arrive now? Perhaps Honest Ed (Mirvish) can start selling these costumes.

Spencer: No, we have no commercial interest whatsoever. We do not accept donations, we even turn back postage stamps. Our foundation is strictly self-sufficient. We've been around for four years and we have over fifty thousand members in the United States and Canada who swear by our constitution.

Stone: You actually think that Jackie Kennedy and Caroline were contributing to juvenile delinquency by riding naked horses?

Spencer: Well, let's put it this way. They could have been a moral symbol that would have given us a giant step forward. For example, if Mrs. Kennedy had put Bermuda shorts on her horse and on Caroline's perhaps people around the country would take up a cry and clothe their animals, just as our fifty thousand members do.

Berton: Mr. Spencer, I have three Siamese cats and six children. The children often try to dress these cats in dolls' clothes.

Spencer: Admirable of them.

Pierre: They want to be good citizens. And they're worried about their morals. But cats object. The cats are nudists and there's nothing we can do about it.

Spencer: I think you're wrong. I don't think you're giving it a fair chance, because children look at small animals and say, "Mother and Daddy are dressed. I'm dressed, but the little cat isn't. Why isn't it?"

Berton: Around our house, Mr. Spencer, I've got news for you. I don't wear any clothes. I live in the country, there's nobody around. If a man can't go nude in his own house, I don't know what the world's coming to.

Spencer: Well, I would evaluate this, that you are interested in the nudist cult, which we are not.

Berton: No, I'm just a bit of a nudist for animals.

Stone: Actually, he's Canada's Gypsy Rose Lee.

Spencer: No, we don't look upon these people with favour—fads like nudism, for example. What have nudists contributed to our culture except perhaps a few good volleyball players?

(It was at this point that Gordon Sinclair could no longer keep his silence.)

Sinclair: Bruce, I'm interested, for example, in the comfort of the dog. You're concerned about his comfort, I take it, when you want him clothed. Now, would this completely wipe out the use of the fire hydrant?

Spencer: Not necessarily. That's a very practical question. We've been asked this question many times. And we say this, that any dog, cat or any animal, can be trained to take his drawers on or off at will with one snap of the jaw. It's all a matter of training. Animals are very smart. They're smarter than children.

Sinclair: Now, I don't suppose that in your wildest hopes you will undertake to have all species of animals clothed at the one time. For example, I'm curious to know which you would like to start with. Would it be perhaps the bull or the cow or...

Spencer: No, just domestic animals. We're not interested in anything that swims or flies.

Sinclair: Bulls neither swim nor fly.

Spencer: I know that. Mainly we want the small animals that are used as pets, around in public view. We will not consider any animal that swims or flies. Certain amphibious animals are under investigation right now. We're not interested in chickens, because a chicken, after all, is neither fish nor fowl. A chicken is kind of neutral.

Sinclair: Most people think it's fowl.

Spencer: No, we're not interested in that. After all, this is a growing movement. We have many, many sympathizers, right here in Toronto and Montreal. . .in Canada we have several thousand members who clothe their animals.

Sinclair: I think you'll appreciate, Bruce, that I'm taking this seriously.

Spencer: Yes.

Sinclair: Unlike our audience.

Spencer: Then you would possibly make a very good member if you could pass the emotional stability test. No, really. I don't mean that facetiously. I'm serious. We have an emotional stability test that permits us to weed out the crackpots and thrill-seekers—no reflection—but there are people who obtain vicarious thrills by belonging to S.I.N.A. They want to belong because they want to belong.

Sinclair: I appear to get comments of this kind from time to time. Now, in terms of cats, for example, there seem to be no visible sex organs on a cat, are there?

Spencer: Well, I would have to disagree with you. I think that it's basically not that the organs are visible per se, but I think it's a matter of morality and consistency. For example, we as human beings are biologically animals. We share our food, our love, our homes with animals, but we won't give them decency. It's illogical, it's unfair and it's against our social customs...

At this point, having expounded his murky philosophy, Mr. Spencer proceeded to sing the S.I.N.A. anthem (unaccompanied) and was prepared to go into a second verse before Fred Davis managed to wrap the interview.

No artificial laugh track could approach the genuine laughter that rocked the studio that night.

Sinclair, always a specialist at stimulating titillating conversations, had another such chance in 1981, on the last show of that year.

This time the challenger was a man named Hugo Vickers, author of a book about the forthcoming nuptials of Prince Charles and Lady Diana Spencer.

Actually, it was guest panelist Alex Trebek who brought up the matter of Lady Diana's virginity, because the British press had already published some comment about her made by one of her uncles. But it was Gordon who pressed the issue:

> **Sinclair:** You indicated that people were vulgar peeping Toms, so to speak, in inquiring as to her virginity. But was not this raised officially as a question?
>
> **Vickers:** I think the problem had been that various girlfriends of Prince Charles had had previous boyfriends who came forward and said things like, "Oh, she'll make him very happy. She made me very happy when we were living together." And in this particular case there are no such people and will not be.
>
> **Sinclair:** Yes, but was there any examination by a gynecologist? You say that an uncle made some statement... But these things are important. Don't think me vulgar. I'm merely inquisitive.
>
> **Vickers:** I think the inquiries were entirely from the press, in fact, and they couldn't believe that they'd got a thoroughly nice girl.
>
> **Sinclair:** They couldn't believe that about English girls?
>
> **Vickers:** Well, I think that it's quite difficult these days...
>
> **Sinclair:** You're quite right about that.
>
> **Vickers:** But on the other hand, you have a girl of this kind, who's been brought up in a good family, and there's no reason to suppose, whatsoever, that she's not a virgin.
>
> **Sinclair:** Thank you.

It might have been a sign of the changing times, but mail reaction to this particular show was not especially high.

In one of her three appearances on "Front Page Challenge," swimmer Cindy Nicholas was grilled by Sinclair, who began by recalling that when he first covered some swimming meets some female swimmers competed in the nude. Then, he asked Cindy why she didn't swim in the nude.

"A bathing suit," she replied, "streamlines the body and I figured there would be more resistance if I didn't using a bathing suit."

"More resistance in the nude?" demanded Gordon.

"Yes."

"Then," pursued Sinclair, "why don't porpoises wear bathing suits?"

Cindy smiled and replied: "They don't have the curves where it counts."

That brought laughter and applause—and an end to Sinclair's questions.

Of course, not all the snappy exchange took place on-camera. Some of the spicier ones occurred backstage, either before or after the program.

The night the noted Canadian industrialist, E. P. Taylor, was on the show happened to be the last show of that season, so producer Drew Crossan held a small party for the panel and guests after the show.

Mrs. E. P. Taylor accompanied her husband to the program. At the party afterwards, Mrs. Taylor walked up to Fred Davis and said: "Hi, I know you. You're Fred Davis. I'm Northern Dancer's mother."

On the first telecast of Front Page Challenge (June 24, 1957) Alfred Scadding, one of only three survivors of the 1936 Moose River mine disaster, in Nova Scotia, appeared as a challenger. When a program panelist turned up early, producer Harvey Hart became nervous, lest anyone on the panel spotted Scadding. He stashed Scadding and the other challengers in a dressing room, where they had to wait for two hours.

After the show, Hart asked Scadding if he and the other challengers had tired of sitting in the dressing room for so long. Scadding, who had spent ten days trapped in a mine before he and the other miners were rescued, said: "No, but I've had some experience."

During Jim Guthro's regime as producer (1957–61), he read press reports that Errol Flynn, the over-the-hill movie star, had returned from Cuba, where Fidel Castro had just toppled Batista's government. Flynn was reportedly now in New York.

"So I got on the telephone," Guthro remembers, "and inside of ten minutes I had Errol Flynn on the phone, on the day after he had returned from Cuba. He was broke and I talked him into coming to 'Front Page Challenge,' and the fee was less than a thousand dollars."

Flynn proved to be a troublesome guest. He insisted on bringing along his "secretary," who turned out to be his girlfriend, Beverly Aadland. Flynn arrived rather drunk, but the program's staff did its best to keep him in line, although it wasn't easy.

By late afternoon, he was sent to makeup. Margaret Epp, the program's makeup artist, was standing over the seated Flynn, leaning toward him and applying makeup, when he grabbed her around the bottom and virtually forced her on top of him.

"Now, isn't that better?" he said, grinning.

Margaret was a bit flustered but she managed to extricate herself from his grip, stepped back and said, "No, Mr. Flynn, I can manage from here. My arms are long enough."

One of the more outspoken challengers on "Front Page Challenge" was the militant American feminist Kate Millett. During the interview, she complained that some societies bind women's feet or strap them in bras, and she called this "female mutilation."

Gordon Sinclair replied: "Well, they circumcise little boys before they even leave the hospital, and that's a form of male mutilation."

After the program, Sinclair extended a rare olive branch, telling Miss Millett he didn't know she had "a Ph.D. on the feminist subject." But the woman was not mollified, complaining that Sinclair had not given her a chance.

"Okay," said Gordon, "let's make up. You show me your Ph.D., I'll show you my circumcision."

Late in 1970, the program visited Halifax for the first time, and one of the guests booked was Sally Rand, the famous, now elderly, fan dancer. She had been doing an engagement in Winnipeg (performing her standard fan dance, even though she was seventy years old) and there was some doubt as to whether she would get to Halifax, due to a snowstorm there.

She finally arrived, to everyone's great relief. The producer, Don Brown, welcomed her effusively. Noticing the ostrich plumes clutched in her hands, he said: "And you've brought your fans. What a wonderful touch of nostalgia."

The little old lady brushed past Brown and muttered: "Fuck nostalgia. Where's the dressing room?"

chapter **9**

SOME CHURLISH
CHALLENGERS

One of the challenges facing television producers is getting a program on the air pretty much as planned. This was not always easy in the case of "Front Page Challenge," due in part to the various eccentricities, swollen egos or bizarre behaviour of some challengers. That drinking sometimes played a part in such behaviour is an established fact; but it wasn't the only cause of problems.

In September 1958, the program began its second full year on the air. One of the headlines to be pursued was the 1943 Teheran Conference, at which Franklin Delano Roosevelt, Winston Churchill and Joseph Stalin met to plan war strategy.

Jim Guthro was the producer. "Of course, we tried to get Winston Churchill," he recalled many years later. "The closest we got was not even his wife, but his son, Randolph."

Randolph Churchill turned out to be one of the most irritating challengers ever booked. Guthro would not soon forget some of the harrowing details of that day:

"Churchill came to Toronto early and stayed late. He started to hang out with a local portrait painter who liked to do portraits of the well-to-do. Well, this person took Randolph to the wrong studio. So, we were up there waiting for Randolph for the rehearsal. And the receptionist down at the old Studio 1 building phoned and said, 'Mr. Guthro, there's a man here who claims to be Randolph Churchill, but he's very drunk.' And I said, 'Well, I think you're right on both counts.' She said, 'He's pounding the desk and demanding to be taken to the studio and he doesn't understand the studio is two miles away. What can I do?'"

Guthro instructed the receptionist to keep Churchill there. Then he dispatched FPC writer John Aylesworth to get in his car, go to Studio 1 and bring Churchill up to Studio 4. No sooner was Churchill in the makeup room at Studio 4 than he demanded something to drink. Guthro sent Aylesworth to the nearby liquor store for a bottle of Scotch.

Actually, he demanded "whisky." Guthro, not wanting to displease the guest by sending for the wrong kind of whisky, asked Churchill what kind of whisky he wanted. "I knew that to an Englishman, 'whisky' meant Scotch, but I also knew he had been in the U.S. and he might want bourbon or even Canadian rye," Guthro recalled. Churchill called him a "damn fool" and added there was "only one kind of whisky," so Guthro sent Aylesworth out to bring back Scotch.

By the time he went on the air, Randolph Churchill was well and truly fuelled.

During the rehearsal, things got worse. Churchill refused to go on the program to represent a story concerning his famous father. He wanted the story to be about him.

Guthro told him: "Your father is the world's most famous Englishman and we can't have a story about you being elected an M.P. for the County of Kent or something, I mean it's Winston Churchill's story."

Churchill finally agreed to do the program, but then tossed in another monkey wrench. He announced that he would walk off the show if any of the panel dared ask a question about the drinking problem of his sister, Sarah Churchill. (Until then, no one connected with the program had even thought of such an idea.)

Fortunately, the structure of the program allowed Guthro to indulge Churchill's whim of iron. After the guessing-game portion of each story, there was a commercial break. Guthro sent Aylesworth into a quick huddle with the panel, warning them to make no mention of Sarah's tippling for fear that Randolph would stalk off the show.

Although Randolph Churchill was the first challenger who threatened to walk off the program unless his demands were met, he was not the last.

In 1963, Marian Anderson, the great African-American contralto who, in 1955, was the first woman of her race to perform at the New York Metropolitan Opera House, was booked on "Front Page Challenge."

Miss Anderson had been the key figure in a much bigger story, however. In 1939, she had been denied permission to sing in Washington's Constitution Hall, simply because she was black. The hall was run by the Daughters of the American Revolution (D.A.R.), an organization that had not yet entered the twentieth century. The outcry over this racist stand was sensational, in part because of the attention focused on it by Eleanor Roosevelt. The president's wife wrote about the issue in her daily syndicated column and subsequently resigned her membership in the D.A.R.

But when Miss Anderson arrived in Toronto to appear on "Front Page Challenge," she flatly refused to discuss that matter on the program. She threatened to walk off the show if the incident was even mentioned. Producer Drew Crossan was forced to give in. He used her debut at the Met as the story and, during the commercial break following the guessing game, cautioned the panel to avoid any mention of the civil rights incident.

In the thirty-eight-year life of "Front Page Challenge," only one guest actually walked out on the show, not long before air time: Pietro Annigoni, a portrait painter who had, some years before, done a mildly controversial full-length portrait of Princess Margaret. (The program had earlier used Georgina Moore, a model who stood for Princess Margaret during part of the process.)

Annigoni didn't have to be brought to Canada from England. He was already in Toronto, working on a portrait of the industrialist Colonel Eric Phillips, and agreed to appear on "Front Page Challenge," though not with much enthusiasm.

One would have thought—or, at least, I would have—that a portrait painter, who demands that models sit absolutely still for hours on end, would understand the meaning of patience. But not Signor Annigoni. On the day of the taping, Annigoni got bored with the studio routine, the amount of time required. When he learned that the program would require an hour longer of his time than he had expected, he walked out in a huff. He simply left, without telling anyone. When he was located at the home of a friend, some fifteen minutes before taping time, he flatly refused to do the show. Fortunately, the program had been planned with three stories, so the producer was forced to stretch the time allotted for each of the other two stories and make do.

That was one of the rare occasions when "Front Page Challenge" was forced to use a "standby" story. The producers always tried to be prepared for this. One story or another, with a challenger who lived in Toronto and could be reached on short notice, was kept at the ready for just such emergencies. If an expected challenger failed to arrive on the day of the show or, as in the case of Mr. Annigoni, wandered off never to return, the standby challenger was hustled over to the studio and the substitute story was used. For a long time, Lorraine Thomson doubled as a standby challenger—her headline dealt with the beginning of television in Canada—but she and the story were never needed.

Georgina Moore's appearance on "Front Page Challenge" occurred in 1958, the second year of the program. Her headline had to do with the controversial Annigoni portrait of Princess Margaret, for which, as mentioned above, Miss Moore served as a kind of stand-in, to spare the princess the drudgery of sitting for hours on end while the artist did the early body work. When word of this harmless subterfuge hit the English popular press, Miss Moore became a temporary celebrity and producer Guthro arranged to bring her over for an appearance on the program.

The model landed in New York the day before the show and blithely told the press there that she was bound for Toronto to appear on a television game show. The story, naturally, went from Associated Press to Canadian Press.

Guthro contacted the two Toronto evening papers of the time and asked them not to run the story because the panel would surely notice it and the game would be ruined. The *Toronto Star* went along with his request, but the *Telegram* didn't. So the program had to do without a "game" and go straight to the interview. Davis simply introduced Moore and let the panel ask her some questions about herself and the experience of posing in place of Princess Margaret. It was not one of the show's more stimulating interviews.

In 1960, the flamboyant Broadway producer David Merrick was a challenger on "Front Page Challenge." Being an actress, panelist Toby Robins knew about a dispute between Merrick and the Actors' Equity Association, the performers' union, and she asked him about this during the interview. (According to Toby, Merrick's answer was evasive and inaccurate.)

The next day, still in Toronto, Merrick was interviewed on a radio program and the interviewer brought up the Equity dispute again. Merrick said he knew Miss Robins and that she had auditioned for him several times. The implication was that Toby had been troublesome on "Front Page Challenge" because he had rejected her for a stage role.

"He lied," Toby insisted. "I had never auditioned for him."

It was in 1968 that Artie Shaw, the former bandleader, was on the program. As a fan of the Swing Era, I was happy I happened to be writing the show at the time and looked forward to meeting Shaw. He was always a fascinating man and a truly absorbing conversationalist.

The much-married clarinet player (musicians used to refer to him as "the cat with nine wives") arrived with a strikingly beautiful secretary and took great interest in every detail of the program. At one point in the rehearsal, he asked to see announcer Bunny Cowan's script, which I had written, to check it over. He spent some minutes going over the script, line by line, word by word, correcting spelling, adding or subtracting commas, quotation marks and exclamation points. When he was satisfied, he returned it to Cowan.

After watching all this, I turned to his secretary and said, "He's pretty fussy, isn't he?"

"Fussy?" she responded. "He rewrites *incoming* mail!"

It was to be seventeen years after Randolph Churchill's visit to Toronto that Sarah Churchill herself appeared on the program, representing a story about the hundredth anniversary of Winston Churchill's birth. She proved to be every bit as charming as her brother, and yes, those rumours about her drinking were true. It seems that neither of Churchill's offspring had inherited his famous tolerance for booze.

Miss Churchill arrived at the "Front Page Challenge" studio in the afternoon, drunk. Lorraine Thomson, by then the show's chief troubleshooter, was assigned to look after her. She took Churchill back to her hotel and tried to sober her up in time for the program.

As soon as they got out of the studio, Sarah escaped, ran out into the street, in a pouring rain, without a coat on, and stood in the middle of Yonge Street, waving her arms. (Some observers thought she was directing traffic, but Lorraine thinks she was trying to hail a taxi.)

Thomson got her own car, managed to recapture her "guest" and headed for the hotel. "She began to hit me with her purse, saying 'I'm not going back to the hotel,'" Thomson recalls.

Once they got to the hotel, Sarah headed for the bar, but Thomson managed to get her up to the room. She called room service to get some food into the guest, but Sarah also ordered a drink. While Sarah was in the bathroom, Thomson poured the woman's drink into a flower vase. Eventually, she persuaded Sarah to take a nap.

Back at the studio, producer Ray McConnell was having doubts about putting Sarah Churchill on the program. But he had no replacement story available on such short notice. Without identifying the guest, he warned the panel that they had a problem—a drunk challenger.

Betty Kennedy remembers the incident: "Ray came back again and told us we were going ahead with the guest and that if we had to wipe the tape we would, and he wanted me particularly to open the questioning and do it gently. I was unnerved by that. I think we were all unnerved."

Thomson described the challenger's return to the studio: "I thought she had fallen asleep, but with that innate sense of timing, she realized she had to get back to the studio and nothing I could do would stop her. So I thought, okay, we'll take her back and we'll put her in the makeup room at the back of the studio and she'll fall asleep there and that'll be fine."

Eventually, Sarah had calmed down, or sobered up, enough that McConnell decided to take a chance and put her on the program. Indeed, she insisted she wanted to do the show.

According to the show's writer, Chuck Weir, she missed the first couple of questions in the game and led the panel "all over the place because she was semi-sloshed, but once she hit the interview chair, she gave a good show." A later viewing of the show indicates that Weir was being somewhat gallant. La Churchill was still fairly sloshed and when Berton tried to get her to answer a question it was like pulling teeth.

Thomson also remembered that the program with Sarah Churchill resulted in considerable mail, much of it criticizing the idea of putting Miss Churchill on when she was "obviously ill." Thomson added: "Of course, we couldn't have told the audience that she was drunk as a skunk."

Booze was also a factor in the 1960 appearance on the program of Brendan Behan, the noted Irish playwright and drinker. On the program, he delighted everyone with his description of critics, whom he likened to eunuchs, who see "the trick" being done very night, know exactly how it's done, but can't do it themselves.

After the program ended, producer Jim Guthro and his wife took Behan out, hoping to keep him out of trouble. They went to a jazz club to hear trumpeter Roy Eldridge, a favourite of Behan's. Guthro succeeded in keeping Behan off the sauce. The Irish writer and the noted black jazz musician hit it off and had a lengthy and pleasant conversation.

In the wee hours, when the club closed, Guthro took Behan to his hotel. The next day, he found out that Behan had subsequently got a bottle of liquor (presumably from an enterprising bellhop), got properly smashed and went out again on a pub crawl of his own. Inevitably, he was arrested and spent the rest of the night in the klink.

Ironically, the headline used the night before on "Front Page Challenge" in connection with Behan's appearance, read: "Irish Playwright Lands in Jail After Spree." (A few years later, Brendan Behan drank himself to death.)

Liquor was a factor again while Don Brown was producing the show (1963–73). The guest this time was singer Ginny Sims, who had been vocalist with the Kay Kyser band. Just before the show, the makeup artist told Brown: "We've got a problem. Ginny Sims is stewed to the gills." Brown said later he thought "she had taken a bath in gin. I went to the makeup room to see her in her chair, weaving while sitting. And she was a nasty drunk."

"You don't like me, do you?" she said, and Brown answered: "Whether or not I like you is irrelevant. All I'm interested in is whether you give us a show tonight." After that, Brown added, she began to sober up and was able to go on the air.

By comparison, the drinking demands of William F. Buckley were mild indeed, even though he had ample cause to feel the need of a bracer.

The erudite, acerbic spokesman for American conservatism was due to fly to Toronto from Florida that day, but he didn't arrive on schedule. By 6:00 p.m., despite assurances from Buckley's New York agent that the challenger would be there, producer Drew Crossan was understandably nervous. He began making plans to use a standby story.

At 7:45, Buckley telephoned, explaining he was in Buffalo and could still get to the Toronto studio in time for the 9:00 p.m. program. He had been travelling all day, having run into all sorts of airline difficulties.

Roger McKean, who was the program's official greeter and some-time driver, had been back and forth to the airport several times that day. He finally arrived—with Buckley—in time to do the program. Buckley mumbled his explanations and apologies and then added a heartfelt request: "Please...a six-pack of Molson's."

He barely had time to get made up and gulp down two beers before he was on the air—poised, articulate, urbane as usual, turning every answer in the interview into a compelling speech.

It wasn't booze but drugs that troubled Ray McConnell some years later, when a well-known Hollywood actress was a guest challenger. "She was sniffing coke backstage," McConnell remembered, "and I was very concerned about that. No matter what she was asked, she would go into one of her scenes from a movie."

Drugs were an issue another time, when a guest was on-camera during the taping of "V.I.P.," Lorraine Thomson's interview show. Lorraine was interviewing the trainer of an RCMP dog called Cloud Two, whose keen sense of smell had helped in the capture of several criminals.

"While I was interviewing his RCMP handler," Lorraine recalled, "Cloud Two kept shifting his eyes left and right, looking at the various technical people standing around, and his head kept darting around. I had no idea what was happening with the dog."

The taping had to be stopped because of Cloud Two's mounting agitation. Studio director Steve Hyde remembered:

"The officer told me, 'Somebody in here has got some marijuana. Tell them, for God's sake, to get out of the studio so the dog can settle down.' So I said, "Whoever's got the grass, piss off because the dog's gone bananas. You're not going to be arrested.' A couple of guys walked away and the dog lay down on the floor and was fine after that."

A somewhat less charming guest was Dr. Timothy Leary, the garish guru of LSD and a controversial figure in the 1960s. I was writing the program at the time and I remember the dinner we had that evening. This time we went to the Park Plaza Hotel. Leary was dressed in a light grey suit and he looked like any businessman or academician having a quiet dinner with some friends. He was quite civil and soft-spoken.

When we returned to the studio, he had makeup applied, as did the other guests, and then we sat in the green room, waiting until showtime. He was to be the second guest on the live show, and we were able to watch the program on a TV monitor. A production assistant came in and informed Dr. Leary that he would be needed in the studio in five minutes. He nodded and then quite deliberately took off his shoes and socks. I had no idea what he was up to. Then he stood up and walked out to the studio in his bare feet.

Nobody was deeply offended at the sight of Leary's uncovered toes, just a bit startled. He simply put on his public costume, bare feet being part of the image of anti-establishment blowhard warriors at the time. For the earlier dinner at the Park Plaza, evidently, he was travelling incognito—with feet covered, that is.

Producer Don Brown long remembered the appearance on "Front Page Challenge" of Veronica Lake, the onetime Hollywood siren whose main claim to fame was the long blond hairdo that always hid one of her eyes. "Her every other word was 'fuck,'" Brown recalled. "I asked her if she would be okay on the air without saying that word. 'Oh, I won't say it,' she assured me, and she didn't. But she started in again as soon as she went off the air. She couldn't form a sentence without using that word."

Another challenger who made an impression on producer Don Brown was Ethel Merman, the veteran Broadway star. What was learned about her was that the old habits of struggling actors die hard. Translation: take the money and run.

She was booked for an appearance during Canada's centennial year. We were to do two shows from Montreal, in conjunction with the opening of Expo 67.

When Miss Merman was booked, she insisted she needed not just a hotel room in Montreal for her visit, but a suite. She had a good friend in Montreal, her agent told us, and Merman wanted the friend to stay with her for the two days she was in town. Getting a hotel room, let alone a suite, in Montreal at that time was extremely difficult, because of Expo 67. But somehow it was managed.

The producer had also been told to have a cheque ready for Merman, for her fee, her expenses and her hotel suite. It was given to her before the show. Miss Merman told us she had no friend in Montreal and hadn't insisted on a suite, but since it was there she used it. The next day, Merman returned to her home in New York. Only then did Brown find out she had skipped town without paying her hotel bill. The program paid for the hotel suite—twice.

Over the years, "Front Page Challenge" had its share of close calls: lost or missing challengers, weather foul-ups, mixed messages, near misses of one sort or another.

Lorraine Thomson once commented:

"Our panelists don't know half the things that go on. The no-shows, the backstage happenings, the folks who wander off on their own when they're supposed to be hiding away at a preshow dinner with us..."

When Gary Lautens was writing the show, he recalled:

"I collected (football star) Joe Namath from the airport. There he was, this gorgeous sex symbol. He rolled down the car windows and every time we stopped at a light, he yelled 'Hi, honey' to any passing girl. Well, nobody recognized him, and all the way in, all I saw were girls giving him dirty looks, thinking he was some yahoo from Scarborough. It was very funny."

The day Ottawa's Mayor Charlotte Whitton was to arrive in Toronto, a limousine was sent to the airport to pick her up, but she had decided to come by train instead.

Journalist/author Quentin Reynolds missed his flight but arrived, breathless, at the studio less than half an hour before air time.

Labour reporter Victor Reisel (who had been blinded by acid-throwing labour racketeers) was expected at Toronto's Union Station but could not be found. He had taken an earlier train and gone to a hotel.

A beauty queen was booked to appear on the program and arrived at the studio in her car, which she parked next to Toby Robins's car. The beauty queen's car was festooned with a banner announcing her identity: "Miss Canada." Fortunately, all the panelists were already inside the studio.

Veteran newsreel cameraman Roy Tash seemed to be the ideal challenger for a story about the collapse of Honeymoon Bridge at Niagara Falls. Since Mr. Tash was hard of hearing, he was provided with a special hearing aid for the program. He was placed behind the panel, but when the story was being introduced to the home audience the announcer's voice was inadvertently fed through Tash's hearing aid and could be heard by one panelist, who, happily, was sporting enough to play dumb.

Sometimes, travel arrangements backfired. In 1967, the noted Dr. Benjamin Spock was a challenger, this time in connection with his outspoken opposition to the Vietnam War. He had stipulated that he absolutely must get out of Toronto that same night. In order to make what he regarded as an urgent appointment in New York the following morning, he had to fly from Toronto to Cleveland, connect with another flight that took him to Newark Airport, then go by limousine to New York. Production assistant Jill Burns went to considerable trouble to arrange it.

The next day Jill turned on her radio and heard that Dr. Spock had succeeded in keeping his appointment: he was arrested for burning draft cards at a public protest. Jill remembered thinking: "I sent him to jail!"

These are the times that try men's souls—or, at least, give production people ulcers.

By far the most trying day ever experienced by any "Front Page Challenge" production team had nothing to do with inclement weather, mixed messages or missed airplanes.

This was in 1958, only the program's second year on the air, and the challenger in question was Igor Gouzenko, the Russian-born Canadian intelligence officer who had made international headlines in 1945 by disclosing the existence of a Soviet Russian espionage ring in Ottawa. Gouzenko was then a cipher clerk in the Russian embassy in Ottawa and had blown the whistle on the entire operation. He became an instant celebrity and, he claimed, a man marked for extermination by the KGB, the Soviet's secret police orgnization.

He had come to Canada in 1943, assigned to work for Colonel Nicolai Zabotin, the U.S.S.R. military attaché in Ottawa. In September 1945, he turned over 109 Soviet embassy documents to the RCMP, exposing Soviet espionage activities in Canada. A royal commission was appointed to investigate the charges and, the following year, supported Gouzenko's claims.

Igor Gouzenko remained a figure shrouded in mystery. He wrote a book (*This Was My Choice*) and his story was the basis of a Hollywood film (*The Iron Curtain*, in which he was portrayed by actor Dana Andrews). He also insisted that his life was in danger and that his whereabouts and assumed identity must be protected, a task the RCMP undertook.

However, a dozen years after these events, FPC producer Jim Guthro didn't have too much trouble contacting Gouzenko with an offer to be a mystery challenger on the program.

In true cloak-and-dagger fashion, Guthro and writer John Aylesworth met Gouzenko and an "adviser" in an unprepossessing restaurant in downtown Toronto to discuss such mundane matters as Gouzenko's fee for appearing and the wording of the headline to be used.

Gouzenko was worried—Guthro called it "paranoia"—about being identified. He insisted he had to wear a hood lest any lurking Soviet agents spotted him. A hood was devised for him to wear on the show. It had two eyeholes in it. Guthro wanted a third hole "for the microphone to pick up his voice. But he didn't want that."

On the day of the program, Gouzenko noticed that Fred Davis was having makeup applied to his face, so he demanded that he too be made up, even though his entire head and face were to be covered by the black hood. To further throw off the KGB, a ring was placed on his finger and a pipe was perched sticking out of the pocket of his suit coat.

Even then, Gouzenko was not satisfied. He was afraid to enter the studio for rehearsal and demanded that the premises be searched first for hidden bombs. Then he wanted his voice disguised, so the microphone had to be filtered.

What with his heavy Russian accent, a hood over his head and the filtered microphone to disguise his voice, it was almost impossible for either the panel or the audience to understand very much of what he said on the program. Guthro said later, somewhat disgustedly, that it sounded like "Bell's first telephone."

Hood and all, though, the audience could still hear and grasp at least some of Gouzenko's answers. Sinclair asked him if he thought there was still a Soviet spy ring operating in Canada.

"Yes," said the former spy. "I definitely think there is."

All things considered, apart from the publicity the show got by having this intriguing guest on, it wasn't a terribly successful program, mostly because the former spy had caused such complications that his "appearance" was pretty much of a dud.

Larry Mann, who used to do the audience warm-ups at the time, had a fascinating footnote to add to the Gouzenko incident.

After the show ended, Mann got into a conversation with the still black-hooded Gouzenko. They left the studio together via the stage door or back exit and walked about half a block along Yonge Street before Igor Gouzenko remembered to take off his hood, which was not exactly an inconspicuous costume for a man supposedly terrified of assassination. However, no lurking KGB agents struck, and Gouzenko continued down the street, unhooded and unthreatened.

These were some of the more outrageous challengers to appear on the program. In fairness, it should be added that they were the exception rather

than the rule. There were, after all, something close to two thousand challengers over the program's thirty-eight-year history. A few of them were
bound to be, well, eccentric.

On the other side of the ledger were people like Perle Mesta,
Washington's most celebrated hostess and party-giver. There was a fierce
blizzard the day she was due to arrive for the program and nobody was
able to contact her to ascertain if she was, in fact, on her way.

"All of a sudden," producer Don Brown recalled, "in the late afternoon,
at the end of the rehearsal, into the studio walks Perle Mesta."

She was exhausted and she recounted the woes she had experienced in
her efforts to get to Toronto—switching flights, changing itinerary, and
so forth, all because of the terrible weather.

Sympathetically, Brown asked why she didn't just telephone and say she
couldn't make it.

Mrs. Mesta replied, with some pride: "I know what a commitment
means, and I wouldn't have let you down for the world."

One of the most charming and urbane challengers I can recall, while
I was writing the show, was Sir Alec Douglas-Home, a former prime
minister of England, who kept us amused at dinner with a steady flow
of stories.

Sir Alec had ordered fish, and when it was brought he was in mid-
anecdote, so he absently picked up a knife and fork and began to separate the fish as he talked. The waiter who had served him, a large man with
a middle-European accent, suddenly reached across and yanked the knife
out of Sir Alec's hand. "No," he scolded, "this not for fish." The waiter then
picked up another knife and thrust it at Sir Alec, saying: "*This* for fish."

The rest of us were embarrassed and stunned, but Sir Alec was the per-
sonification of aplomb. He merely took the knife from the truculent waiter,
said "Thank you," and then went right on with his anecdote.

There were yet other challengers, whose behaviour was neither boorish nor influenced by liquor, but whose appearance on the program was
remembered, especially by those involved in the program.

One such was Ed Sullivan, then almost seventy years old, whose long-
running CBS variety program, "The Ed Sullivan Show," had recently been

cancelled. The veteran New York columnist and host of one of television's most enduring variety shows had been displaying signs of growing senility for the past couple of years, but he still carried on valiantly until the CBS axe came relentlessly down.

Lorraine Thomson remembered that Sullivan was slow of speech "and you had to remind him of what he was doing and where he was going."

And Jill Burns, the production assistant, remembers that when she asked him to sign his contract, so he could be paid, he signed it:

"To Jill, Ed Sullivan."

chapter 10

THERE'LL BE SOME CHANGES MADE

As noted earlier, of the people chosen to make up the original "Front Page Challenge" panel, the biggest surprise was Toby Robins, simply because she had no journalistic background.

As mentioned earlier, Toby was an actress, talented as well as beautiful. When she was only fifteen, Mavor Moore, the well-known playwright, actor and director, cast Toby in a Shakespearean play. From there, she went on to a number of stage roles, and with each one she grew as an actress.

However, Canadian actors in those days—and before, and after—also learned that working in the theatre was a precarious occupation. Things were fine when you were cast in a role, but that didn't last too long. And there was often a long time between calls. That was surely a factor in Toby's decision to try out for the panelist's job on "Front Page Challenge." If nothing more, the job meant a bit of extra income—though not all that much—to tide her over until the next acting role. And, of course, the regular exposure on television could only help to increase the public's awareness of her, a vital part of any actor's struggle towards stardom.

Even after she had begun to make regular appearances on "Front Page Challenge," she continued her acting career, always careful to avoid

conflicts with the TV program's schedule. In the fall of 1957, for example, she appeared in a good television drama titled "Ice On Fire," written
by Len Peterson, playing opposite the versatile Bill Walker. The following
year she was part of an all-star cast (John Drainie, Barry Morse, Jane
Mallett, Robert Goulet, Jack Creley and Austin Willis were the others) in
a Toronto stage production of Gore Vidal's comedy *Visit To a Small Planet*,
produced by Toby's husband, Billy Freedman.

The others on "Front Page Challenge" were journalists first and panelists second. Robins was an actress first and second a panelist. While
the panel show helped extend their public recognition, all the panelists
continued in their other careers.

However, by the end of her second year on FPC, the novelty was beginning to wear thin for Toby. She sensed that just as actors sometimes run
the risk of being "typed" for certain kinds of roles, she was being typed
as a-panelist-who-also-acts instead of an-actress-who-also-appears-as-a-
panelist. She felt that she was being passed over for acting jobs because of
her association with "Front Page Challenge." Therefore, she reasoned, she
would have to be paid more by CBC to continue on the panel show if she
was to justify the potential cost to her acting career that "Front Page
Challenge" represented.

As early as August 1959, I ran this item in the daily entertainment
column I wrote for the *Toronto Telegram*: "The war of nerves between Toby
Robins and the CBC continues. She's still holding out for more money on
Front Page Challenge, and the network and sponsors are getting nervous."

When Toby showed no signs of yielding, the CBC began giving serious
consideration to the idea of replacing her. This, however, turned out to be
not so simple a task.

One of the possible replacements approached was journalist June
Callwood, who had already proven herself as a strong guest panelist on
numerous "Front Page Challenge" shows.

"I knew that I was high ranked to replace her (Robins)," Callwood told
me later. "And I felt that if I did, it would be a little bit like walking through
a picket line. If I took it at $400 (the amount Toby had been getting per
show), it would be undercutting something she had tried to do. We weren't

feminists in those days, but I felt a loyalty to a younger woman. I felt that her position was right. I think she was being paid less than the men; I'm not sure, but that was my impression. So I let it be known that I would not do it under those conditions, that if they would offer me more money I would be glad to compete for the job for more money, but I wouldn't do it for the money that she had refused."

Once again, a compromise was reached and Toby signed on again. But each year the problem was the same. In the summer of 1961, when the program had completed its fourth year on the air and was making plans for the fifth, Toby told an interviewer:

"As far as I'm concerned I'm through and negotiations are over, unless they're willing to meet my price...."

Despite attempts by CBC spokesmen to suggest they were confident things would be worked out, Toby left the show, to return only as a guest panelist, now and then, in later years. When she returned to acting full-time, she and her husband, Billy Freedman, moved to England, where he turned producer and she continued to work on the stage.

Long after the events, June Callwood told Knowlton Nash (in *Cue the Elephant*): "Toby quit because she found out she wasn't getting as much money as the men. They told me I would get her slot, but I said, 'I want as much as the men, too.' Toby and I were friends and I didn't want to take less money than she wanted. I said, 'You have to give me the same as Pierre and Gordon.' They said, 'Well, no.' I don't know what Betty got, but she got the job. Maybe they gave in—or maybe she didn't know."

Some twenty years after her departure from "Front Page Challenge," I had a conversation with Toby about her experiences on the program and, more particularly, about her quitting:

"When I left the show," she told me, "I suppose I made money the issue, but I had only done it (the program) always as a temporary thing and, you know, it was like a golden cage—it was marvellous and you were famous and everything, but you were famous for the reasons that I didn't want to be famous for. And I felt it was getting in the way of acting, so I used the money (as an excuse for leaving). I mean, the money wasn't a large amount either way, but I always felt I should leave.

"In fact, I felt I should do the show for two months (the first summer season) and then go. But, you know, it was one of those things. It became such an easy way and an interesting way of working that it was difficult to leave. So I was pushing to leave because I felt I was an actress and that's what I must do."

(It may strike some readers as curious that Toby Robins was unwilling to do the program for $400 a show, less than the male panelists were paid, but was amenable to making later appearances as a guest panelist—a role that paid no more than $200. Guest panelists were always paid less than regulars.)

Nevertheless, the job of replacing Toby Robins presented some considerable problems. No rash decisions were made; numerous people were under consideration before a decision was taken.

"When Toby left," Fred Davis recalled, "they nearly made the horrendous mistake of booking people who looked like Toby, which would have just reminded the country that we didn't have the real thing."

The "Front Page Challenge" producer at the time was Bob Jarvis, and he was fully aware of the delicacy of the matter.

This item was in my column on August 17, 1961:

"Every female from nineteen to fifty is trying to convince Bob Jarvis she's just the girl to replace Toby. But Jarvis is being cagey. He has no intention of trying to replace Miss Robins. Instead, he'll use guest panelists, female, of course, for a while at least. Should one of them prove successful, he may sign her for the season—and then again he may not."

During the early part of the 1961–62 season, Jarvis did try out a few potential women panelists, the CBC once again indulging in what amounted to on-the-air auditions.

"There was a great deal of concern (at the CBC) and it was sort of two-edged," Jarvis told me later. "On the one hand there was concern that the show would be weakened if they did not replace Toby with a personality as magnetic as Toby was. On the other side was the feeling that they perhaps couldn't replace her, that there wasn't someone that they were aware of who could replace her. So it would be safer to go with several girls."

Among those who tried out were June Callwood, Lorraine Thomson, Barbara Moon, Mary Helen McPhillips, Libby Christenson, Clare Olson, Mickey Moore and, of course, Betty Kennedy.

"There were, in truth, so many girls who were good and each one had one thing or another in her favour," Jarvis told me later. "Also, in considering someone to go in as a permanent replacement you have to take into account the others on the panel, and it's my recollection, at this distance in time, that Gordon in particular had a very warm spot for Betty (they both worked at Toronto radio station CFRB), as he had had for Toby, of course. And he would defer to her sometimes, where he would not to some of the other women. And I think this grew and developed as they worked more often together."

When it was agreed that Kennedy was the best candidate, Jarvis favoured making a public announcement naming her as a regular panelist on the program.

"I said, 'If we're gonna do it, let's do it and let's give her all the help we can. Let's make something of it. Let's promote it," said Jarvis. "But the CBC didn't want to do that, in case we'd made a mistake. Again, as the CBC often does, we sort of snuck into it."

The choice of Betty Kennedy would seem, in retrospect, to have been a fairly obvious one. Over the first four years, she had appeared several times as a guest panelist and proved her value. (During that period, the three women who had been guest panelists most frequently were June Callwood, Lorraine Thomson and Betty Kennedy.)

Like Callwood's, Kennedy's journalistic credentials were impressive. Born and raised in Ottawa, she was doing both newspaper and radio work before she was fully grown-up. She married Gerhard Kennedy in 1948 and, after a spell in Calgary the couple moved to Montreal, where Betty was soon appearing on a TV magazine show called "Around the Town."

The Kennedys moved to Toronto in 1959 and she was promptly hired by radio station CFRB, starting her long-running afternoon program, "The Betty Kennedy Show." One of the countless celebrated people she interviewed on her daily radio show was Buckminster Fuller, the brilliant but

eccentric architect and philosopher, a man not unaccustomed to being interviewed. In the midst of the interview, Fuller declared:

"I just want to say something about your interviewing me here. I don't
think I recall a conversation where anybody has been quite as logically sensitive as you are about these questions you ask."

Logic and sensitivity were to become hallmarks of Kennedy's skills as
an interviewer, both on CFRB and on "Front Page Challenge."

In 1975, after twenty-seven years of marriage, Gerhard Kennedy died
of cancer and Betty soon afterwards wrote a book about him, titled *Gerhard*,
which spoke of his career and their life together. Not quite a year later,
she married Allan Burton, then the head of Simpson's department stores.
The Kennedys and the Burtons had known each other for years and Burton's
first wife had died, also of cancer, only a week before Gerhard. Inevitably,
some of the more straitlaced viewers of "Front Page Challenge" sneered
at what they regarded as her unseemly haste in remarrying.

One friend who stood by her staunchly was Gordon Sinclair:

"When she married Allan Burton, I think she was a little frightened....
A lot of people were ready to pick Betty apart. And I did a piece here
(on CFRB) on the 'Let's Be Personal' series, called 'Life is for the Living,
Not for the Dead. He's Gone.' The reaction was very strong, very favourable,
and I think she appreciated that."

It was at CFRB that Betty got to know Gordon Sinclair, who had been
one of that station's top attractions for a good many years. He was also,
by then, on "Front Page Challenge."

"I had been a guest panelist several times," Betty told me some years
later, "and I had been absolutely petrified, terrified. I don't know that I
was even able to say my name straight. You know that terrible feeling you
have that everything's gone by in a blur? Well, that's what it was like.

"And then when Toby was leaving, I think Gordon told me that they had
been doing what was in effect on-air auditions... So, then Gordon told
me that I was being considered, and I heard first that I had gotten it (the
job on the panel), and then I heard that I had not gotten it. So, you know,
it was a roller coaster, emotionally."

Bob Jarvis, the producer who had a hand in selecting Kennedy, later assessed her value to the program:

"I think one of the strengths that Betty had, and still has—I mean she's obviously intelligent, but more than that—she projects warmth, at the same time she is interrogating or interviewing. And I think that was apparent. The viewers very quickly accepted her, and I think that was partly because once she had the opportunity to shine, she did."

Announcer Bunny Cowan made his own insightful comment:

"Betty is a member of the board of directors of many large corporate institutions. She flies by private jet to board meetings, she's chauffeured to the studio and home in a Rolls-Royce. She is one of the most beautiful women, I think, we have in Canada. And it is a beauty which is consistent with her intellect and her perception of what's going on in the world today. And strangely enough, she projects the big-business image on the show, not Gordon and not Pierre."

Producer Don Brown summed her up this way:

"She has class. She's a very experienced journalist. She brought dignity, a femininity, a cool, controlled intelligence. I guess she would be the kind of panelist on 'Front Page' that most female guest panelists wished they could be."

Betty Kennedy herself looked back on her evolution as a "Front Page Challenge" star this way:

"Despite the fact that I knew Pierre and I knew Gordon—I knew Gordon better than Pierre—don't forget they're real giants in the business, and so to suddenly be a part of that panel, of course you felt like the new kid on the block, and it took quite a while, a long time really, before I began to feel quite at home there.

"Gordon was a great help. He's a friend, anyway, and I would see him every day at CFRB. So that Gordon, to me, has never been particularly intimidating, whereas to many people he is. I've never felt that way about him. I think somebody else coming in (to the show) who didn't know Gordon, who really wasn't working with him here might have found it more difficult."

Kennedy talked later about a side of Sinclair most people never saw or heard much about. (Fred Davis said Sinclair hated to have stories told about him where he had done some act of kindness.) Betty remembered Sinclair seeing a man coatless on the street outside CFRB on an extremely cold winter day. Sinclair asked the man, "Why haven't you got a coat on?" The man answered, "Because I don't own a coat." "Here," said Sinclair, "take mine." And he gave the man his coat.

Like the others, Betty Kennedy grew to appreciate the team-effort attitude of the panel:

"I think that people don't realize just how much of a team effort it is, and you'll see some stuff written that we're at one another's throats or that there's great rivalry and all this jazz, but when you look at it, every question, if it's well asked, eliminates a whole category. So that if you ask your question well, you've eliminated whole areas just right off the bat. And the other thing I think is missed sometimes is that the game is one of pace and movement, and if you've got a two-minute game and you've got four people on the panel, you've got thirty seconds to ask your questions— that's all."

Kennedy also assessed her own role as a panelist and especially as an interviewer:

"I bring a kind of balance. If Gordon is going to be particularly outrageous, I'll bring something that will be gentler. If he's going to be deliberately humorous, I'll be the other side of the coin and take it into, perhaps, the human, poignant aspect of the story. I'm a good balancer.

"And I think you do it instinctively and you do it with a feeling of the tempo of the show. If a certain area has been covered or is beginning to drag, when it gets to your turn you introduce some other element. And the elements that generally interest me are the human ones. How somebody felt, or what it meant in their career. The kind of thing which oftentimes people are not as reluctant to answer with a woman as they are with a man."

Don Brown said Betty had "class." Fred Davis said when he thought of Betty he thought of "the three C's—calm, cool and collected." Berton said

Kennedy was "every woman's idea of a lady." Berton added there was another side to Betty Kennedy that was rarely seen by audiences: "She's
got quite a temper, if she wants to use it. I've seen it."

And Allan Fotheringham, a frequent guest panelist over the years, said:
"Do I know Betty Kennedy? I'm not sure anybody does... Betty is a sur-
prising person in that, down behind those blissful good manners, there's
a backbone of steel. When she gets mad, she can't be pushed around. She's
a very tough lady underneath."

As he had with Toby Robins, Sinclair formed a lasting friendship with
Betty, perhaps more so because they used to see each other every day at
the radio station, as well as every week on "Front Page Challenge." That
close friendship lasted until Sinclair's death in 1984.

Betty's association with the program was to last for some thirty-four
years, from 1961, when she became the third regular member of the panel,
until the program's sudden demise in 1995.

Only once during Kennedy's years on "Front Page Challenge" was there
any thought given to replacing her. That was Don Brown's recollection.
Brown took over as producer in 1964. By that time, Jim Guthro, one of
the show's earlier producers (1957–61) had become head of the Light
Entertainment Department. Guthro went to him, said Brown, and said;
"I want you to fire Betty Kennedy." Brown's reply was: "Sure, I'll fire her
as soon as I find someone better to replace her." He adds: "I never did."

The "Front Page Challenge" panel was to remain constant, except for
the guest panelists, until Gordon Sinclair's death, on May 17, 1984. (Sadly,
two years later, Toby Robins died of cancer in London.)

Gordon Sinclair was the ultimate self-made man. A high school dropout
(where he was reported to have been good in English, bad in grammar and
terrible in spelling), he worked as a clerk before turning to journalism,
where he soon made his name. Later, he made his money.

His work took him around the world several times. He liked Paris. "If
I should become a lonely widower someday," he once mused, "I think I'd
like to live in Paris." But he later proclaimed Toronto his favourite place to
live—except on Sundays.

"I am what I am," said Sinclair, the ardent nationalist. "I am a Canadian in my own country. I'm even a rich Canadian in my own country, and there is nothing much better than that."

The public and press reaction to Sinclair's death was quite remarkable. So many of the readers, listeners and viewers who had spent a lifetime hating Sinclair suddenly realized that his death was a loss even to them.

Understandably, the *Toronto Star*, where he had worked for so long, did the fullest coverage of his death. The headline read: "Tributes to Sinclair Pour in from Friends Around the World."

Among the "friends" was U.S. president Ronald Reagan, who had become aware of Sinclair, as had many Americans, after his 1973 broadcast in defence of Americans, which was widely rebroadcasted and was later issued as a record, titled "Americans," and became an international hit.

The *Globe and Mail*'s coverage included one of Sinclair's lines reflecting his scorn of heaven and hell: "Asked once what his reaction would be if he found there was an afterlife, he replied, 'I'll say, Sinclair, you're in one hell of a mess.'"

In *Saturday Night*, Robert Fulford wrote: "On his good days his writing had a rushing sense of wonder that few journalists ever achieve."

At his funeral service, Dr. Stewart B. East, a retired minister in the United Church, mentioned Sinclair's professed agnosticism and suggested that by then he had probably arrived at the place he thought didn't exist and was saying something like, "Well, Sinclair's here. What are you going to do about it?"

chapter 11

ON THE ROAD

In one sense, "Front Page Challenge" was decades ahead of American television. Even in the 1960s, the CBC began experimenting with the notion of taking the show on the road. Over the next thirty years, Canada's most popular panel/game show turned up for tapings in Canadian cities from coast to coast. This practice proved tremendously successful, not only in gaining additional viewers for the program but in giving Canadians across the country a sense of identification with the show.

Not until the 1990s did American television's two most enduring game shows discover that this business of taking the show on the road—long a practice with theatrical attractions—could be applied to television.

In the past decade, "Wheel of Fortune" and "Jeopardy," the two top American TV game shows, have turned up in cities across the United States, from Las Vegas to Boston. As with the Canadian experiment, this proved a wise move, adding more viewers and giving people in those cities visited a stronger sense of identification with the programs.

It was during Don Brown's nine-year reign as producer of "Front Page Challenge," between 1964 and 1973, that the idea of taking the program on the road, even in a limited way, was first tried. The destination was

Vancouver and the time was the summer of 1966. The plan was to tape four programs for use during FPC's next season. As writer of the show, I went along with Brown and other production personnel.

Brown later recalled that he learned a valuable lesson from that trip:

"We did the shows from the Queen Elizabeth Theatre there, and everyone was happy. We shipped our set out to Vancouver and they put it up on the stage of the theatre and it looked fine, but when the show went on the air I saw what I should have been smart enough to realize before: the show could have been coming from the Toronto studio. It looked exactly the same.

"We never did that again. From then on when we travelled, we had a local (set) designer in whatever city design a set. We told him what we needed and then let him go ahead and have a chance to do his bit."

In that way, the show looked just different enough in each city so that the larger home audience would be aware that it was emanating from a different locale on these occasions. This was sensible not only for "Front Page Challenge" but for the CBC as a whole. There was no point, after all, in going to the trouble and expense of taking a television show on the road if people watching it at home couldn't tell the difference between a show taped in Saskatoon and the usual ones done at Toronto's Studio 4.

"For whatever reason," producer McConnell said, "it became politically desirable for the show not to originate from Toronto at all, and be known as a regional show. So, therefore, for the last almost five years, I never did a show out of Toronto, there was never a show done out of Toronto. All our shows were done out of the regions. And this was specifically asked of me, to do this. I think the reason was more economic. I think it also enabled that half hour a week to go on to the regional credit. That was as good a reason as any, and there's nothing wrong with that."

This politically desirable goal of being perceived as a "national" broadcaster was not new at the CBC. Even in the mid-1970s, the Corporation signed Montreal pop singer René Simard to do a weekly TV variety series. But then the Corp. flew young Simard from Montreal to Vancouver each week or so to tape his shows there, thus presumably mollifying an increasingly grumpy western Canada.

The shows taped in Vancouver in the summer of 1966 were reasonably good ones. Among the challengers were three well-known authors: Alex Haley, who had collaborated on *The Autobiography of Malcolm X* (but not yet written his magnum opus, *Roots*); Jessica Mitford, whose book *The American Way of Death* had created some controversy; and Barnaby Conrad, whose best-known work, to that time, was *The Death of Manolette*. Other challengers included Melvin Belli, the flamboyant American criminal lawyer, and the witty stripteaser, Gypsy Rose Lee.

Emboldened by the moderate success of that first venture out of town, Brown planned more the following year, Canada's centennial year.

Early in 1967, there was a trip to Ottawa, mostly for the purpose of getting Prime Minster Lester B. Pearson to appear on "Front Page Challenge" again.

In the summer of 1967, after Expo had opened, we went to Montreal to do a few shows, the most prestigious of which featured former prime minister Louis St. Laurent. It was on that same trip that Ethel Merman stiffed the CBC for her hotel suite (see chapter 9 for more about this incident).

Whatever problems going on the road entailed, all concerned agreed that it was worth doing from time to time, and that included Fred Davis and the panelists.

One bonus of the travel was the startling, and gratifying, realization by those connected with the show that they were recognized and welcomed by people wherever they went.

Pierre Berton told me, some years later:

"You know, you don't see this too much in Toronto, where everybody's blasé and you see all these people around... I was in St. John's last week; well, for Christ's sake, you'd think I was the prime minister. Everybody comes up to you and talks about the show. And they'll see the show and then they all say the same thing: we feel we know you, we feel we know you."

Production assistant Carroll Hicks worked on "Front Page Challenge," under several different producers, for many years. She, too, expressed enthusiasm about the boost in morale that came once the program took to the road:

"Travelling with the show we are so completely accepted as a Canadian show—it isn't Toronto-based anymore. Whether we're in Vancouver, Halifax, St. John's, wherever it is, it's "Front Page Challenge," it's travelling and it belongs to everybody. It's a wonderful feeling."

Fred Davis remembered a trip to Winnipeg in 1971:

"You have to book these places months in advance, and Winnipeg was delighted to have us. It was a departure, we were going to be in their beautiful Centennial hall, a 2,700-seat auditorium.

"About four weeks before we were to appear there, the hockey schedule suddenly determined that that night was going to be a Stanley Cup playoff night—not in Winnipeg, but Winnipeg is a real sports town. And I thought, geez, we're gonna be playing to an empty house... Well, the place was packed. And I made reference to the fact that the husbands had brought their transistor radios. And I said, 'I hope you'll keep us informed of the score.'"

In 1979, "Front Page Challenge" visited Quebec City for the first time, during that city's Winter Carnival. It was the twenty-fifth anniversary of the carnival.

"We were a little apprehensive about going," producer Ray McConnell remembered, "because 'Front Page Challenge' has never been carried on the French network. It had been carried in Quebec, but only on the English network. And we were to be in a huge theatre that held something like 2,500 people. We had a packed house and the panel was just knocked out. The fact that here in the centre of French Canada, 'Front Page Challenge' was every bit as popular as it was anywhere else in Canada, made it memorable."

Betty Kennedy seemed to have mixed feelings about the travel, and this was back in 1981, when the trips weren't as frequent as they were to become:

"Going out of town sometimes creates a problem, because then it takes two or three days, depending on where you're going, and you've got to travel out, be there a day and travel back. That's a little more of a problem. But you can solve it and I do. I usually tape a show or two (for radio) ahead. And I'm on a number of boards and occasionally that runs into some problems.

"You don't often get a chance to see a place, stay for a few days. The last time we went to Vancouver, some of them did go and stay for a week. I couldn't because I had an annual meeting in the States, and that turned out to be a real bear of a thing, because it meant that I came back from Bermuda, got on a plane and flew out to Vancouver, did the show, came back on the midnight red-eye; and the corporation (board of directors) that I'm on in the States, they always send a private plane for me, so I got in on the plane in the morning, went home, dumped my clothes, picked up fresh clothes and back out on another plane that afternoon. That's a little more than I like to do, but that was just the luck of the draw."

In his later years with the program, Gordon Sinclair spoke freely about how tiring the travel could get:

"I don't think I can stand any more of the long trips—the three-hour time changes, like going to Vancouver. I was disoriented there last April, and then I was invited by several people, strangers, to have a drink with them, which I foolishly did, and so I got all mixed up there. You see, all the others at that time were with their wives or someone like that. I was alone, an old chap alone, and so on a three-hour time difference it is not very good.

"So I don't think I could take any more three-hour changes. Maybe two, if we're going to Edmonton, say, or Calgary. Certainly the East is no problem, going to Halifax or Newfoundland would be no problem, but I don't think I could take another three-hour thing..."

In the same interview, he said at one point that he didn't want to retire, he wanted to keep active. Later, he mused about the potential pleasures of retiring:

"If I ever did retire, I would still live in Toronto. I don't know if I'd go south even in the wintertime, but...I would try to redevelop some hobbies I once had. I was pretty good once as an amateur ornithologist or bird-watcher... I was also a pretty good photographer, I illustrated my own books, and if I had the proper cameras in those days I think I could have made some real good pictures..."

Yet even Sinclair admitted he found the nationwide recognition enjoyable. He also recalled one trip that he had enjoyed:

"I remember one time I was in Halifax and I was going to go out on Air Canada and the weather socked in, so I met an old pal named Champagne and, well, naturally, we called him Fizz. Fizz Champagne. And he was a flyer, had his own machine there. And I said, 'Jesus, Fizz, I'm anxious to get out. Are you going?' He says, 'Yeah, I'm going up to Montreal.' I said, 'Well, I'm with you, come on.'

"So we took off from Halifax and the weather was really bad, so we had to come down in Kingston, Nova Scotia. So we came down on a little bit of an airport and they phoned up and got us a cab and we went up into the town, Saturday night in the town, Kingston. Geez, you walk along the streets, you know, 'Hello, hello, hello. Oh, that's Gord Sinclair.' Jesus. Amazing... Here I'd come out of the sky and the fog, Kingston, Nova Scotia, in the Annapolis Valley. I'd never been there in my life. Saturday night. 'Come have a beer. Come on in.' That was the first time I was aware of the impact of television."

That incident took place in the early 1960s. It was in 1970 that Sinclair had a "serious angina attack," as he later described it. The place was again Nova Scotia.

Fred Davis recalled the incident to me almost a dozen years later:

"It hit him and he turned like the colour of that wall (grey). Lorraine Thomson and I were sitting just behind him on the bus. It was an ungodly hour and he'd really worked on the trip, just done too much. He couldn't get his breath and was gasping and we're on an airport bus, we'd just stopped at the Holiday Inn in Dartmouth and we didn't know what to do. None of us are St. John Ambulance types.

"It (the angina attack) lasted about a minute and then he broke out into a cold sweat and he relaxed. So I said, 'Do you want to go to the hospital, Gordon? We'll get this guy to drive us anywhere. You know, let's miss the plane.' And he said, 'No, I'm all right. If I could just get a stimulant, you know, some liquor.' And this is six-thirty in the morning. So we get to the airport. There was no bar in Canada open at six-thirty in the morning and nobody could find a key.

"There wasn't even a drop of liquor on the plane, because it was a morning flight. And he seemed to be all right, but we were on tenterhooks. You

Larry Mann warmed up the studio audience for several years.

After Mann departed, he was succeeded by actor Paul Kligman.

Bernard ('Bunny') Cowan was the program's announcer for three decades.

Irish playwright Brendan Behan (with Sinclair, right) was as pugnacious as his reputation suggested. He wound up in jail that night, picked up as a drunk.

Fred Davis and challenger Harry Belafonte were amused at the panel's struggle to identify the guest.

Feminist Betty Friedan was a lively guest challenger.

Hockey superstar Gordie Howe delighted in the fact that the panel never guessed him—not in five appearances.

Conservative writer William F. Buckley charmed both panelists and viewers.

The program's 25th anniversary called for a celebratory cake, which Betty cut.

Edgar Bergen (minus dummies) delighted panelists Sinclair, Kennedy and Jack Webster.

The last addition to the panel was Allan Fotheringham,
seen here with Pierre, Fred and Betty

Studio director Steve Hyde going over some program
notes with Fred Davis.

Lorraine Thomson, once
a frequent guest panelist,
later became program
coordinator.

Gordon and Gladys Sinclair's Christmas card in the late 1960s.

Sinclair, guest panelist Libby Christenson, Alex Barris
and Pierre Berton were baffled by Jayne Mansfield—
especially in the interview following the game.

Lorne Green points out to Fred Davis a picture of the first class to graduate from Green's Academy of Radio Arts. Davis was in the class.

Davis was especially proud of the night he led the band behind singer Dinah Shore, at a Toronto ball.

Fred and Joy Davis,
photographed in 1990.

Alex Barris with Fred Davis, photographed shortly
before Fred's death.

know, is it worth going?'We'll forget about the plane, Gordon, we'll stay over,' I said. 'No, I'll be all right, but I would like a drink.' I don't think he ever did get his drink."

The road schedule began to intensify in the late 1970s, by which time Ray McConnell had been the "Front Page Challenge" producer for several years. During his nineteen years as producer, he took the program around Canada, from coast to coast.

There had been a few trips in the earlier days (such as the ones to Vancouver and Montreal) but now McConnell decided to make more forays into the regions. "We were getting so many requests and it was such a big moment, especially in the life of a small community, when we arrived," McConnell explained.

The program originated from Saskatoon, Whitehorse, Corner Brook, Quebec City, London and many other Canadian locations.

"I know there were over thirty-nine locations. The only place we missed was Labrador," he recalled in the summer of 1997.

In 1984, there was a plan to take "Front Page Challenge" overseas for the first time, to Lars, Germany, to tape two or three shows before an audience of Canadian Forces members. By then, however, CBC budgets were coming under severe pressure, so the overseas junket was postponed, and eventually cancelled altogether.

In August 1982, yet another development in the history of "Front Page Challenge" caused some ripples, at least among the people most intimately involved in the long-running series.

Stan Colbert, then head of CBC-TV's Light Entertainment Department, under whose jurisdiction FPC fell, came up with the idea of a daytime spinoff of Canada's most popular quiz/game show. This show was to be called "Daytime Challenge" and it was to begin airing late in September.

Colbert, an energetic, if not always practical, leader, persuaded Fred Davis to become moderator of the daytime program, but none of the other regular panelists were involved.

Many years later, Ray McConnell, the "Front Page Challenge" producer at the time, recalled the new spinoff:

"I wanted nothing to do with it. It was not a good idea. At no time did anybody come to the producer of the show and say, 'What do you think of this?' We always had this problem of a we-they relationship on management's part."

He said the CBC's decision to put the new show on the air created an awkward relationship between Fred and the panelists, "especially Gordon," who thought Davis had "betrayed" the panel. (Sinclair eventually cooled down.)

Although McConnell had nothing to do with Colbert's new project, he recalled that he had earlier proposed rerunning some of the "Front Page Challenge" shows in a daytime slot. The CBC had rejected his proposal. Later still, Berton recalled discussing with CBC brass the possibility of rerunning FPC programs and indicated a willingness to work out a pay schedule that would be more than reasonable for the Corporation. This idea, too, was rejected.

However, in 1997, the CBC finally decided to allow some of the old "Front Page Challenge" shows to be reshown, but leased the rights to the new History Channel.

Colbert's daytime version of the show, according to a CBC press release of the time, said it would adopt the same general format as "its venerated parent" but would deal with "inside page" guests and stories—those that were lighter, more entertainment-oriented and "more fun."

"Daytime Challenge" was to air twice weekly, with a rotating roster of panelists that included Roger Abbott, of "Royal Canadian Air Farce," actress Jayne Eastwood, *Toronto Star* columnist Gary Lautens, singer Diane Stapley, actor Jonathan Welsh and pop-music critic Peter Goddard. The producer was to be Cynthia Grech and I was hired to write the show, likely a suggestion made by Davis.

But the daytime spinoff never quite managed to spin. The show was dropped after about a dozen weeks, mostly unlamented by all concerned, except possibly Stan Colbert.

Other factors, however, affected the real "Front Page Challenge." By the early 1980s, the CBC was facing the first round of serious financial cutbacks, some in radio but even more in television. Over the next few years, inevitably, budgetary problems became more acute. To counter them, Ray McConnell devised a new production schedule.

Normally, when all the shows were produced in Toronto, the most effective method had been to do two shows in an evening, every other week—one taped for future use, and one live. McConnell decided that when the program went out of Toronto, it would do three shows in one evening—two taped for future use, and one live. That approach helped to keep the costs of travel under control, for the time being.

Of course, McConnell and others involved in the program were well aware of Gordon Sinclair's heart condition, after the angina attack in Nova Scotia. When travel was involved, Ray McConnell made sure that either he or Betty Kennedy went with Sinclair. Gordon's bosses at CFRB were also aware of his health problems and tried to make things easier for him. It was suggested that he do his radio broadcasts from home, but he flatly refused.

According to Scott Young's revealing biography of Sinclair, *Gordon Sinclair—A Life...And Then Some*, the curmudgeon even refused to have a limousine drive him to and from the studio.

"When the day comes that I can't drive my own car, get myself to work, then I'm not fit to come to work and should quit," snarled Sinclair.

Kennedy, by now a longtime friend of Sinclair's, was sensitive to his mood swings. "He was very moody," she said. "I would go and see him and take him flowers, and he would say, 'I've had it. I'm finished. I'm done.'... He could get down in the dumps. My guess is that he probably did have what today would be called clinical depression. He would be gone like that for three or four days until we'd persuade him to come back to work and tell him he was needed."

But Sinclair's health continued to deteriorate. He would grudgingly take a little time off, rest, then bounce back to work, certain he was as good as new.

On the morning of May 15, 1984, he took a driving test, required annually because of his age. He passed the test and made that little victory the subject of his "Let's Be Personal" broadcast later the same morning.

Betty Kennedy dropped into his office just after his 11:50 newscast. They chatted briefly and she asked him if he remembered that they were scheduled to tape two "Front Page Challenge" shows the next day.

"No, I didn't," he said. "Okay, darlin', I'll see you there."

He didn't make it. He collapsed later that day and was dead two days later, a few weeks short of his eighty-fourth birthday.

When he started with "Front Page Challenge," in 1957, he was paid $60 a show. By the time of his death, he was making $2,000 a show, as were the other regular panelists.

Everyone involved in the program was well aware that "Front Page Challenge" had suffered a grievous loss. Replacing him would be no easy task.

Three years before Sinclair's death, announcer Bunny Cowan had mused: "I've been asked about Gordon Sinclair... what would happen to 'Front Page Challenge' if something happened to Gordon? And I can't conceive of that, it's just not reasonable. He's going to go on forever. But if, God forbid, something happens, I'd have to say we'd be making a terrible mistake to assume that Gordon Sinclair is 'Front Page Challenge' or 'Front Page Challenge' is Gordon Sinclair. No, I think that the show performs such a valuable function in the context of today's programming requirements, that it stimulates people in such a creative way, that it would be a terrible mistake to assume that any single element of 'Front Page Challenge' is responsible for the total picture... We'll never run out of stories. We'll never run out of people, until they drop the bomb. And when they do, 'Front Page Challenge' will go on the air and tell the world what a mistake that was."

So, replace him the CBC must. The little summer show that had by then been running for twenty-seven years was not anywhere near finished yet.

Producer McConnell spent the summer of 1984 mulling over that large issue.

chapter **12**

GUESS AGAIN

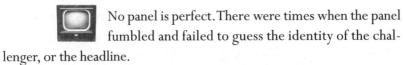 No panel is perfect. There were times when the panel fumbled and failed to guess the identity of the challenger, or the headline.

Show business challengers didn't always work out too well, surprisingly enough. When Groucho Marx was on the show, for example, the expected hilarity didn't really occur. This was partly because Groucho was in a relatively "serious" mood (the headline dealt with his papers being turned over to the Library of Congress), but also because the panelists were afraid of walking smack into the destructive Marxian wit, thus becoming the defenseless butt of one of his barbs.

Comedians were generally troublesome for the panel, as illustrated by an incident that Betty Kennedy recalled:

"Victor Borge was good. I had done Borge myself (on radio) and I got him off the kind of comedy thing for a few minutes and he had some very interesting things to say. But not on 'Front Page Challenge'—there he saw an audience.

"The comics are the hardest of all. And they are the hardest people to interview whether you are on a game show or whatever, for the simple reason that you're playing the straight man, only you don't know what the script is. I don't mind playing straight man, but I sure would like to know what the script is."

Even Fred Davis fell into Borge's comic trap:

"As we got to the end of the interview, I wrapped him (Borge) up and cut him off and didn't give him a chance, because if you did he was gonna take us to the network cue. We went to a commercial.

"During it, he leaned over and said, 'Is there any more time at all?' I figured he was hot on something. I said, 'Can you do it in thirty seconds?' Then I got the studio director and said, 'Borge has an ending for us. Can we drop the closing credits?' So we cleared decks, dropped the credits, everything was all set. They told me, 'He's got forty seconds before we're off the air.' So I come up and say, 'Well, I know we've said good night, but, Mr. Borge, was there something else that you wanted to say?' He says, 'No.'

"And I fell off the chair laughing. It was the greatest put-on. I shouldn't have enjoyed it that much, because the audience didn't know why we were laughing. I thought it was a great inside joke, which was not very professional of me."

The panel always tried to outguess the producers, but it didn't always work. Betty Kennedy recalled one such incident:

"You know how we sit around and say, 'What'll we have while we're in Halifax? We'll probably have one show business story and there are several movies being made, and Patricia Neal is here making a movie. She's a good bet, we might get her.'

"So, on one show, there was a woman's voice (the hidden challenger) and the minute she began to talk, Pierre said: 'I would recognize that voice anywhere. You're Patricia Neal.' And she said, 'No, I'm not.' And it wasn't."

The hidden challenger was Joan Fontaine. Some months later, Patricia Neal was on the show, but nobody mistook her for Joan Fontaine.

During the program's first summer on the air, actor Don Ameche was a challenger. He disguised his voice so effectively that panelist Toby Robins blurted out: "Are you Jane Russell?"

The panelists found themselves with egg on their faces again when the challenger was Robert Clary, the French-born actor and singer who was then appearing on the U.S. television comedy series "Hogan's Heroes."

The panel tended to resent the appearance of a challenger whose con-nection with the headline was tenuous. In this case, Clary "represented" a story about the liberation of the surviving prisoners of Buchenwald. The ensuing interview was somewhat bumpy.

At one point, Clary made mention of a revue called *New Faces of 1952*, in which he had made his Broadway debut. One panelist admitted he didn't remember Clary in that show but added he had enjoyed Clary on the "Jack Paar Show."

Clary pointed out, somewhat testily, that he had never appeared on the Paar program. As usual, good old Fred had to smooth things over. That was one of his specialties; nobody could match him at that.

Errol Flynn baffled the panel by disguising his voice so effectively that he sounded like a woman. In the interview that followed, the Flynn charm worked on panel and audience alike.

As mentioned earlier, when he arrived in Toronto, he was accompa-nied by his girlfriend, Beverly Aadland, for whom he had insisted FPC provide a second airline ticket. That same year, a film called *Cuban Rebel Girls* was released, to uniformly unfavourable reviews. It starred Flynn and Aadland.

The same Miss Aadland turned up again on "Front Page Challenge" nine years later, in connection with a story about Flynn's death, which occurred a short time after Flynn's appearance on the panel show.

Don Brown remembered calling Aadland to invite her to appear on the program. On the phone, she asked him if "this program" was in good taste, and he assured her that it was.

"Miss Aadland came on the show. Betty asked her if anyone had objected to her travelling with Flynn. She said, 'Oh, no. Oh, well, I suppose Mrs. Flynn did.' And at the end of the interview...someone asked her if she was now married. And she said, 'Yes, and I've got a roast in the oven.' And pat-ted her stomach. And she was asking *me* about good taste!"

Another challenger was David Frost, who arrived with a retinue of lack-eys, and his lady friend of the time, the singer/actress Diahann Carroll. Lorraine Thomson remembered that "everybody was more interested in Diahann Carroll than we were in David Frost."

The "Front Page Challenge" panel were, to begin with, knowledgeable, curious, articulate journalists, and few things annoyed them more than being faced with political figures who simply stonewalled them, or hedged as long as possible. This sometimes resulted in an acid-toned interview.

Berton recalled being annoyed at former British prime minister Clement Atlee "because he wouldn't answer any question except with yes or no."

Another man who irked Berton was the French prime minister, Pierre Mendès-France. Here was the leader of a country noted for its wines and "for some reason (he) wouldn't talk about anything but milk." Sinclair also remembered Mendès-France: "He would only talk on milk. Nothing else. He was opposed to the French wine industry. He was a very strange one."

Some noted challengers succeeded in throwing the panel off stride. When Indira Gandhi was on the program, guest panelist Peter Worthington asked her about the chances that she would become the prime minister of India.

"I don't look forward to such a prospect," Mrs. Gandhi said. "In fact, I'm against it."

About a year later Mrs. Gandhi became the country's prime minister.

Any challengers who declined to discuss the very stories that had made them people of interest to the panel were a source of annoyance to the panel. Another instance of this was Marian Anderson, whose 1939 snub by the Daughters of the American Revolution reverberated throughout much of the world. Her refusal to discuss that incident frustrated the panel, and resulted in a bland interview.

The "Front Page Challenge" panel was also annoyed with challenger Ruth Carter Stapleton, sister of Jimmy Carter, who had then recently been nominated to run for the U.S. presidency. The panel understandably wanted to learn about her brother, but all she was interested in discussing was being a born-again Christian.

"That was really disappointing," recalled Carroll Hicks. "She really got miffed, she wanted a platform for her religious beliefs and all they wanted to do was ask about Jimmy Carter. Nobody got what they wanted."

Sinclair made no secret of his scorn for religion. This got to be a back-stage gag. The show's band members would taunt him mischievously just before a program by saying things like "God be with you, Gordon" or "God bless you, Gordon."

Late in 1964, a Canadian missionary, Rev. Hector MacMillan, was killed in the Congo. A couple of months later, producer Don Brown persuaded his widow, Ione MacMillan, to appear on "Front Page Challenge." After the panel guessed the story, Brown recalled hearing the panelists in conversation (during the commercial) talking about who would begin the interview. Mrs. MacMillan was now seated in the interview chair in the centre of the studio.

"They were deciding who should ask the first question," Brown said, "and Pierre said to Gordon—which we could hear in the control room—'Gordon, you'd better start the questioning, this is right up your alley.' And Gordon said, 'No, you know what I'm like on these religious questions.' And the guest, the little widow, turned to Gordon and very piously said, 'Don't worry, Mr. Sinclair. I won't be too hard on you.'

"Well, the horns came out and Gordon did start the questioning and he kind of wiped the floor with her, and she deserved it. But of course the audience didn't know why. All they knew was this was a poor widow and Gordon was being very unkind to her."

The following year, "Front Page Challenge" taped the only show in its illustrious history that was never aired. It was March 30, 1965. The challenger in this taped show was Leon Balcer, a Progressive Conservative M.P. from Quebec. Mr. Balcer and his political party had publicly disagreed over some matter of policy. In the interview, Balcer was asked if he was going to quit his party and sit as an independent. Mr. Balcer hedged, saying he couldn't release that information, he hadn't quite decided. It was news in the making, a broad hint that he was going to break with his party.

The taped show was scheduled to air the following Monday night, but Canada's annual love affair with the Stanley Cup playoffs interfered and "Front Page Challenge" was pre-empted. By the following week, the fact that Balcer had indeed left his party was announced in large-sized headlines. And the show on which Balcer had hinted at his future plans was now obsolete.

Ten years after Sinclair tangled with Mrs. MacMillan, he faced Father Daniel Berrigan, the radical priest. As mentioned above, Sinclair never had any use for religion and, at the moment, wasn't too keen on radicals, either. At one point in the interview, Sinclair pointed to the cross Father Berrigan was wearing and asked if it "was not an instrument of torture and execution in Jesus' day." The priest agreed that it was.

Sinclair went on: "Do you think you could establish a religion today based on the firing squad, the electric chair and the hangman's noose?"

The priest grew angry, said that he could. Sinclair then went on to question the biblical version of Christ's resurrection. Fred Davis tried to calm the waters by moving along to the next panelist.

Producer Ray McConnell said later: "That's just Gordon. We don't put any muzzle on him and we don't edit the show."

Victor Podoski, a former Polish minister to Canada, was a challenger on a story about Polish art treasures that had been stored in Ottawa and Quebec during the Second World War. After many years, Ottawa had returned some of the treasures, but Quebec declined to, presumably because Poland was by then under communist rule.

At one point in the interview, Podoski was asked if Quebec premier Maurice Duplessis was justified in keeping the art treasures. The challenger seemed to be answering; his lips moved but no sound came out. The producer and the sound crew, and Davis and the panel, were thoroughly confused. They thought, understandably, that a microphone had gone dead. The eventual explanation was simpler: Podoski had merely chosen his own method for avoiding an answer to a delicate question without openly refusing. He moved his lips as if speaking, but made no sound at all.

Another challenger who failed to charm anyone on the program was Elsa Maxwell, the social gadfly and party-giver.

"I thought she'd have been the epitome of fashion and supposedly what glamour was all about," Toby recalled. "But she was aggressive and seemed dirty, actually; her dress was all stained. She was rather pathetic."

Producer Jim Guthro felt the same way: "When I saw her, it reminded me of the time she was on Jack Paar's show and Paar said to her, 'Why don't you pull up your stockings? They're awfully wrinkled.' And she said, 'I have no stockings on, Jack.' That just about sums her up."

During all the years that he was on the program, Gordon Sinclair had no trouble maintaining his reputation as outspoken, blunt, sometimes outrageous. When Wayne and Shuster were on as challengers, Sinclair, predictably, demanded to know how much money they earned for their TV appearances on Ed Sullivan's variety show. Just as predictably, they stonewalled him, refusing to discuss their income. (Shuster quipped that Sullivan gave them "carfare.")

Like the other panelists, Sinclair was occasionally peeved when the producers came up with obscure stories and equally obscure challengers:

"We had a few things that totally and absolutely bewildered us, because they didn't seem to be on any front page anywhere in Canada. I remember one, there was a man who got stuck in a chimney in Moncton. Well, now, what kind of a story is that? How are we going to guess a man who got stuck in a chimney in Moncton?"

In 1968, Dr. Norma Helen Verwey, of Vancouver, a proponent of vasectomies as a means of sterilizing men, appeared on the program. The highlight of the show was Gordon Sinclair, in high dudgeon, announcing that he certainly wasn't going to stand for anyone robbing him of his manhood, and otherwise giving Dr. Verwey a fairly vivid picture of what he thought of this method of birth control.

Despite the occasional beefs by the panelists about uncooperative challengers or obscure headlines, they all treasured memories of challengers they enjoyed meeting.

One that Sinclair remembered was a woman whose name he could not recall, but whose story had stayed with him:

"She was shipwrecked and got into a lifeboat with thirteen men. She was the only female. And her big problem was urination. She had to talk about having a pee. And we couldn't get her stopped. She was on this one subject and there was some anxiety, you know...about this woman wanting to have a pee with thirteen men (there) and she was saying how courteous and how understanding they were, and it made a beautiful show, really."

Anyone who watched "Front Page Challenge" over the years knows that one of the strongest aspects of emotional involvement for the audience is a subconscious wish to see the panel fall on its famous face. The real name of the game—this one or any other—is Beat the Panel. Any producer of a game show knows this and can be relied upon to make good use of it, now and then.

Just to keep the panelists on their toes, the producers sometimes played Machiavellian tricks on them. One effective way of doing this was to invite a mystery challenger to the show who was very close to somebody on the panel. This device was used a number of times.

The first time was in December 1958, with a headline about the first Grey Cup game played in Vancouver. The challenger, who had covered that game, was Gord Sinclair, the Montreal-based son of Gordon. The elder Sinclair did not recognize his own son's voice, but Toby Robins guessed the story.

Only a few weeks later, Laura Berton, mother of Pierre, was a challenger in connection with the Yukon gold rush. This time, it was Pierre who failed to recognize a familiar voice. But the panel still managed to guess the headline.

An even more devious way of tricking the panel was to have one of the panelists on as a challenger. This approach was also used several times, and it required a lot of scheming.

Berton was on as a challenger several times, as was Sinclair. On one such occasion, Berton had gone to Australia but, by arrangement with the producer, Don Brown, had returned earlier than he was expected. Brown told the other panelists that Berton had been delayed and booked a substitute panelist. The headline dealt with the completion of the transcontinental railway, a subject about which Pierre had written a book.

On an earlier occasion, in 1958, Berton was a mystery challenger representing a story about the Headless Valley, a western Canadian legend about which he had also written.

Berton was supposedly away that week, in Quebec; in fact, he was secretly brought into the studio to throw the rest of the panel off. The stunt backfired, however, when Sinclair spotted Pierre in the corridors of the studio building. Convinced that some trickery was afoot, although he knew not what it might be, Sinclair took producer Jim Guthro aside and told him he'd seen Berton. It was too close to air time to make any changes, so Guthro told Sinclair to say nothing to the other panelists and also not to make use of his knowledge of Berton's presence. Gordon went along with the producer's instructions, although it undoubtedly bothered him that the viewing audience would think him useless during the game.

On another show, there occurred one of those rare but inevitable breakdowns in the program's security system, the objective of which was always to keep the panelists from learning in advance the identity of the challengers.

An American friend of Berton's, the writer Robert Crichton, happened to be in Toronto and tracked Pierre down to the CBC's Studio 4 on a show day. Crichton went backstage to see Berton in the early evening. After they'd exchanged greetings, Crichton asked, "What in hell is David Susskind doing around back there?" That chance remark, of course, alerted Berton to the fact that Susskind was to be a challenger that evening. As was the custom when these incidents occurred, Berton disqualified himself from that particular story.

Gordon Sinclair was a challenger four times, and on one of those occasions he didn't know he was the challenger until after the game was over. This was in 1958 and the story was the assassination of Huey Long, the colourful, controversial Louisiana governor, a 1935 story Sinclair had covered as a reporter.

On that occasion, Fred Davis answered all the panel's questions, including Sinclair's, on the legitimate but sneaky grounds that the panel would recognize the "hidden" challenger. The panel did not guess the story.

When it was revealed, Sinclair was asked to move over to the interview chair and, without any advance notice, answered all questions about the assassination.

Another time, with Sinclair serving as both panelist and unknowing challenger, writer Chuck Weir was standing behind the panel, wearing a Gordon Sinclair mask and answering questions. On a different appearance as challenger, announcer Bunny Cowan wore the Sinclair mask.

In 1966, Sinclair returned to the program after an illness a week before the rest of the panel expected his return. This time, he served as a mystery challenger to mark the approaching tenth anniversary of the show. Not an earth-shaking story, to be sure, but a neat, and inexpensive, way of tricking the panel.

Some years later, Jack Webster was a hidden challenger, representing a story about a prison riot that he had covered. "I spoke in an imitation French accent," he told me. "I answered '*Oui*' and '*Non*.' That was a riot."

Another device used by producers when they had someone closely associated with a panel member on the show as a challenger was to have that panelist begin the questioning, a decision that was always controlled by the producer and Fred.

Thus, when Pierre Berton's mother was the challenger, Fred asked him to start the game. The logic was solid: he had to start doing the spadework, narrowing down the time, place and type of story. Also, if the questioning started with someone else, this would have given Berton more opportunity to hear, and possibly recognize, the familiar voice of his mother.

Producer Jim Guthro recalled yet another trick played on the panel, one that he clearly relished:

"There was a dog story, a good topical dog story. I forget what the story was, but we got the dog and we had the dog in a cage and it was up there (behind the panel) and when Gordon would ask 'Is this an important story?' we'd take a close-up of the dog. The studio audience (seeing the dog on a TV monitor) would just fold up with laughter. And Gordon would say, 'What are they laughing at?' Take another close-up of the dog. Then another laugh. The dog would yawn, and so on. I forget the story—the dog saved someone's life, I think, but it doesn't matter. But I'd get laughs from the live audience because the picture of the dog was making fun of the panel."

Bob Jarvis, who produced the show in the early 1960s, remembered another instance of trickery used against the panel. He recalled a period when the show's props man, apparently a born prankster, suggested "accidentally-on-purpose" leaving items on the table in the green room that would arouse the panel's curiosity.

"He would do things like this and there would never be an explanation," Jarvis said. "He'd get a plastic fish, or something, and leave it there for the panel to 'discover' when they came in. And, of course, Gordon, who was like a great big kid, would come screaming into the green room and pounce on this, and try to figure out what it meant."

In 1961, while Guthro was the show's producer, he dreamed up yet another tricky scenario for the "Front Page Challenge" panel. There had been a U.S. presidential election the previous November, the one in which John F. Kennedy defeated Richard Nixon, and Guthro felt this story was certainly worth covering, in some way.

Obviously, he couldn't get either of the principals in the headline to participate. To settle for an American newsman who had covered the election was acceptable, but not especially novel. Guthro kept trying to come up with an angle, and it finally came to him.

He remembered that the U.S. election involving Kennedy and Nixon had been the first one in which computers were used to project results. So he contacted International Business Machines (IBM) and arranged to have a computer (the IBM Ramac 305) installed in the studio, with the computer panel up behind the program's panelists. In his preamble to the game, Fred Davis explained that the challenger was "not able" to answer questions about the headline, so he would supply the answers. Inevitably, the panelists assumed the "challenger" was a dog or some other such animal.

It turned out to be an amusing game, but the best fun came later. Since there could obviously be no interview in the conventional sense, Guthro and his staff dreamed up still another switch. Under the guidance of IBM computer experts (Dr. Eugene Lindstrom was in charge), the computer was programmed to answer a series of questions on trivia. Information was fed into the computer and Davis conducted a contest between the panel, acting individually or collectively, and the computer, to see whether the panel or the computer could come up with the answers first. Some of the questions, Guthro recalled, concerned when the first steamboat crossed the Atlantic, when Quebec was first settled, and so on.

"I'll tell you the truth," Guthro told me, "when it was finally over, the awful truth is that the panel was faster than the computer, because they were all trivia people, especially Toby Robins."

But Jim Guthro had one more card left to play. The final trivia question was about the bust, waist and hip measurements of Marilyn Monroe. The correct answer had been fed into the computer, and while the panelists were debating whether the numbers were 36–24–36, or whatever, the computer printed the correct answer.

To make it even more fun, the computer had been programmed to print out the statistics, plus the word "WOW." That added touch convulsed the studio audience, who enjoyed the notion that a computer could express what seemed like a human reaction.

"We must have got a thousand letters on that," Guthro added, wearing a smile aglow with the happy memory.

chapter 13

MORE
CHANGES

At the time of Sinclair's death, May 1984, the producer of the program was Ray McConnell, who had joined "Front Page Challenge" eleven years earlier, having come from Winnipeg, where he had done mostly public affairs shows.

McConnell had been producing the show for eleven years when Sinclair died. He knew that replacing Sinclair would be a difficult task, so he lost no time in tackling it. He soon had compiled a shortlist of possible replacements. Topping that list, surprisingly enough, was the name of Pierre Elliott Trudeau, who had been on the program as a guest challenger.

"Trudeau loved the show, and he loved coming on it, as a challenger," McConnell recalled. "But also he was very comfortable with the panel, and I think he liked what the show stood for."

At the end of June 1984, Trudeau stepped down as Canada's prime minister, and was, theoretically, at least, "available" to do whatever he wished. There were some gingerly negotiations, and it was McConnell's impression that Trudeau was titillated by the prospect. He eventually decided against accepting the invitation, however. Trudeau evidently made the question of money the issue, but those involved believed he merely used that as an excuse to back away from making a commitment to become a regular panelist.

Thus, McConnell went back to his shortlist: Gary Lautens, Allan Fotheringham and Jack Webster. "I wanted to get a journalist involved in the show. That was my prime consideration," said McConnell. "The CBC had always been interested in getting Webster, but he was still under contract to CTV."

McConnell decided that Gary Lautens was "good, but wasn't what the show needed at that time. I also wanted someone who would have immediate national impact. Also somebody who would continue that relationship that the show had always had with politicians, in that it wasn't lightweight and fluffy."

So he settled on Allan Fotheringham, who joined the program as a regular in the fall of 1984.

Some time later, Fotheringham commented on the fact that he was the CBC's second choice to take Sinclair's seat: "I don't really mind being second choice to Pierre Trudeau. But can you imagine? Every one of his questions would have been twenty minutes long."

It was Ivan Fecan, then head of CBC-TV Variety, who announced at a press conference the choice of Fotheringham as the permanent replacement for Sinclair.

At that press conference, Fotheringham said: "I'm not here to fill the shoes or the kilt of Gordon Sinclair. No one will ever be a Gordon Sinclair in this country. It will take me a while to fit in with the panel."

Even after he had Fotheringham on his regular panel, McConnell still had another evolution in mind. By this time, the program was travelling all the time (For more about this, see chapter 11.). That is, none of the shows were being done in Toronto, where the program had been born. McConnell had no qualms about that. The CBC had decided that the program should originate in different cities across the country, but not Toronto.

"As a matter of fact," McConnell remembered, "I had requested to do a couple of shows in Toronto and that was denied me. They wouldn't let me do shows from Toronto, for all the reasons that they came up with, you know, studio space and political reasons, all that stuff."

One lesson McConnell learned from "travelling" the show was that finding appropriate guest panelists was not easy. Because of budgetary pressures in the CBC, it didn't make sense to fly guest panelists to Saskatoon or Halifax, so McConnell had to use "local" guest panelists in each city the program visited, and this presented yet another problem. "It's not that they weren't good," McConnell said, "but they didn't have national recognition."

The producer's ideal solution to this continuing problem was to have a regular four-person panel, thus eliminating the need for finding acceptable local guest panelists.

At this point, Jack Webster's contract with CTV ran out and he was theoretically available. McConnell decided to take advantage of the opening in Webster's schedule.

When McConnell told his superiors he wanted Webster and would have to pay Webster the same amount the other panelists were getting, the brass at CBC approved his choice. It was announced that Jack Webster would be joining the panel and Webster was flown to Toronto from Vancouver for the launch of the fall season.

"But," McConnell remembered, "they neglected to tell me that my budget was not going to be increased to pay for Webster's salary. So I had to eat his salary for the whole goddamn thing. And that hurt the show to a degree. That kind of belt-tightening, which was happening throughout the CBC at that time, didn't do the show any good."

(The difference was not insignificant. Even this late in the program's run, guest panelists were still being paid $200 per appearance. But the regular panelists were now earning some $2,000 a show, and this rate would now apply to Jack Webster. That meant an additional cost of some $1,800 per show for McConnell, but his budget was not increased accordingly.)

Jack Webster said that when he had been a guest panelist he was "paralyzed with nerves." It wasn't easy "for a wee boy from the West Coast to come out and sit beside the great Berton."

The Glasgow-born Webster had paid his newspaperman dues in Scotland and then England before emigrating to Vancouver in 1947. He started working at the *Vancouver Sun* the day Pierre Berton left that same paper.

Berton informed Knowlton Nash that Webster told the *Sun's* managing editor that he wanted to be the next Pierre Berton. Added Berton: "But I don't think Webster could be the next anything. Webster's unique. You wouldn't want two of them. One is plenty."

Before long, Webster had switched to radio and by the 1960s, he was the most provocative radio hot-line host in Canada. In time, Cameron Bell, then the head of news programming at BCTV, lured Webster away from radio and into television. He soon had one of the most popular TV shows on the West Coast. Webster also became the West Coast correspondent for "This Hour Has Seven Days," the CBC's hard-hitting public affairs show of the time.

Webster and Bell did not always get on well together, as both later admitted, but Jack's television show was successful enough to run for nine years. It could probably have gone on longer, but at the age of seventy-one he decided to slow down.

(Ironically, the next time Webster's path would cross Cameron Bell's was during the last three years of "Front Page Challenge's" long and hitherto happy life, when Bell became the last producer of what had long since become one of the CBC's most successful programs.)

"We went along for a number of years with 'Foth' as panelist, still using guest panelists, and then it got to the point where I was having to fly guest panelists in all the time because there's a limited supply of people to choose from in the regions, not because they're not good or anything, but because they're not national figures," said McConnell.

"And then one day Webster became available. He and I had always had a very warm relationship, he was a guest panelist two and three times a year, and I had said to him, 'Look, let me know, give me a tipoff, because I may want to make a decision,' and it all came to a head at that point, where I could get Webster, and I did."

But by the time McConnell called him with an offer to become a regular panelist, he forgot his earlier nervousness and accepted the post, despite his avowed intention of slowing down. "I'm always nervous," he commented. "I am not secure. I think that if you're a fully secure person, you're not much of a reporter."

Webster had no trouble fitting into the "Front Page Challenge" panel, readily trading good-humoured jibes with Berton and Fotheringham.

It might be said fairly that it took two tough, outspoken but vastly different journalists—Allan Fotheringham and Jack Webster—to replace the seemingly irreplaceable Gordon Sinclair.

From the late 1980s until the demise of the program, in 1995, there were no more changes of personnel on the "Front Page Challenge" panel—although there was talk of some changes in the program's last year or so.

chapter 14

THE BUDGET
SHRINKS

Budget cutbacks at the CBC started in the early 1980s and, inevitably, television was affected more than radio was, if only because TV was always, by its very nature, the more expensive service.

By the middle of the 1980s, the budget cuts were becoming more and more difficult to cope with, for virtually all CBC television programs, with the possible exception of news and sports coverage.

"Front Page Challenge" was still being produced by Ray McConnell, by now a past-master at cutting costs wherever possible. His scheme of taping three shows instead of two at each session helped, but not enough.

"The kind of belt-tightening which was happening throughout the CBC at the time didn't do the show any good. I couldn't afford some guests that I wanted. The other thing was that airline fares and hotel rates were going out of sight, the old days when you could fly people in from Europe and so on were long gone, because if you had to (fly them) first class, and a lot of these people insisted on it, you couldn't afford it."

McConnell was quick to note that both the panel and moderator were always cooperative and understanding with regard to his budgetary problems.

"But it got more and more expensive to do the show," McConnell said. "Talent fees always increased, airlines, hotels, especially. Originally, the panel always flew first-class, and they were magnificent. I called them one day and said we're at the point now where if I honour my agreement that you fly first-class, which is in your contract, the show will suffer. And without a moment's hesitation, they said, Oh, well, don't be ridiculous, we'll fly business class or whatever. So we did that immediately and all that money went back into the budget."

The producer says he never had trouble negotiating with the panel. He would simply tell panelists what he could afford and they would pretty well take his word. On an earlier occasion, he recalled, because of tight budgets, they actually took a kind of pay cut. That is, they had a two-year contract that called for a small incremental raise in the second year. When he told the panelists how tight the budget was, they volunteered to forgo the increase.

Another time, McConnell took a different approach when it was time to renegotiate with the panel:

"I said to the panel, I can't get you a raise next year unless, perhaps, I can get you a raise if we give a second release, within, say, one week. And they thought it over and they said, 'Yeah, we think that's a good idea. Sure, we'll take it.' And, honest to God, the raise, you wouldn't believe it, the raise was $50 or something. But it was a token raise, with the ability to run the show twice. Whoever was in charge of those decisions (at the CBC) in those days, for their own political reasons, wanted to do something different, and that was crazy... They could have got it (a second run) for peanuts, and the Corporation rejected it."

Yet another cutback helped keep the costs in check: Bunny Cowan, who supplied the voice-over narration that accompanied the filmed re-creation of the news event featured on the show, normally travelled with the program, but McConnell arranged to have him prepackage his narration in Toronto. This saved a return fare, plus hotel and meal expenses.

McConnell added another element to the continuing survival of the program by arranging with various charitable or public service organizations to have them sponsor local tapings of "Front Page Challenge" and raise money for their charities by charging admission to the tapings. This approach was taken in Winnipeg in aid of the Canadian Mental Health Association, with tickets for the "Front Page Challenge" taping going for $100 a seat.

"We get a big cross-section," McConnell told a Vancouver interviewer at the time. "We've done shows in some cities where the tickets were sold for $10 with the proceeds going to a charity, and in Calgary people were scalping them. In Regina, people drove fifty miles through a blizzard to see the show—good audience in Regina." The Calgary taping netted $48,000 for a charitable cause there.

However, such measures were aimed at attracting public attention to the FPC appearances across the country, rather than saving money out of the show's budget.

One thing that always irked producer McConnell was that he was not allowed to make deals with airlines for free tickets in exchange for an on-air credit to the airline.

"It was terribly unfair," he commented. "Shows that were produced outside of the CBC for the CBC could employ these credits and we—in-house productions—couldn't. That was hard to swallow, but that's what happened."

McConnell was forced to find other ways to cut the costs of the program. One of the first cuts he made was to drop Paul Kligman, who had been the program's warm-up man for many years. (For more about Kligman, see chapter 7.)

"I always felt badly about that. I had to examine my budget, and that's going back to probably 1982. We had to make budget cuts and I made two cuts. One of them was dropping the number of live musicians in the band. And the only other place I could cut that, in my opinion, was not going to be felt on the air was the warm-up person.

"Let's suppose you hire somebody for $25 to do warm-ups, and he does warm-ups for twenty-five years. You've got to give them the odd increase, so, all of a sudden, twenty-five years down the road, you're looking at, boy, that's an awful lot of money that I could be putting into the show. And so what I did at that time was I said, 'Okay, whoever the writer was would do the warm-ups.' So that's what happened."

And still the budgetary cloud hovered over the program.

McConnell looked for yet more ways of cutting costs. One possibility that occurred to him was the show's music, composed and conducted each week for almost three decades by the prolific Lucio Agostini. (For more about Agostini, see chapter 7.)

(Incidentally, it's a peculiarity of the CBC that "Front Page Challenge" had live music to begin with. Most quiz or panel shows on U.S. television got by nicely with either canned music or no music at all.)

In 1957, when "Front Page Challenge" was born, the Corporation had a contractual arrangement with the musicians' union to the effect that variety shows would include live musicians, which was sensible enough. But "Front Page Challenge"? Well, it was produced by the Light Entertainment Department, and therefore came within the purview of the agreement with the musicians' union. Had the program been produced by Public Affairs, the musicians' union would have had no jurisdiction.

In the early days, when budgets were fatter and costs lower, this posed no problem. Over the years, however, Agostini's orchestra for the program had swelled to twelve musicians. With the drastically tightened budget, this area of program costs seemed to offer some hope.

When McConnell began producing the show from various Canadian cities, he took only Agostini along and picked up local musicians in each city. Unfortunately, this approach proved ineffective: more rehearsal time was required and the quality of the orchestra varied from place to place.

So McConnell went a step further: he had Agostini and the orchestra pre-record all the music for a whole season in Toronto, and then he used the recorded music. Agostini came up with various thematic pieces, reflecting different moods, musical punctuations to accompany the introduction of a mystery guest and musical transitions going into and coming out of commercial breaks.

"We did that for quite a number of years," McConnell explained. "And then the money kept shrinking and shrinking, and combine that with the fact that the age of electronic music was now here."

What finally allowed McConnell to solve the problem of musical costs is attributable again to the CBC agreement with the musicians' union. The Light Entertainment Department wanted to produce a noontime variety show, with a live orchestra, but didn't have enough money in the budget for that. Since McConnell had already established his need to cut down his musical costs, the CBC and the musicians worked out a compromise: McConnell could cut down the size of the "Front Page Challenge" orchestra provided the money was still paid to musicians—the ones in the orchestra on the new noontime show. The last few years that McConnell was producer, the program's music was supplied by one man: Lucio Agostini, using a multi-track approach.

By now, Ray McConnell felt as if he were using a sardine tin to bail water out of a lifeboat that had sprung a large leak.

In those same years, roughly the 1980s, another curious factor had an effect on the fortunes of "Front Page Challenge." This was the practice of shuffling the program around the schedule.

For most of the first quarter century of its life, the program had aired on Monday nights. Quite apart from the merits of the show, regularity was significant in building a large and loyal audience. Early in the 1980s, however, the CBC bumped FPC to a Thursday-evening spot, then again to a Saturday-evening time slot. Somewhere along the way, the program was taken off the full network, to be made available to only thirty-two stations, and not always on the same night or time slot.

Pierre Berton commented on this:

"The constant changing of the time slot, that didn't help at all. It kept our ratings going down. People could not find us, and I was upset about it. We used to talk about it, and I think Ray (McConnell) agreed with us. But it wasn't his fault. This was the powers that be, kicking it (the show) around because it had been on a long time and didn't count anymore. It's what I call the Don Messer syndrome." (The CBC's seemingly arbitrary cancellation of the popular "Don Messer's Jubilee" in 1969 is still perplexing to many.)

By the mid-1980s, the Corporation's practice of shunting the program around to different nights and time slots elicited some objections from the *Toronto Star's* Sid Adilman in 1986:

"Why is CBC-TV so mean to Front Page Challenge, the longest-running, most successful panel show on (any) North American TV network?

"The show aired on the full CBC network until two years ago and regularly drew ratings of at least 1,500,000 viewers a week, despite carping from some critics who complained that it creaked of old age and should be axed.

"CBC then quietly and abruptly moved the show off the network, to air only on 32 stations on Saturday night but at different times in different provinces..."

Viewers naturally became confused, then fed up. Lorraine Thomson felt this was a factor in the program's decline:

"It was a money-maker. If they (the Corporation) hadn't screwed around so much with where they were putting the show in the schedule... I don't think that the fight to keep it in its proper time slot was carried to where it needed to be carried, which was Scheduling (department) and the people who made the scheduling decisions...It was the changing of it (the program's time slot). Even as a viewer you lost it. That was a frequent viewer complaint."

In fairness, shifting programs around on the schedule was not exclusively a CBC practice. Other networks, both in Canada and the United States, indulge in it, sometimes moving a struggling program to a spot where it would immediately precede or follow a more successful show, on the theory, one supposes, that gilt might rub off by association. Moving a successful program, however, and more than once, hardly seemed a prudent approach, if the object was to help its ratings, which is the only defensible reason for moving any program.

It all suggested a growing lack of confidence in "Front Page Challenge" on the part of somebody in the Corporation. The worst of this situation is that such an attitude often speeds up the process of disintegration, so that the program shunted around goes downhill, thus justifying the network's lack of confidence in it. After a while, it's a chicken-and-egg thing: which came first, the slipped ratings or the faltering confidence?

In any case, the shuffling around didn't help "Front Page Challenge." Nor did the endless budget cutbacks.

chapter 15

EGOS AMONG AMIGOS

Ego makes up part of most people, but perhaps especially in those who are celebrated and in the public eye, such as film stars, highly paid athletes, rock idols, vote-seeking politicians and, not incidentally, nationally recognized television panelists.

Helen Slinger, assistant to producer Cameron Bell (Bell succeeded Ray McConnell as producer of FPC), admittedly not an ardent fan of this particular panel, described them all as "towering egos." She said:

"Berton is a towering ego, we know that. Foth is a funny little sexist with a towering ego. Jack is a towering ego, but a sweet, lovable man and, you know, Jack is worried about when he's going to be on and when he's not. And Betty is a towering ego inside a smart woman. I had a lot of respect for Betty. I had a lot of respect for all of them, but I don't think they're Gods. Sometimes, I think you were supposed to bow a little more than you wanted to."

The remarkable thing about the stars of "Front Page Challenge"— Gordon Sinclair, Pierre Berton, Toby Robins, Betty Kennedy, Fred Davis, Allan Fotheringham and Jack Webster—is that they almost always managed to check their egos on their way into the studio.

Part of this, of course, was due to the fact that they were consummate professionals, and that, on the whole, they liked and respected one another. Certainly their public utterances about each other reflect that, again and again. Everyone on the panel had a high regard for Fred Davis. Betty adored Sinclair, Berton had the greatest respect for Betty—and before her, Toby. Webster looked up to Berton and Sinclair. Fotheringham held all his confreres in high esteem.

But however expertly they were concealed, the egos were still there and could occasionally erupt without warning. This might happen backstage, when no outsiders were around. On the rare occasions that it happened on the air, the target was more often a disagreeable challenger than a fellow panelist.

Betty Kennedy remembered an incident when Sinclair went ballistic in a confrontation with a left-wing politician, following an Ottawa taping:

"We had on a prominent NDP member of Parliament as a guest panelist, and after the show we were backstage and for some reason Gordon went on a rampage. 'You're the fella who would insist that in my house I would have to have so many other people living there because the house is too big for me!' he shouted. He worked himself up into a towering rage, and this poor man just sat there. He hadn't said any of those things at all. I don't know what provoked it (Gordon's outburst). Then Gordon got up, laughed and walked off."

In his later years, Gordon was touchy about his age. Actor Bruno Gerussi would sometimes act the part of an old man on a CBC-Radio skit by imitating Sinclair. This never failed to enrage Gordon and he was never reticent about expressing his displeasure.

Once, during a television interview, Jack Webster referred to Sinclair as "an old man who made his fame by standing in a desert in India with his foot on the head of a tiger he had just shot."

The next time Webster turned up as a guest panelist on "Front Page Challenge," Gordon tore into him.

"I was sitting in the little green room," Webster recalled to Knowlton Nash, "and boy, oh, boy, Gordon steamed into the room, took one look at me, and said, 'You horrible son of a bitch! How dare you say things about me like that? How dare you suggest that I'm old because to be old is to be near death, and I'm not near dead! You are a loudmouth clod and stupid!'"

Webster said he felt demolished. "I apologized, and when he finished harrumphing at me, he said, 'All right. It's all over now. Forget it. Just don't do it again. We've got a show to do. Let's do it.' After the apology, we became friends. The real Gordon Sinclair was delightful and courteous."

The other matter that offended Sinclair's vanity was his increasing baldness.

"He had one hair on top," remembered Ray McConnell, "and it had to be just right. He wanted (the viewers) to be reminded that he had at least one hair."

Davis added: "What hair Gordon had, he dyed, and he had his teeth fixed as well. He told me, 'I'm in show business, so why not?'"

During the 1962 Cuban Missile crisis, Sinclair was doing one of his regular radio broadcasts on CFRB when his program was interrupted by a news bulletin. When Sinclair came back on the air, he roared:

"What the hell is going on? Yankee propaganda. If those bastards ever break in on me again, I'm through. I'd never come back. Goddamn fools!"

Fred Davis felt the sting of Sinclair's wrath early in the history of "Front Page Challenge." In his role as general peacekeeper, Davis apologized for something evidently indelicate or possibly actionable that Gordon had said during a show.

"He could hardly wait to get off the air," Fred recalled. "'Don't you ever apologize for me!' Sinclair shouted at me. 'I know more about libel laws than you'll ever know, you young whipper-snapper.' What bothered me was that everybody else was around, and he was using some fairly free language and I guess my pride was hurt. I said, 'You can't talk to me that way in front of these people.' So we had a screaming match."

Davis was then also doing a television interview show called "Open House," with Anna Cameron. Soon after the aforementioned screaming match, Sinclair referred to Fred, publicly, as "a cream puff interviewer. When they next met, Sinclair didn't exactly apologize, but he said: "I think

I overreacted and I don't think what I said was called for. Let's shake hands and forget about it."

By his own admission, Pierre Berton developed a hide as thick as an elephant's. In his early days on "Front Page Challenge," though, he came to the conclusion that Fred Davis didn't like him. "He thought I was a son of a bitch when we first knew each other," said Berton.

But Berton took it in his stride and they later became good friends. Berton was used to being considered haughty; it didn't bother him much.

"Pierre is very shy," Betty Kennedy has said. "He doesn't have that war chest of small talk. He's not very good with strangers at cocktail parties. He often comes off aloof, and he may pass you without saying hello. Half the time he doesn't see you because he's very short-sighted."

Fotheringham echoed the same sentiments:

"Betty Kennedy threw a farewell dinner when 'Front Page Challenge' was cancelled. And I took a young lady who was seated beside Pierre. Later she told me, 'That's the most arrogant man I ever met. He said hardly a word to me (during) dinner.' I get this from a lot of people, especially at a party. 'That tall, imperious look...that arrogant bastard.' Actually, I think he is quite shy."

Foth has had his run-ins with Berton, too. He once attacked Berton in his own *Vancouver Sun* column. "In my youthful arrogance," Foth said later, "I said in a review on his book, *The Comfortable Pew*, 'Come on, Berton, what is this junk?'"

On his part, Berton once threatened to sue Fotheringham for libel. "He said I got a fat fee for travelling around the country for Canada Day," Berton said. "I didn't and I tore a strip off him. I saw him in a bar in the Georgia Hotel in Vancouver having a beer. I said, 'You son of a bitch, I'm suing you for every nickel you've got.' I had no intention of getting into a court case with him, but I thought I'd scare the hell out of him, and I think I succeeded." Foth said he'd been sued so many times that threats no longer worried him.

Berton has ping-ponged from regretting his public shyness to defending his arrogance. "It's time some Canadians were arrogant," he once said. "We need more arrogance."

Fotheringham has commented: "Pierre has never said, 'On the other hand' in his life."

Then there was the running mock rivalry between Webster and Fotheringham, which went on for several years when both men were on the panel.

For example, Foth has said: "Webster's a born ham and a very good ham. And I suspect he was hired by 'Front Page Challenge' to fill the blustering bombast role that Sinclair had."

Long before that, Foth had nicknamed Webster "Haggis McBagpipe, the mouth that roars."

When Webster became the fourth regular panelist, there emerged a kind of rivalry between Fotheringham and Webster, mostly on the question of who had been the program's first choice to succeed the late Gordon Sinclair.

As mentioned earlier, in 1984, the program tried to interest Pierre Trudeau to take the post. When he declined, they signed Fotheringham.

"I had a secret to myself that when Gordon Sinclair died they'd ask me to take his place," Fotheringham later said. "He died in the spring of 1984 and I didn't hear anything. Months and months went by. Then in the summer of 1984 Southam asked me to go to Washington as a correspondent. I was in the shower in my hotel in Washington and the phone rang and a voice says, 'This is Ray McConnell of "Front Page Challenge."' I said, 'What took you so long?'"

The CBC obviously thought highly of Fotheringham and his value to the "Front Page Challenge" panel. He had just begun his Washington assignment when McConnell called. The Washington job lasted for five years and during that period Foth was flown from Washington to Toronto (or whatever other city FPC was being taped in) and back, at the CBC's expense.

When he joined the panel, Fotheringham recalled, "the son of a bitch (Webster) has an ego bigger than Prince Edward Island, and he used to go to parties and everything and say, 'Well, you know, Fotheringham was the second choice, behind me.' And I would hear this and so I would go to a party and I'd say, in front of him, 'You lying son of a bitch, I wasn't the second choice, I was the third choice. You were the second choice, after Trudeau.' So that shut him up."

Betty Kennedy was always held in high esteem by her colleagues on the show, but they were also aware of her steely interior. Kennedy said in one interview, "I think I'm a very agreeable person, but don't push me around, don't make the mistake of thinking you can push me around. It will be a mistake, believe me."

Producer Ray McConnell said:

"The last thing in the world I would want to do on any show was run out of time before Betty had a chance, because I would have heard about it. She was always conscious that she should have her fair share of time. She felt she deserved as much time as the men, maybe altogether."

McConnell also said about Kennedy:

"She has claws. She's a very strong person. You see it in disagreements that might arise in meetings about the show. You see it in her being very conscious of her own turf and her own stature. Put yourself in the middle of those 'Front Page Challenge' personalities. Betty had to be made of pretty stern stuff to survive."

Lorraine Thomson also remembers Betty's tenacity on the show:

"She did love to hog the question time. So Don (Brown, the producer) used to say he was going to put a buzzer under her chair, so when she would ignore the light (to pass to the next panelist), she'd get a little shock when it was time to pass. But I don't think it ever happened."

Elaine Saunders, makeup artist to the "Front Page Challenge" panelists and guests for years, told Knowlton Nash:

"When she had her baby or when her first husband was dying, she kept working. She never stopped for a moment. She's a trouper, although she can be a very cold person and aloof. She's tough, as tough as Pamela Wallin or Hana Gartner. They're tough women. They're going to survive, no matter what."

Even Cameron Bell, who tended to downplay the importance and effectiveness of the panel he inherited, voiced some praise for Kennedy's tenacity as a questioner or interviewer.

Bell also could find no fault with Fred Davis.

"Fred was a pro's pro," he said. "It's those butterflies that kept him up there. They gave him the energy. He sweated his script and his timing was exquisite.

Davis was always careful about his appearance. "We were always waiting for him," commented Berton, "because he took longer than the rest of us to get ready. He was always late."

June Callwood, a frequent guest panelist, remembered a time when even a prime minister was kept waiting because of Fred's concern about his appearance.

"One time, Toby Robins and I were told there was no makeup person for the show, so we were doing our own makeup," she remembered. "The prime minister (Lester Pearson) was going to have to leave the House of Commons to do the show, and we had to begin the minute he was there. Fred came in and said, 'I'm a professional and I'm going to have professional makeup.' Almost at that instant the makeup person showed up and Fred sat there very calmly and kept the prime minister waiting while he got his makeup on. It's not critical of Fred, but I learned something from that. When a woman does something like that, she's said to be a bitch. When a man does it, he's a professional."

Davis defended his attitude:

"I make sure my tie is straight, my suit fits, my makeup is good. I don't want to inflict the Fred Davis face, with the jowls and lines, on the country."

He was also proud of his rich, naturally brown hair. "I've never had a brush cut and it's never been dyed. My barber gets this all the time. 'Sandy, would you give me that dye job that you give Fred Davis because it looks so natural. I won't tell anybody.' Nope, I never did dye it. With all the trouble involved, why the hell would I bother?"

Davis's concern about his image was put to the test once when the program was being done from Vancouver, having arrived there from the B.C. interior. The panelists were using Betty Kennedy's hotel room as a meeting place and dressing room before the show.

The program's wardrobe woman came in and asked if anybody needed anything pressed. Davis told her he had been sitting in his trousers on a plane for three days and he'd like them pressed.

"I go back to my room," Davis recalled, "take a shower, and there's a knock on the door. I wrap a towel around me and, dripping wet, answer the door. Just across the hall an old couple was going into their room and looked over at me half-naked. And the wardrobe girl said, 'Oh, Fred, sorry to bother you, but you left your pants in Betty's room.' I prayed they didn't know who I was."

chapter 16

THE OUTSIDE INSIDER

Lorraine Thomson is in the unique position of being able to view "Front Page Challenge" both from the inside and the outside. In the earlier days of the program, she was one of the most frequent guest panelists.

Then, in 1971, Don Brown, the show's producer at the time, asked Lorraine to become program coordinator, with the chief responsibility of finding and booking guests.

Her first reaction to the offer was: "Oh, my God, I can't be a guest panelist anymore."

She admits that she loved being a guest panelist. "I liked the surprise element. But I knew what I was going to do. The most difficult was sitting next to Betty Kennedy. She is very competitive, too, and she would not give up the questioning. I felt too embarrassed to leap in and say, 'It's my turn.'"

But she accepted Brown's offer and did the job for some twenty years, first with Brown and then his successor, Ray McConnell.

For ten of those years, she also hosted "V.I.P." This was an interview show, taped the same nights as the "Front Page Challenge" shows. In that series, she did some eighty-five half-hour programs. Once "Front Page

Challenge" began doing all its shows away from Toronto, the "V.I.P." program was phased out.

After the first six months as program coordinator, she took on the added chore of booking guest panelists.

"The whole point of hiring me," she said, "was that I was an interviewer, and therefore, when you were talking to a guest, you get a much better idea of what kind of guest they would be."

Thomson also had a lot of good contacts, and these often became vital in her later years on the job, because of budget cuts.

"When I first joined the show, we had a thousand dollars that we could spend a few times a year (for challengers)," she said. "It doesn't sound like much in today's money, but that was enough to bring a first-rate challenger from England or India or wherever," she told me. "When I left the show we were scraping together $250 per guest. We had to pay them an ACTRA minimum. The last eight to ten years you really had to talk people into doing the show."

Looking back over her years as FPC's program coordinator, Thomson recalled some "disasters" that occurred:

"The panel didn't always ask the right questions. I often wished that Fred was allowed to jump in, because Fred sometimes knew, and I would share with Fred. We sometimes gave them questions, but the panel had their own mind."

Another aspect of her job as program coordinator was looking after the challengers, both before and after the shows. Sometimes, she would go out for a drink with them after the show, and Thomson sometimes had to "stroke" the challengers—"because the panel was sometimes mean to them." She found it helped to reassure them, tell them how well they had done. But she took it all in her stride. Some challengers (like both Randolph Churchill and, later, his sister Sarah) were difficult to deal with. (See chapter 9 for more about this.) Others, she found charming and/or fascinating.

Thomson had good memories of former Progressive Conservative leader Joe Clark, who she said revealed "rather an offbeat sense of humour."

"There have been terrifically funny guests," Thomson said, "but pretty moving ones, too. I think the one who stands out is jockey Ron Turcotte.

He rode Secretariat to the Triple Crown, then was paralyzed in a racing accident."

On the subject of hiring a fourth regular panelist, Thomson didn't agree with the idea of hiring Jack Webster for the position. She said:

"I felt the guest panelist was a very important slot for the show. I know the (regular) panelists always used to make fun of the guest panelists and they could be rather cruel to them, not assisting them in any way, particularly when it was someone who was new to the show. They would not help them."

When I mentioned the argument, made by McConnell and Berton, that it was difficult to find guest panelists on the road who were good enough or well-known, Thomson said:

"Bullshit. They weren't known to the panel. They were known to the audience in whatever city they were in.... One of the points of 'Front Page Challenge' being on the road was for public relations. It made CBC's very presence in a given city very important, and they gave that up. It also gave Canada an opportunity of seeing some young journalists or broadcasters who were popular in their regions."

Thomson had several disagreements with Ray McConnell and, when the chance of a different job, completely outside television, came along, she decided to take it.

Lorraine left the program in the spring of 1989, after working some fifteen years with Ray McConnell.

"My biggest problem with Ray was that he was busy, he was doing other things and you couldn't get him when you needed him. We couldn't find him, it was always frustrating. But he had a great sense of humour. Ray always had a great deal of energy and was always up, but you couldn't find him to make decisions."

"What happened in my last years with the show," she said, "and I was very proud of this, we became almost all-Canadian. We had to. We had not the money to bring in people from overseas or even the United States. Canadians were thrilled to be on 'Front Page Challenge.' We had Canadian heroes, notorious Canadians."

She still has the fondest memories of Gordon Sinclair:

"While Gordon would often be bombastic, he would be the only one of the panelists who would come to me after the show was over and ask, 'Did I hurt that person? Have I injured them? Are they okay? Will they be all right? You know, I'm not really a journalist. I'm an entertainer and this is show business.'"

To her, the program was a winner for the CBC. One thing Thomson liked was the interest shown by viewers.

"We never had under a hundred letters a week," she said. "Frequently, there were more than that. Very often they were from friends, they would write regularly, they would send clippings, send in ideas for stories. We got papers from all over Canada, so I had national ideas for stories. But it was mostly the letters.... We couldn't keep up with answering all the mail. Fred would thank them on the air."

Another aspect of her job that she remembered with fondness were the dinners with guests.

"They were fabulous," she said. "Gary Lautens (the show's writer for several years) and I took an oath at that time never to write about our guest dinners. Boy, was I sorry. I never kept my notes. Such great stories, but they were never used."

One day she and Don Brown were talking about those dinners, and Lorraine said it was so frustrating that they had wonderful guests but got only five-minute interviews with them on "Front Page Challenge." That was how the idea for "V.I.P." was born—the awareness that these people were already here and available for further interviewing. Their fares and expenses were already paid, by "Front Page Challenge," so all that was needed was to establish a format in which Lorraine took many of these guests into an adjoining studio and had longer conversations with them.

Lorraine Thomson looks back contentedly on her long career with "Front Page Challenge," both as a guest panelist and as a program coordinator.

"It was a wonderful experience," she said. "The people I met, and the travel—seeing all of Canada."

chapter 17

CHANGE OF COMMAND

As had been his custom during his long reign as producer of "Front Page Challenge," McConnell went to his superiors at the CBC in March 1992, with his proposal for the program's next season. At this point, he had been with the CBC for thirty years, nineteen of them as producer of FPC. He had worked for the Corporation first in Winnipeg, doing mostly public affairs programs, and had been moved to Toronto in 1973. He had initially agreed to do "Front Page Challenge" for only two years.

How was he regarded by the people who worked with him during those nineteen years with "Front Page Challenge"? Pretty highly, according to the regular panelists. Of the seven men who served as producers, McConnell filled the post the longest and was considered by the panel as being among the top two or three. His dealings with the panel had always been amicable, most notably, perhaps, when it came to negotiating each year and even in getting their cooperation in the matter of keeping program costs under control.

At the end of his nineteenth season, McConnell knew the program was facing a serious crisis. Because of the constant belt-tightening, he had come to the conclusion that one of three approaches had to be taken if "Front Page Challenge" was to survive:

Plan A was to do all the shows in Vancouver.

Plan B was to do half the shows from Vancouver and the other half from Toronto.

Plan C was to do most of the shows from Vancouver, with a couple of token trips to Toronto.

He felt that only by adopting one of those plans could the show be brought in on budget.

"So, I had already put that (approach) in and I was waiting," McConnell remembers. "And then I started getting interesting little phone calls from the panel. 'So-and-so wants to have lunch with us. Do you know why?' And So-and-so was George Anthony (creative head of the newly formed Arts, Music, Science and Variety Department). And I said, 'I haven't got a clue.'"

Then he learned that Anthony had had a series of lunches with the panelists individually.

"I never did ask them what they talked about, and I wasn't interested in what they talked about, because I assumed that if he was having his little individual lunches with the panel, I didn't like the order, but I assumed he was gonna have a little lunch with me. I would have preferred it if he had the little lunch with me (first) and then the panel. But that never happened."

Betty Kennedy remembers:

"We got a call to attend a meeting with George Anthony. I thought this was the end, he's just calling us together to tell us the show was finished. But he told us about doing all future shows in Vancouver, with a new production team. I didn't mind that, because I have a son who lives there, anyway. We were to go out there every second week to do shows. But I called Ray (McConnell) and he didn't know anything about it. That was stupid."

Then McConnell was summoned one day to a meeting with Susan Steves, administrative head of in-house productions.

"And I walked into this meeting with Susan Steves and one of her assistants—they were both females, and both had very long faces on them, so I tried to make light of it and said, 'What's happening?'

"She said, 'Well, the decision has been made in the program area'—taking herself out of the mix, obviously—'that the show would be moved to Vancouver.' Which didn't surprise me a hell of a lot because I had already put that in a proposal that the budget could be met if we did this. And she said it's been decided that it would be done with a new production unit out of Vancouver. And at that point, I thought, 'Well, is she telling me that they don't want me to executive produce it out of here or have anything to do with the show?' And I just went right to it, and I said, 'Well, has any thought been given to me executive producing the show out of Vancouver?' And she said, 'No, politically, we made a decision it would be better if a Vancouver producer did it.'"

When he realized he was being forced out of the show, he cracked: "Well, now I know why all those meetings have been going on."

McConnell admits that he felt hurt, not that he was being moved off the show, because networks do that from time to time. He felt, having done the show for nineteen years, it would have been nice if he had been consulted, in some way, as to the program's future, or been asked to help in the transition period. He was simply out, as far as "Front Page Challenge" was concerned.

"It was, like, you know, 'Let's keep him out of here, don't anybody meet with him, one on one'... And I didn't get angry. I let them know that I was very disappointed because after all these nineteen years with the show and also the ratings weren't bad, the ratings were still up there. So I said I'm disappointed that I wasn't at least involved. And also, as a sideline, I never ever was contacted by CBC management to discuss where the show should go and all the rest of it."

McConnell remembers a degree of embarrassment on the part of the panel about the way things had been handled.

"At the same time they were meeting with me," McConnell remembers, referring to the meeting at which he learned he was being removed from the show, "they (CBC officials) were meeting with the panel and (Cameron) Bell. No one had seen fit to find out what my thoughts might be regarding the future of the show."

The CBC told the panel that McConnell would be doing a major special about "Front Page Challenge" and that there were other projects that he would be kept busy with.

"I ended up doing a couple of other things after that," he says. "I did the special, 'Front Page Confidential,' and I did a Karen Kain thing. I did a 'Juliette' special, but that was basically it. That was starting in 1992 and then I guess in '94 I received a silver handshake. I refer to it as a silver handshake as opposed to the golden handshake. Nothing was ever golden at the CBC. It was silver."

McConnell added:

"My only regret in that period of time is the fact that there was a less than desirable relationship between me and the program people (at the CBC) regarding what should be happening to 'Front Page Challenge.' And I still have that regret. And I made it a point not to watch a 'Front Page Challenge' show out of Vancouver."

He only looked at the Vancouver-based programs several years later, well after his retirement as a CBC staff producer, when he was contracted, by the same CBC, to create a database of the complete library of "Front Page Challenge" programs, from 1957 to 1995.

On the very day that Ray McConnell learned he was no longer to be connected with "Front Page Challenge," CBC management people were meeting, in Toronto, with Cameron Bell, the Vancouver-based producer who had already been hired to succeed McConnell.

All other considerations aside, the panelists were not altogether unhappy about the show's being moved to Vancouver. To begin with, they were already accustomed to visiting Vancouver frequently, especially during the latter years of the program, when many of the shows were taped there. In addition, Berton and Fotheringham were both former British Columbia residents and Webster still made his home there. Betty didn't mind the Vancouver shift, either.

From the very beginning, however, there were hints of trouble ahead. At that very first meeting the panel had with Cameron Bell, in Toronto, on the same day McConnell was being given his walking papers, Bell began talking about editing the program.

His plan, as was later confirmed by the panel, was that on any program that was being taped, it might be useful to overtape a show—that is, let it run longer than it would on the air—and then edit out any weak spots. This would result in stronger, tighter shows.

In addition, according to the panel, Bell indicated that even during a taping, the taping could be stopped and the producer (or his delegate) might confer with the panel to make sure that the right questions were being asked, to steer the interview in a way that would elicit the particular angle on a story that the producer felt was most important.

Alarm bells immediately went off in the minds of the panelists. They all urged Bell not to adopt that approach, not to even think of editing the show. The panel argued that this business of stopping tape in the middle of a program would only confuse, and possibly alienate, the studio audience, who would have no idea why the program was being stopped in midstream. It would certainly be a source of some embarrassment to the panelists.

Betty Kennedy remembers: "We all urged him not to edit the shows. Every one of us."

Perhaps because the panel's opposition to the idea was so strong, Bell evidently decided to leave the matter of editing future programs in abeyance. In any case, no more was said on the subject at that first meeting. However, it was soon to become a serious problem—one of numerous serious problems—both for the panelists and the production staff, once the move to Vancouver took place.

chapter 18

THE NEW ORDER

Whether they knew it or not, the panelists who arrived in Vancouver were like four square pegs about to be hammered into four round holes. The result was bound to be both painful and messy.

To be fair, this was a classic case of failure of communication. There were, it developed, two totally different visions of what "Front Page Challenge" was—or should be.

Remember that the people who comprised the FPC panel were not only journalistic icons to the public and celebrated personalities, they had been with the program for many years. Pierre Berton was on the panel from almost the very beginning, in the summer of 1957. Moderator Fred Davis began his stint in the fall of that year. Betty Kennedy had been a guest panelist since the fall of 1961. Fotheringham had become a regular panelist shortly after Gordon Sinclair's death, in 1984. And Jack Webster had joined the panel a couple of years later.

They had made "Front Page Challenge" a hit, and the program had made them stars across Canada. It's understandable that they should have a proprietary feeling about the long-running series. In the process, of course, the panel, and Fred Davis, had become good friends.

It's true the program was owned and operated by the CBC. The panelists were never consulted as to who would produce it or write it and, of course, had no say in who the guest challengers would or should be. By the same token, the Corporation recognized their value to the program and the wisdom of keeping them contented.

Much of this happy relationship was soon to change, and not merely because of the move to Vancouver, but because of the differing visions of the show's purpose, content and direction between the panel and the new production bosses. (Fred Davis, it should be added, was far less involved in all this; he simply continued to do what he had always done so expertly, no matter who was at the program's helm.)

Cameron Bell, who had been a successful producer both in radio and television in Vancouver, was hired by Ivan Fecan, then vice-president of CBC English Language Networks, to take over "Front Page Challenge."

"My mandate," Bell told me, "was to give it (the program) some edge. They had contemplated cancelling it and they had, I think, reached the point where they—the senior CBC and the cast—were seriously concerned about the program, and the cast apparently was beseeching the CBC to make some changes. So I was called in and I was asked if I would do it. I took a walk around the block from the Sutton Place Hotel (in Toronto) and came back and said, sure, I would like to, I'd be thrilled to, and I could think of two or three changes that I would like to do, and that's where it began."

That, indeed, is where it began, because the changes that Bell had in mind were decidedly opposed to the panelists' understanding of what FPC should be, always had been.

Bell's position was that the television landscape had changed over the years. When FPC was young, famous or distinguished challengers like Eleanor Roosevelt or Indira Gandhi or Errol Flynn were regarded, by the viewers, as a great attraction, a good reason to watch the program each week. But those days were gone. The plethora of TV talk shows—Donahue, Geraldo, Oprah, et al.—made the appearance of celebrities on television routine, thus robbing "Front Page Challenge" of part of its appeal.

In an interview with Knowlton Nash, Bell said:

"My task was to revive a television show that was failing. I had to bring more than simply the personae to the public. We could not run the show on celebrity alone. That's where the friction was. Their favourite guest would be wearing an Order of Canada pin. They wanted the official Canadians."

Still, Bell spoke glowingly of the absolute genius of the program's format, but he felt it was no longer respected as a journalistic enterprise. He added:

"It was still one of the best formats that was ever invented and because of that there was room for the game, there was room for the profile and still room for really good interviewing. If we could have got them (the panel) to go there... If it had been respected as a journalistic-enterprise vehicle as well as an entertainment vehicle and a vehicle for those four people, we could have got people of greater stature, of greater celebrity."

Unquestionably, the new skippers of "Front Page Challenge" felt one of their challenges was to lure younger viewers to the program. Their feeling and, no doubt, the CBC's, was that the program now depended on older viewers, and all the demographic surveys indicated that such people were not the ones who buy the products advertised by sponsors: cosmetics, health foods, sports cars and rock videos. The audience the show must attract were in the eighteen-to-thirty-five age group. To do that, the program had to present more contemporary stories and, if possible, add at least one younger panelist.

When I talked to him, Bell agreed with only part of this analysis. "I don't believe the program failed on commercial grounds," he said. "It failed because it was losing audience and also there was gonna have to be a cast change."

Bell and his aide, Helen Slinger, also felt that what the program had to do now was *make* news rather than cover or recall it. They felt that if the program could offer lively interviews on controversial subjects, "Front Page Challenge" itself would be in the next day's newspaper headlines. To that end, they sometimes sought out not front page stories but what they considered important issues that should be discussed: domestic abuse, sex discrimination, child abuse, and the like.

The panel, on the other hand, felt that what was important was having challengers who represented front page stories. What they were getting, they complained, were unknown challengers representing obscure stories, however worthy the issues might be.

One of Bell's first acts upon assuming command of what he regarded as a floundering ship was to hire Helen Slinger, a former CBC News executive producer in Vancouver. She tracked down, wooed and booked the guest challengers she and Bell felt were needed. Another of her jobs was to supervise what had once been the film re-creations of the headline stories, only now they had become mini-documentaries, sometimes running two minutes or longer.

Pierre Berton summed up his attitude toward Bell's efforts succinctly: "He was trying to produce 'The Fifth Estate.'"

"I think (Ivan) Fecan wanted to improve the show, to spice it up," Berton added. "His idea was to make it like a new show, make headlines every week. Bell said we're going to make headlines every week with this show. I said, you're not. I had a bet on it, which I won. One bottle of Scotch. I said you won't make three or four headlines. He bought me the Scotch. They didn't make headlines, because it wasn't that kind of show."

Helen Slinger gave me her version of the producers' difficulties with the panel. The matter of issue-oriented, as opposed to headline-oriented, stories was "the heart of the real debate," she said.

"There was definitely a real sense of what the panel felt, and this is where I think there was a generational thing. I think it was about having a woman on who was abused, as a kid, by her father, and who won a landmark case, the first case in Canada that said the statute of limitations does not run out. To me, it remains a huge front page story, it was in fact a front page story in the *Globe and Mail*.

"I think some were not event stories and they (the panel) were less comfortable, they were sometimes downers, the panel didn't like to deal with downers. But I still think there are a number of social issues that are front page stories in this decade, and I think they wanted so much to cover events that were much more in the spirit of the game, and much easier in the spirit of the game. Only in this decade issues like sexual abuse,

recovered memory and AIDS—they are the front page stories today, so
I think there was an inevitable conflict about their comfort zone, and
about what's a legitimate front page story and what isn't."

Berton also told me:

"The whole secret of 'Front Page Challenge' is that we ask the questions, we're all journalists, we know what questions to ask. I got fed up
with Bell telling us what to ask. It flummoxed Webster. It just threw him...
We used to have these long, boring postmortems, telling us what we did
wrong. 'We want to help you.' I finally phoned up and said, 'That's the
worst postmortem I've ever seen.' So they didn't have any more."

The panel's disdain for the kind of challengers Bell and Slinger were
coming up with sometimes spilled over onto the air. On one show, when
the identity of a mystery challenger was revealed—after the panel had
failed to identity her—Berton turned to Fotheringham and asked: "Who?
Who's she?" This exchange was, of course, edited out of the show, thus
perhaps justifying Bell's policy of editing shows.

But Pierre Berton's anger still came through on the air, during the interview with the celebrity. The challenger in this case was Lisa Brokop, a
twenty-one-year-old Canadian country singer whose headline dealt with
the fact that her latest record was a matter of dispute because two of its
three co-writers were Americans rather than Canadians.

After the commercial break, the mini-documentary was shown, including a music video of Lisa Brokop's song.

When it was Berton's turn in the interview, he attacked:

"I wanna know why you consider it necessary to change your accent
from a good Canadian accent to a Tennessee accent when you sing?"

The flustered Ms. Brokop asked: "Do I?"

"I just heard you," Berton argued. "'Wanna be mah baybay.' That is how
you sing."

"I don't do that on purpose," Brokop said defensively. "I don't really notice that myself."

"You do it," shouted prosecutor Berton, "because you're down in Nashville
listening to those guys talk in that phony accent."

In the control booth, Cameron Bell sighed resignedly.

Berton remembered that incident:

"I got in a fight with somebody over the fact that she was singing with a Tennessee accent, this girl. I didn't get in a fight with her. I just said, 'Why don't you sing with a Canadian accent?' Well, I got hell over that. 'Why did you do this?'... They (Bell and Slinger) would say things like, 'Well, what you said, that's a very unpopular thing to say.' What do you think the show was about, for Christ's sake?"

Allan Fotheringham was equally outspoken in his disagreement with where Bell and Slinger were trying to take the show:

"Cameron Bell was hired by Ivan the Terrible (Fecan) to sort of put a new skin on the show. Helen Slinger... was sort of in charge of selecting the guests, and I guess they were trying to make it politically correct or incorrect or something. So they were selecting people that no one had ever heard of but they had interesting causes, like wife battering, that sort of thing, to the extent that at the end of the first season when we had a sort of gangbang with the people in Toronto, I said Helen's idea of the ideal guest is a one-legged black Indian lesbian whose husband beat her... It got so bad that Pierre said to Bell, 'Don't let that woman (Slinger) come down onto the floor.' She used to come down in between stories and she used to drive Pierre... She would come down and we'd go to black for five minutes and she would try to say you should have asked so and so. You're trying to tell Pierre Berton how to ask questions? Christ! He went bananas... And so the guests they would bring in, Pierre used to rail against: 'The name of the fucking program is "Front Page Challenge." You know, from the Halifax explosion to some celebrity. And they would bring on people no one has ever heard of. The stories were sort of relevant, if you're a feminist producer, but no one had ever heard of the people... all these people never made a headline."

When I asked Helen Slinger about the incident when Berton demanded she be kept out of the studio, she said: "I don't remember any moment when he ordered me out of the studio." (In fact, she would not necessarily know about it, because Berton had gone up to the control booth and talked to Bell about it, rather than to her.)

But Cameron Bell said he did remember this particular incident, although he could not recall what had sparked it.

Another point on which Bell's and Slinger's recollections differed was the matter of ratings. Slinger told me that the ratings had started to improve again after a while; Bell said no, they hadn't. "They were below 500,000," he recalled.

Berton disputes this:

"The last show we did was 700,000 rating. That's very high, greater than Adrienne Clarkson. But Bell was the wrong man for the job. He wasn't a bad guy. He was hired for the job. (Ivan) Fecan told me, he said, 'You know, we keep trying to kill "Front Page Challenge," but every time I look at the book the ratings are pretty good for it.' He said that to me."

And Betty Kennedy said:

"Bell told us the numbers were going up again the last year."

When I told Helen Slinger that Fotheringham had referred to her as "a card-carrying feminist," she laughed and said: "Oh, what's wonderful. Please report back to him that I still consider him a card-carrying sexist."

Slinger's feelings about the panel were similar to Bell's. She thought they all had "towering egos," although she felt Betty Kennedy was less guilty of that than the others.

Kennedy, however, had a different view of Slinger:

"She was very bright and capable. She was a strong personality, but she also had an ego. And when we disagreed with her, she'd say: 'Well, that's your egos talking.'"

Slinger's strongest criticism was saved for Foth. She quoted him as saying: "If I don't think it's a story and Berton doesn't think it's a story, it's not a story." Added Slinger: "I don't accept that."

Betty Kennedy's memories of those three years in Vancouver were mostly unhappy ones:

"The show changed dramatically. In the first season, all the stories were somber, black, downers. They wanted the show to make headlines... They would interrupt a show, come down to the floor with four and five pages of questions. We'd say there was no time to read all that stuff, and they'd say, 'Oh, you want time, take all the time you want.' But the show lost its momentum.

"We had Roberta Bondar, Canada's first female astronaut, on the show. And they wanted her to talk about gender discrimination in the Armed Forces. But she was a smart woman, she wasn't going to go on national television and make such charges. So, of course, she didn't say what they wanted. And then they told us we didn't ask the right questions. It was three very unhappy years. Everybody voiced their concerns. They (Bell and Slinger) felt we were just a bunch of prima donnas."

Kennedy related the same incident to Knowlton Nash and added: "They (Bell and Slinger) would have been perfectly happy to have scripted every word we said. We were all angry."

Bell said he believed the panelists had gone to George Anthony (then head of CBC-TV Variety) and suggested changes be made on the panel, but he added: "You'll have a hard time proving this."

(When I interviewed Fotheringham, he remembered a talk he'd had with Ivan Fecan. "He asked me how we can keep this show going, and Pierre and I said, 'It's obvious, bring in a couple of bright, funny, attractive women to attract younger viewers. One, anyway.' So they brought in Jack Webster, who's a friend of mine. But that wasn't the right answer.")

Bell said, too, that during his tenure as the program's producer, "there was never any discussion of changes (to the panel). But I wouldn't have supported it because it was my experience by then that the program had only one audience—the older audience. And it was my further belief that the panel was not prepared to countenance the changes that I was recommending."

Nevertheless, he said that he and Slinger "made a list of about seventy-five people who could be replacements for the existing panelists, but we never raised it, did not go anywhere with it because we were told by George Anthony that 'Front Page Challenge' was the cast."

He did "raise a plan," he said, whereby the panel would "try to turn it (the show) over to a second generation in a mentoring process that would happen on the air.

"The idea would be that we would come up with some younger people, like Vicki Gabereau or Carole Taylor...and that we'd kind of start to incorporate them in, maybe as a fifth panelist, and find a way to basically have these four (the panelists) sponsor the younger ones. Maybe do a week and come back in three weeks, or something. So there'd be a kind of process of gradual change. It didn't happen. I do remember raising it with the CBC but I don't remember it being any more than just an idea."

Slinger remembers this idea, too. The way she explained it, one or another of the four regular panelists would take a week off, to be replaced by a younger panelist. In this way, new (young) panelists could be tried out, without any of the veteran panelists being dropped permanently.

"I'm not sure that there couldn't have been a transition to another generation. The show did change dramatically," she said. "To some extent the panel did buy into the new approach. To some extent I think the panel did change. If they had changed a bit more, the show might still be alive today."

She also said there was never any serious thought given to changing the whole panel:

"But certainly we all discussed the overall notion that if the show was to survive, one of the things to be put on the table was a discussion of building another generation of panelists and doing that not by dumping anybody, but by beginning to bring new people in for a number of shows a year, so that every panelist would still do a number of shows, still be a continuing player but not a constant player, in the sense that Berton may want to think he's immortal, but he isn't."

The basic idea of getting a younger person on the panel was not rejected by the panelists. Fotheringham told me he thought that adding Jack Webster as a fourth regular panelist was "a mistake," although he added that he and Webster were good friends. He felt that what the panel needed was a younger addition, not an older one. Berton, too, felt that someone like Vicki Gabereau would be an asset to the panel, and he was sure Betty Kennedy would not have minded. Even if this had come about, however, there's no doubt it would have led to other problems.

Bell indicated to Knowlton Nash that he had been told Berton and Fotheringham "were of the opinion that with two other panelists they would have a stronger program."

That wasn't the way Berton remembered it:

"I was approached about Betty and Webster and I said, 'Look, these people are my friends. I'm having no part in all this.'"

It eventually developed, and Helen Slinger confirmed this to me, that although the regular panelists—and Betty Kennedy, in particular—would not have been devastated if the show were cancelled, as long as it was on the air, they wanted to continue doing it.

So any ideas or plans about rejuvenating the panel were necessarily doomed.

As week followed week and taping followed taping, the hostility between the producers and the panel became more evident, though not on the air. The situation was exacerbated in the second Vancouver year, when Bell and Slinger went ahead with the editing of shows, knowing full well that the panel were opposed to this practice.

On the question of editing the shows, Bell remembered:

"In our very first meeting, with (Ivan) Fecan in the room, I raised this notion, that we could improve the program a great deal by editing. Pierre went off like a Saturn rocket and unburdened himself of a lecture on journalism ethics, and in his case the performance generally backed his speech."

At another point in our talk, Bell said: "I guess I, with the CBC's support, was trying to redefine the job and they (the panel) were trying to tell me that the way they got to where they were was the way they did it. And I was saying, 'Well, look where you are. The plane is landing.'"

It's interesting to note that the matter of editing "Front Page Challenge" had come up once before, almost three decades earlier, when Don Brown was producing the program.

At that time, in the mid-1960s, the CBC's hottest public affairs program was "This Hour Has Seven Days." According to Brown:

"They were booking the biggest guests and they'd bring them into the studio and tape an hour with them and then use thirty seconds on the air, and this frustrated so many people. Then I would call someone (to appear on 'Front Page Challenge' and say who I was and they'd hang up in my ear."

This bothered him until he figured out why:

"It was because the other show was doing that. They were editing, making people say things they didn't mean."

Brown's solution was to promise any such guest that "your appearance on 'Front Page Challenge' will be treated as a live one, it will not be edited, you say what you want to say."

That solved Brown's problem—and settled, until 1992, the question of editing "Front Page Challenge."

Cameron Bell's recollection is that the editing of shows began partway into the second season. Bell said the panel "had great resistance to any editing, that came out of the very first meeting we had. And the notion of stopping tape so these people could become more briefed than they were from their oracular positions simply wasn't going to fly. And we did finally end up with some editing. We had to for cosmetic reasons."

What Bell meant by "cosmetic reasons," he told me, was that Jack Webster was having "a bit of trouble focusing. At one point, he asked questions of the second guest that had been prepared for the first. And some of his asides, his bon mots, made no sense. It wasn't that they were ribald, they just didn't make sense. And it was for him that we had to edit. The fact was that Jack was losing it."

Jack Webster had known Cameron Bell some years earlier, when both worked at BCTV. "We weren't good friends or anything," Jack recalled, "but I was able to work with him. The thing that really got me was this editing the program. Towards the end it happened regularly."

The muted hostility between Bell and Webster kept surfacing again and again during those last three years in Vancouver.

Webster remembered an earlier incident at BCTV, in Vancouver:

"I was sitting around the desk one morning, and we were having quite a jolly little time since we'd had a good program. Cameron swaggers over and says, 'What the hell have you got to giggle about?' I said, 'Listen, you son of a bitch, get out of my way.' I went up to management and screamed my head off about him."

Bell acknowledged that he and Webster had had their differences:

"There was one problem about a cameraman assignment. He didn't take kindly to my questioning something, and he issued some kind of arbitrary order. So we had a rather large and colourful discussion. Other than that, he and I got along, I thought, quite well."

"Cam was nominally Webster's boss," Fotheringham said, "but Webster was a star and wasn't going to have any kid push him around."

Despite Webster's comment that he was "able to work" with Bell, Fotheringham told me there was "bad chemistry between Jack and Cameron... Bell started editing Jack out. Jack lost his confidence. He was losing his memory; Bell broke Jack's confidence."

Like the others on the panel, Webster disliked receiving "far too much background, five or six pages of background. This is in the commercial break, and they would occasionally suggest questions, but not very often. I don't think any of us used the prepared notes."

Also like the other panelists, Webster hated the idea of editing the shows:

"I was the first one to be cut out altogether, and I couldn't bloody well understand it. I bitched about it but nothing happened. When they did it with Fotheringham, the shit hit the fan. You can't have a guy up in the introduction and then not be seen again. The editing took every piece of zip out of the program. Cam acted like a dictator. He wanted to teach us the lesson that he was the boss."

Webster also said:

"We don't need questions at our age and experience. And also you can't do suicides and buggery in Newfoundland for more than a short time, otherwise it becomes depressing."

Fotheringham recalled: "Pierre used to say, 'The talent is the reason why the show is there, why it's lasted thirty-eight years.' I used to say to Cam, 'You're going to tell Pierre Berton how to interview? Come on now!' If they could have scripted the whole show, they would have."

Bell told me what things were like when they started editing programs:

"We didn't have a meeting to discuss it. I think we told them we had done it. Once we established it, we did then start letting the interviews run a little long, which gave us some flexibility. And there was no real bitching until Foth got cut out of a show and behaved like an asshole."

Bell said Foth had been cut out of one interview:

"He asked only one question, it was irrelevant, it didn't go anywhere, and it was in my judgment not up to the program's standards."

Fotheringham remembers it differently:

"They started editing and Pierre and I went bananas over this thing, and they made me look completely stupid at one stage. They cut out something, you know what it's like, you can chop a statement in half, change the meaning, and at one stage they had a guest on and you'd go from Webster to Betty to Foth to Berton, and they cut me out of this one sequence because they thought my questions were either distasteful or risqué. And Pierre, as you know, held that show on his heart, and he said, 'This is not what this show is about.' He said, 'Gordon made the most outrageous statements, talked about Tampax with Elaine Tanner, and if you guys were in charge you would have edited out the Elaine Tanner menstruation thing.'"

Fotheringham recalled another incident that illustrated the differences on "Front Page Challenge" caused by the shift to Vancouver and the switch to a new production team.

"The very first show when they hired me (as a regular panelist) was in Yellowknife," he recalled. "This was when they were going around the country. The first guest on the first show was David Crombie, the tiny perfect mayor (of Toronto), who had just been elected as a Conservative M.P. and was made, in the Mulroney government, minister of Indian Affairs and Northern Development. And so, since Fred (Davis) knew that I knew something about politics, I led off the interview. And he (Crombie) said how proud he was to be and really wanted this portfolio and everything. And I said, 'Mr. Crombie, you know perfectly well why you got this portfolio. It's because in the leadership race when you ran against Mulroney and you got like twenty-nine votes or something on the second ballot and you should have dropped out because they needed to build up momentum and this really put Mulroney in a desperate position against Joe Clark, he punished you and he sent you to this no-account goddamn place up in the North.'

"Well, Crombie went bananas. He said, 'Fotheringham, what have you been smoking?' And then we had to break before the second show, and we went into the green room and Berton said, 'Foth, why don't you get over your shyness?'

"And we got on the plane the next morning, and Mr. and Mrs. Crombie are sitting there and as I go by, the steam is still coming out of her ears, and I said, 'Did you see the morning paper, you guys are in the headlines.' She said, 'Yeah?' I said, 'Yeah. Cabinet Minister Accuses Fotheringham of Smoking Dope.'

"Now, if that happened in Vancouver under Bell they would have cut it all out. But Cameron Bell and Helen Slinger, they just didn't get it. As Pierre said, they thought they would be in effect the stars of the show. They would construct a show and what they didn't know was that the show was the four stars."

When I talked to Cameron Bell in 1997 he was outspoken in his criticism of Fotheringham and Berton:

"You have to ask Foth what he thinks is important. And there are some Canadians who believe that who Foth had lunch with on Parliament Hill is really interesting. There are another few million out there who were unfranchised, disenfranchised single parents, victims of abuse, and as long as the Fotheringhams of the world are in charge of the media these people aren't gonna get a whole lot of exposure. Every one of the stories Helen (Slinger) brought forward, the stories we brought were stories in which the central figure could tell a human story. There were some wife abuse things and there was a woman who had been artificially inseminated and got AIDS. And we explained to them (the panel), look, these people have dealt with it. We know it's a big surprise to you, you're suddenly dealing with a person who's got AIDS, you feel uncomfortable. Please trust us, it works. So Foth can't get there, right? Foth has sniped at me in his column a few times. He's really chickenshit. Once while we were doing the program, in *Maclean's*, he took a shot in *Maclean's* and he took a shot in his column in the *Financial Post*, he referred to me as somebody who'd never been east of the Fraser River. Just small-minded. And he would interpret those kind of stories as not being legitimate because they weren't people that he'd ever encounter in Rosedale, or on Parliament Hill or flying first-class back and forth to wherever (his editor) would send him. You know, that's his view of the world."

The Vancouver producer's feelings about Fotheringham apparently hadn't cooled much, even three years after the event. He told me Foth was at times "less concerned with the quality of the program and more concerned with the exposure."

Fotheringham, said Bell, would go to "what passed for production meetings with a laptop computer and write another column. He more than once reported that he had been the one who had replaced Sinclair and has been instructed or somehow had come to believe that his role was to be the curmudgeon and we politely suggested he be Allan and go to his best stuff, because when Foth is on, which happens every ten or fifteen years, he could do great work."

Fotheringham said of Bell and Slinger: "They thought we'd become prima donnas, big shots from Toronto."

Bell countered: "They all had professional personae. They are where they are today as a result of carefully currying those personae."

Betty Kennedy felt that Bell and Slinger wanted "to have complete control, take it away from the panel."

Bell also cited an instance where he found Berton at fault:

"We did schoolyard violence. There's a guy here, a black guy from California, about whom a CBS movie had been made. He was a school principal and he had become the guy who could solve violence in the schoolyard. He was here for a conference, there had been a couple of incidents of schoolyard violence. We spotted him in the papers and we put that story on. Berton came off (after the taping) and declared there is no schoolyard violence in Canada. He attacked us after the program, he attacked me, on the grounds that it is not relevant, it doesn't happen in Canada, it does not happen here. Well, what are you gonna say? So, we contemplated faxing them (the newspaper stories) to him. Then, we figured, what's the point? In Pierre Berton's world there is no schoolyard violence. And a black guy from California who can fix it is therefore of no interest."

The ongoing discontent was evident on both sides. As Berton said:

"Our unhappiness, I think, showed. They were bugging us all the time. They would stop the tape—with the audience there—and harangue us. They were trying to tell us what questions to ask. We revolted. So they were upset."

Bell also voiced some criticism of Webster:

"He would rarely go to his strength," said Bell. "His journalistic ability is to extract information from people in a friendly way. The width of his brogue is inversely proportional to the depth of the story. When there is nothing happening, he'll put in the burr, but when there is something he wants to bring out, he's excellent. Sometimes, you could see flashes of it, but he was, I think, very much intimidated by the others."

Fotheringham remembers that "once in a while Cam would take him (Webster) off and talk with him like the kid trying to tell the teacher."

Davis said Webster was "intimidated by the producer, Cameron Bell. They were kind of tough on him. Jack's value on the show was a sort of curmudgeon, a gruff Scot who came up with some very funny stuff. In a sense, a replacement for Sinclair. Whereas with Cameron there were times when Jack was cut out of the show entirely. Foth was once, too. It really upset the panel. We had a knock-down, drag-out fight about that with Cameron. Jack was always being put down and criticized, which was a shame. They were missing what he could bring to the show."

There were frequent arguments not only about guests who were used, but some who weren't.

Pierre Berton:

"The choice of guests had a sameness to it, there was no jump. He (Bell) didn't want any big shots. He didn't want Lewis McKenzie. He said, 'We don't want any generals.' We said, 'Where's Lewis McKenzie, he's the hottest guy, he'll have lots to say.' Bell said, 'Oh, he'll just say the same old stuff.'"

Berton had other complaints:

"I'll tell you a typical story of what was wrong. They were trying to run the program, tell us what questions to ask, you know, editing everything, to which we were all violently opposed. And one day, somebody, maybe me, said: 'You know, it's not fun anymore.' And Slinger snapped: 'It's not supposed to be fun.' And I thought to myself, if it's not supposed to be fun, why the fuck are we doing it? That's the secret of the show. That it's fun and the audience sees that it's fun. But they (Bell and Slinger) tried to run the show in every way. They really tried to tell us what questions to ask. They'd give us three or four sheets of paper, you couldn't even read it during the commercials, so they'd stop the tape (during the commercials) which is terrible for the (studio) audience and terrible for everybody. You lost the tension. You did that by editing, too. If you know it's going to be edited, you say, 'Well, I'll take a little more time on this thing.' It slackens out, there's no tension."

There was another confrontation when the producers booked Elaine Tanner for yet another appearance on the program. During the commercial break, Bell suggested to Pierre that he not bring up the menstruation incident immediately but "give it a while," that is, let the interview go along before mentioning that famous event.

"I'll never forget him saying, 'All Canada is waiting for me to ask that question,'" Bell said. "No, they're not, Pierre. Nobody watching knew Gordon Sinclair. That was thirty years ago. They were nine years old."

Bell's feelings about the panel and, more particularly, his numerous disagreements with them during those three turbulent years in Vancouver, still suggest a kind of bitterness.

He felt hurt that "they went behind my back" with complaints to the CBC brass about his handling of the program:

"What I can remember is learning that they went behind my back and that I had said at the beginning that the only demand I was making was if there's a problem come to me… And they all sat around and nodded and then went behind my back. When I learned about that I saw red, and I don't remember what the CBC said about it, but I do remember that I didn't learn about it until long after it happened, so I don't think the CBC came back to me the next day and said, 'Oh, by the way, do this now.'"

The reference to the panel going behind his back was probably related to the fact that Pierre Berton wrote a letter to George Anthony (head

of variety programming), back in Toronto, objecting to the amount of editing that was being done.

Betty Kennedy recalled Berton writing a letter "about the editing (and)
about Foth being cut out of a show." She added that Pierre had sent a copy
of his letter to Cameron Bell, "who was very upset about the letter."

Berton, too, recalled the incident:

"They cut out Foth once. They cut out Webster, and I raised hell. I wrote
a letter to George Anthony, and he wrote back saying, 'No, the producer
is in charge.'"

In his letter, Berton said:

"I must tell you that we are disturbed and indeed offended by the producer's insistence that they have carte blanche to edit the interviews in
such a way that one or more of the panelists is cut right out."

He cited two instances of panelists being cut out of the show, one involving Webster, the other Fotheringham.

"None of us, as you know, are very happy about the editing of the show,"
he continued. "We've gone along with it but these last two incidents have
our backs up. We don't want to be protected by editing. We want to be allowed to ask our own questions... All of us have strong egos. We wouldn't
have got where we are if we didn't. As longtime experienced journalists
we don't want to be told that a question thrown at a guest isn't right for
the program. We think we know as much about the interview technique
as the producers."

When I interviewed Bell, he told me: "It wasn't the CBC's idea to get rid
of (Ray) McConnell, in my opinion. It was the panel's. Ask them about that."

I later did, and they denied it.

Betty told me: "No. I don't recall that at all."

Fotheringham: "We never talked to anybody at CBC to get rid of him.
We never said to anybody, 'Get rid of him.'"

Berton: "No. We never did that."

Both Berton and Foth acknowledged that they felt McConnell had been
doing the show for a long time and perhaps had become a little jaded, but
they emphatically denied having any discussions with the CBC about replacing McConnell as producer.

Fotheringham also expressed his distaste for the way the brass dumped McConnell: "Typical CBC. They handled it so badly."

Since Bell said that it was his "opinion" that the panel had been instrumental in removing McConnell, and given their expressed sense of shock at his removal and the way in which it was handled, it seems at least possible that Bell was mistaken in this "opinion."

In fairness, by this time Bell was pretty disenchanted with the "old" panel he had inherited. When I talked with him, he said he found "an irony" in the panel:

"They had convinced the CBC that they were the program, and by convincing them and believing that they were the program they built the concrete that they couldn't crack to make it continue, so the program that they had was dying and I think the panel knew they couldn't get an audience. My real frustration was that I couldn't get them to see the opportunity that existed. I guess their frustration was that somebody kind of poured something on their red carpet and stained it.

"I know that in the history of 'Front Page Challenge,' I'm going to be wearing the black hat. Because I was the guy who got to ride it off into the sunset. And I don't care."

It was Bell's belief, when he took over the show, that it could survive "indefinitely…if the four Canadian journalists who were, arguably, the highest-profile and probably among the four best on television would…demonstrate their journalistic skills a few times, and (we) could deliver the newsmakers who would play under these circumstances and we could have turned it into a show with real edge and still be entertaining and not offend the format. And the show would be running today."

This statement seems diametrically opposed to his, and Slinger's, earlier argument that the program was no longer capable of attracting celebrated people to the program because of the glut of TV talk shows that were by now luring all these celebrities, and that having such celebrities on "Front Page Challenge" was no longer much of an attraction to FPC's shrinking audience.

Towards the end of my lengthy interview with him, Bell said his one regret about the end of the series was that he had hoped to have John

Aylesworth, who invented the program, as a guest challenger on the "final show."

But there was not to be a "final show," at least not in the sense that Cameron Bell intended.

chapter 19

PULLING
THE PLUG

On December 3, 1994, the *Toronto Star* ran a column by its entertainment columnist, Sid Adilman, in which he chatted with two top CBC executives about the status of "Front Page Challenge." They were George Anthony, head of the Corporation's variety programming, and Phyllis Platt, executive director of arts and entertainment programming. Both Anthony and Platt seemed generally upbeat, which is what network executives are supposed to do, of course. Among other things, Anthony said:

"Despite the travel (to and from Vancouver) by Fred, Betty, Pierre and Allan—they get special hotel deals—'Front Page Challenge' is not a costly show. That's a big factor."

The *Star* columnist also asked Platt and Anthony why "Front Page Challenge" was being done in Vancouver rather than at the new CBC centre in Toronto.

"There's no studio space there," said Anthony. "We're all booked up with 'Rita and Friends,' 'The Royal Canadian Air Farce' and 'Side Effects.'"

In his piece, Adilman commented: "Ironically, more national CBC shows these days come from the network's cramped Halifax studios than from the larger, better-equipped Vancouver premises."

Adilman then wandered into the area of "Front Page Challenge's" future. The program was then nearing completion of its thirty-eighth year on the air.

Both Anthony and Platt told him that decisions regarding renewal of programs would not be made until the following January or February.

"Shows are judged on a number of factors, not just on performance, not just on ratings," he quoted Platt as saying. "I try to make decisions on a year-by-year basis."

Then she added: "Front Page's ratings are not bad at all for (what CBC calls) available time."

For his part, Anthony said that "Front Page Challenge does not have a divine mandate," but he added: "I do like round numbers. Forty (years) sounds good."

The implication was that he favoured continuing the program for another two years, when it would have reached the "round number" of forty years on the air.

Evidently, sometime between winter and early spring, feelings somewhere at the CBC changed. On Friday, April 14, 1995, the Corporation announced that "Front Page Challenge" would not be renewed for a thirty-ninth season. The afternoon before, Platt evidently attempted to reach the various panelists by phone to inform them of the impending cancellation.

"It feels sad to be doing this," Phyllis Platt, who made the announcement, was quoted in the next day's papers. "Front Page Challenge has had a terrific run—thirty-eight years is a record."

"This year, we're also looking at issues of financial constraint, and new expectations from the CRTC... Writ large, we're having to review our entire programming strategy."

The *Globe and Mail* quoted Pierre Berton as saying he wasn't too surprised at the announcement, since "its demise has been predicted for the last thirty-five years."

He was inclined to blame the decision on the CBC's "trouble with money," but he said he was surprised that the plug was pulled at the end of a successful season.

"The network had indicated to us that they were going to keep us going until our fortieth season, but I guess they decided against that," he added.

He was less sanguine when I talked with him about the demise of the program:

"You know how I found out about it? Somebody phoned the office and got Elsa (Franklin, Berton's chief aide) and said, 'Tell Pierre "Front Page Challenge" has been cancelled.' That was it. I never got a phone call from anybody.

"If you have a long-running show, why not use it for publicity, why not have a big thing, give a party, have a big send-off, and then fine, no hard feelings...But that was no way to go out. It was not classy. There's no class to that."

Allan Fotheringham was somewhat less restrained in his reaction:

"I heard about it in the usual classy CBC style—on a speakerphone. The boss, George Anthony, was conveniently out of town. (The announcement came) very cleverly on a Thursday before the long Easter weekend, when few newspapers were publishing the next day."

Foth later recalled that day to me:

"I was upstairs in my study, up there doing my little computer junk, and I get the phone call one morning and it's Phyllis Platt. And she said, 'Alan, could I talk to you.' I said fine. She said, 'Would you mind, I'm on the conference phone'—and she's got some guy (who) used to be sort of a lawyer figure, and obviously he was there to monitor the call. And she said, 'We're sorry about this, but we're gonna cancel the show...at the end of the season.' And she said, 'We're gonna have a lunch' and all that sort of stuff.

"So, I was so fucking mad that I sat down and I wrote the most vicious letter I've ever written, and I'm an authority on vicious letters. I wrote to George Anthony and I said this is the most despicable thing I've ever heard of. I said I don't care about me, I'm the teenager, but for what you did to Pierre and Fred and Betty, I said all you had to do was call us all in and have a nice lunch, raise a bottle of champagne and say, Guys, it's been great but it's over. Instead, you took the old horse out behind the barn and you shot it in the dark.

"And you know what they did as a result of my letter? They cancelled the lunch. Anthony cancelled the lunch."

Betty Kennedy heard about the cancellation in a roundabout way, too. Allan Burton, her husband, phoned her and told her he had heard on the radio that the program was cancelled.

"Later, Phyllis Platt called me to tell me and I told her it was on the radio already. She said, 'I had hoped get to you before the word got out'... I never did get so much as a letter from her."

Kennedy didn't think much of the way the cancellation was handled:

"I've been on lots of boards of directors, and when someone leaves after serving for some years, they always handled things with class—a farewell dinner, a parting gift. It's standard practice. When I left Standard (CFRB) after all those years, they were wonderful. But this, the way the cancellation was handled, had no class."

Ironically, the cancellation of the long-running series was given greater press coverage than anything the program had done in its thirty-eight years on the air.

The *Globe and Mail* ran the cancellation on its front page with a picture of Fred and the panel, and the lengthy story was continued on an inside page.

The *Toronto Sun*, which rarely had a good word for anything the CBC ever did, ran true to form:

"So this is the way 'Front Page Challenge' goes to its reward," wrote the paper's Jim Slotek, "quietly, like some old movie star you weren't sure was still alive. It's last word might as well have been 'Rosebud.'"

In the *Vancouver Sun*, Jack Webster was quoted as saying: "I'm sorry to see it go. It was good fun. And you couldn't be that stupid, you had to keep your wits about you, especially with Fotheringham and Berton on the panel."

The Vancouver story also quoted Cameron Bell as saying that while the show still had an audience and was relatively inexpensive to produce, it fell victim of changing times in broadcasting.

"I believe it has less to do with Front Page Challenge," it quoted Bell, "and more to do with whatever the CBC is going to be able to do when the smoke clears...Their problem is not Front Page Challenge, their problem is building a new CBC."

Newspapers in Montreal, Calgary and many other cities across Canada also carried stories, mostly via Canadian Press. The Calgary story quoted Phyllis Platt: "We didn't make this decision lightly (but) concluded thirty-eight years is an incredibly long run. I'm sure there will be a number of disappointed viewers."

Conspicuous by his absence from most of the press stories covering various reactions to the CBC announcement was any comment from Fred Davis, who had been with the program as long as Berton had, and far longer than any of the others.

The Canadian Press story published in the *Calgary Herald* included this brief comment from Fred:

"We're sort of letting down the hundreds of thousands of Canadians who have stuck with us over the years." While acknowledging that the over-fifty set didn't carry much clout in the marketing departments of the 1990s, Davis added that "Front Page Challenge" was inexpensive to produce and still attracted a substantial slice of the viewing audience.

The *Toronto Star* featured a full story, again with a picture of the panel, that was headlined: "Everybody Famous Wanted To Be On." The headline came from a quote attributed to Ray McConnell, the program's producer for nineteen years. McConnell was asked how he felt about the cancellation.

"Sad, that's how I feel," McConnell said. "The concept was wonderful, particularly when CBC was the only game in town. Everybody famous wanted to be on it."

In that story, Jim Bawden, the *Star*'s television critic, also wrote that Cameron Bell, the program's producer, said he was "tipped off several months ago" about the CBC's decision to kill the show after its thirty-eighth season.

The Edmonton *Journal* story also mentioned the business of the program's producer being "tipped off" several months before. It quoted Bell as saying: "We were put on CBC's 'watch list' for shows deemed cuttable because of low ratings."

But when I interviewed Cameron Bell a couple of years later he made no mention of being "tipped off" in advance. Indeed, he indicated he was taken as much by surprise as everyone else involved.

"I got a phone call around six o'clock in the evening," he said, referring to the evening of April 13, "from Phyllis Platt. Urgent call. They were going to make an announcement tomorrow... She said they had been thinking of it and they appreciated what I had to say on the subject, and that the program schedule (for the next season) would be coming out and that 'Front Page Challenge' would not be on it. And I said, 'Okay. I'm not surprised, while I'm disappointed, I'm not surprised.'

"I said I'd like to make some calls, but she said 'Don't call anybody.' I said I'd like to call Helen (Slinger). But she said, 'No, don't call Helen. I'm gonna call everybody.' And I said okay.

"So I waited till the next morning and I phoned Helen and I said, 'So, what do you think?' and she said, 'About what?' So, I told her what I'd been told and she said, 'Well, I'd better phone the cast.' And I said, 'Well, I was told not to.' She said, 'Well, I'm going to call anyhow,' and I think she made a couple of calls."

Then I told Bell that it was generally felt (by the panel) that the matter was handled clumsily.

"Yes," he said. "I think after that length of service that they ought to have been given some kind of farewell... These people made a tremendous contribution. They are true Canadian celebrities."

At long last, after three years of monumental disagreements and constant bickering, Cameron Bell and his reluctant panelists found something on which they could agree: the clumsy manner in which the Corporation had handled the cancellation of "Front Page Challenge."

However, even in this conversation, Bell continued to express his disagreement with the panelists' attitude about the program during his three years of working with them:

"With the exception of Fred and generally the exception of Betty, they clung to a program that was doomed. They would not, or could not, or I could not be effective in getting them to see where 'Front Page Challenge' could go for the next thirty years, and I guess I offended them when I said that we can re-establish them in Canada's mind as Canada's principal journalists..."

The body of "Front Page Challenge" was barely cold before a different sort of press reaction surfaced. In the *Toronto Star*, media reporter Antonia Zerbisias wrote a piece for her column, "Channel Surfing," which bore the headline: "26 Million Canadians Won't Even Notice FPC's Gone."

In her acerbic piece, Ms. Zerbisias began:

"There was much beating of breasts last weekend over the sudden death of CBC's Front Page Challenge, 'the longest running panel show in North America,' certified Canadian institution, 'tribal statement,' fill in the epitaph of your choice.

"So it's gone. So what?

"Some of us were kicking around its demise in mournful tones. I was unmoved. Not because I didn't appreciate its value as Canadian nostalgia but because the show and its stars had long passed it."

After listing the ages of all the principals—from Betty Kennedy at sixty-nine to Jack Webster at seventy-seven—she continued:

"That single statistic was enough to make 'Front Page Challenge' an edge of the seat show lately. One of these nights, the correct answer really truly would be the 1956 sinking of the Andrea Doria and one of the FPC stars would keel over in shock, hand clutching heart."

Zerbisias went on to point out how much Canada had changed in the years since "Front Page Challenge" first went on the air, ending that section with:

"The country and its people have changed, for better or worse, but FPC remained hopelessly mired in its 1950s white-bread gentility."

Then the writer managed to drag the Charlottetown Accord into her diatribe, ending this section:

"But let's not dwell on that. Charlottetown is ancient history now, as is Front Page Challenge, as is that Toronto that no longer exists in the minds of anyone who rides the subway beyond Eglinton. For that alone, CBC should be applauded for pulling the plug."

Maclean's magazine caught up with the story a week later. Its coverage, headed "The End of a Good Run," also featured a picture of Davis and the panel. It began:

"Not with a bang, but a whimper—that is how the end came for the long-running stump-the-panel TV show Front Page Challenge."

A couple of months later, *Saturday Night* magazine ran an article headlined: "Front Page Challenged." It was written by Terry Gould, who was hired by Cameron Bell as the program's writer for what turned out to be its last season of existence.

Gould, then aged forty-five, paid lip service to the various journalistic achievements of the panelists, but seemed obsessed with their age and increasingly aware of their "grumpiness."

Understandably, Gould's piece reflected his admiration of Cameron Bell and Helen Slinger:

"Since he'd come aboard as boss in 1991, hiring as his lieutenant the aggressively innovative Slinger…several proposals to revivify the show had circulated among FPC's staff. For the sake of continuity, most of the proposals advocated retaining on the panel the gracile Kennedy… But Berton, Foth and Webster, it was suggested, should be replaced with well-known personalities whose ages were equivalent to Berton's when he first joined the set in 1957. While the proposals were supposedly confidential, the panel had an idea they existed, and the implicit judgments became the subtext to so much of what went on in the dressing room, a hurtful dagger buried deep in every legitimate criticism or request."

His supposedly in-depth article merely showed that Gould was out of his depth, at least as a competent researcher. For example, in a sketchy historical section, he wrote that "By the early sixties, two million Moms and Pops were shushing the kids every Saturday night to sit before the Philco to watch Gordon Sinclair, Pierre and Betty spark the tubes."

But the fact is that in the early 1960s, "Front Page Challenge" was not on the air on Saturday nights, it aired on Mondays for a good many years.

Gould had a way of sprinkling praise for the panel here and there, but sometimes there was jagged glass mixed in with the compliments:

"Not surprisingly, these giants of journalism were adored by the half-million or so senior citizens who watched the show, and every conversation Bell had had with the CBC brass back east had given him the clear impression that, while he could spruce up the set, have (Helen) Slinger produce edgy introductory videos on the mystery guests, and bring to the program challengers known only to the high-spending eighteen to thirty-four crowd, he could not touch the panel. The CBC was quite simply petrified of risking a grey-power boycott, and no one wanted to take the responsibility for mistakenly torpedoing Front Page Challenge while seemingly trying to save it.

"Problem was, brilliant as the men were, in the last few years the crew at FPC had been dismayed to see one or the other occasionally act as grumpy on camera as they did in the dressing room, especially when challenged by a young headliner they'd never heard of, who represented a hole in their omniscience that they found hard to admit existed."

Gould continued:

"Wielding her axe on that Black Thursday before Good Friday, 1995, the CBC's arts and entertainment director Phyllis Platt would explain that 'the rapidly changing TV environment' had leapt ahead without FPC; that viewers could now flip to a dozen other venues to see newsmakers interviewed. But the notion that fighting talk shows are no longer in vogue is absurd: they are all the salacious rage. FPC stood still because the CBC brass dithered for three years on proposals put forward by FPC's staff. No one even seriously asked the panel if they agreed it was time to move on..."

The closing of Gould's piece suddenly turned sentimental as he recounted the last taping and his farewells to the panel:

"They all smiled and wished me well, and, looking down their line, I felt a surge of love for each one of them, understanding perfectly well why no one could ever have told them to retire. My only regret now is that I landed on their mythic peak just as the sun was setting, but I still got to play with the gods."

Perhaps the last published comment on "Front Page Challenge" (until now, at least) came from Knowlton Nash, who wrote in his book *Cue The Elephant*:

"Front Page Challenge marched triumphantly onto the nation's screens in 1957 and ended thirty-eight years later, slinking off amid recriminations and rancour."

Also in his chapter about the long-running series, Nash wrote:

"No Canadian network weekly TV program has lasted so long or seen such a panorama of high-profile guests, iconoclastic panelists, and rampaging egos as those who strode before the cameras of this grand old lady of all Canadian TV shows. Beginning as a summer replacement, it received applause from its audience and yearly obituary notices from its critics before finally being killed with a management indifference that bordered on brutality."

After mentioning that the final producer of "Front Page Challenge" had described the program's format as "just brilliant," Nash added:

"Sadly, that brilliance disappeared from the screen unhonoured and unmourned by the CBC."

Phyllis Platt, the CBC's executive director of arts and entertainment, was not in that position when the decision was made to move "Front Page Challenge" to Vancouver, but she was aware of the various elements that went into that decision: the availability of better studio facilities in Vancouver, the feeling that the show needed to be revitalized, and so on

As to the cancellation of the program, three years later, she was part of the decision-making process that reached that fateful conclusion.

When I spoke with her, she went over again the various elements that went into that decision: the program's slipping ratings, the demographics that showed the program's apparent inability to attract younger viewers in large numbers, the program's long and distinguished history, the Corporation's feeling that the panel had served Canadian television extraordinarily well, the feeling that if the series had to end, it was probably better to take it off while it still had respect rather than watch it dribble away.

"I felt personally very sad about it," she added. "It's never a happy thing to have to say goodbye."

There were two more people I wanted to talk to: Ivan Fecan, who was in command when the decision was made to move the program to

Vancouver, but had since moved on to Baton/CTV; and George Anthony, who was "creative head" of CBC-TV Variety when "Front Page Challenge" was cancelled and is still at the CBC.

They were, as the saying goes, unavailable for comment.

chapter 20

THE FRED WE NEVER KNEW

To her many readers, she is known as Joy Carroll. She has also written as Joy Brown, Margeurite Ford and Heather Hill. Carroll is the name by which she is best known. Joy Carroll was the name on *Proud Blood*, probably her most successful book, which has sold some three-quarters of a million copies. At last count she had written eighteen books, all but two of them fiction.

She became Joy Carroll after she married writer and journalist Jock Carroll. They had four children and when Joy wrote "a couple of so-called sexy novels," her husband didn't want their children seeing their mother's name on those books. That was when she became Heather Hill, for a while—two books' worth.

Eventually, she became Mrs. Fred Davis, but she still writes as Joy Carroll, a name that is now so firmly fixed in the minds of her public.

Joy Carroll Davis is a pleasant, soft-spoken woman, in her late sixties, perhaps a foot shorter than Fred was. She is an interesting mixture of 1990s chatelaine, career woman and mother. She speaks plainly, occasionally slipping into slang, but never vulgarity.

She lives now, as she and Fred had done since 1986, in a spacious and attractively, tastefully furnished condo that offers a breathtaking view of

Lake Ontario. Among the numerous comforts of the Davis household are three pianos. Both Fred and Joy enjoyed playing the piano.

"I play popular music," she told me. "He wasn't really a jazz pianist, he played what you might call cocktail music. But he had a good ear. And that was his second or third instrument. He had a horn (trumpet) and a flugelhorn. He only practiced when he was going to do a little appearance. But he did play the piano a lot, and when we had guests he always played for them. And for years we had an organ, an electric organ with all the trimmings. He was very good on the organ. Terrific. And then three months before he died he bought a digital piano, now we had three. It had all the bells and whistles. And he loved it, he would practice away on it."

She showed me a picture that she said Fred was especially proud of. It shows Dinah Shore singing in front of a band at some Toronto banquet. Behind Dinah you can see Fred, playing trumpet.

Fred and Joy were together since 1983, but they didn't marry for three years because of "problems" caused by Fred's ex-wife, whom Joy sometimes refers to as "Madame DeFarge."

"They were married for twenty-five years," the last Mrs. Davis told me. "They had a big party for their twenty-fifth anniversary and then a few days after she announced she was leaving."

In contrast, according to Joy, her years with Fred were free from rancour. "We never raised our voices to each other. If we had a disagreement...we'd have a debate or we'd have a talk or what I called a meeting, and then we would discuss it. But he never raised his voice in my experience in thirteen years. So, I know that Fred had no more temper than any average person."

"Fred wanted to move in here," she remembered, referring to the condo, "and I was very doubtful, because I don't drive. I had lived right downtown. So he made me a promise. He said, 'If you'll move in here, I will drive you, when I'm in town, I will drive you anywhere you want to go. I will pick you up anywhere you are. When I'm not here, you'll have to take cabs or do whatever you can, if you have friends to pick you up, that's fine. But when I'm here, I'll take you everywhere.' And so he took me shopping every time, maybe twice a week. And I had him trained to go to the best butcher. He'd go pick it up if I phoned ahead."

When they were having guests, he would ask her what he could do to help. "He couldn't cook anything, because I wouldn't allow him to. But there were lots of things he could do. He could sharpen knives and cut the roast…"

They bought the condo a dozen years ago and very soon after they moved in, Fred was asked to serve on the owners' board of directors. "Fred was on the board for ten years, he was still on the board when he died. He was always going to quit but he never did."

Joy recalled an incident that happened in their building:

"Fred was very good about doing things that people (outside) wouldn't have expected him to do. There was a couple who were in their sixties and the woman's mother—she was about ninety-five—was having a birthday. Now, this woman didn't know Fred personally, but she knew who he was and she got it into her head, she told me this, 'I realize I'm being kind of pushy,' she told me 'but I thought I'd try, because I knew my mother would just think it was heaven if Fred would come to the birthday party.' So she said she did stop Fred in the elevator and said, 'Would you consider coming.' He just had to get on the elevator. So she asked him if he would just come up and have a cup of tea and say hello to her mother. And she couldn't get over how nice he was.

"And he came down after he'd met her and said, 'This woman wants me to go. I don't really want to go but I really should because I know from what she said, it would mean something.' And so he did. He didn't know the people.

"But for Fred, you know, it wasn't just getting on the elevator and going up. It took him two hours to get ready, and he had to have three suits laid out on the bed and six ties and three handkerchiefs, and decide which shoes. I had to help him decide. We had a meeting about everything, and so he got dressed and he went up. And he told me afterwards, 'It meant so much to her mother.' He was wonderful with elderly ladies because they all thought he was perfection.

The business about Fred needing two hours to decide what to wear for the old lady's birthday party was another side of Fred that Joy talked about:

"When I bought clothes, Fred sat there," said Joy. "If I was being fitted, he was just the way he was with his own tailor. He'd say, 'No, that's not right, that sleeve is not right.' And they didn't mind, because he had excellent taste. He knew material. Or, he'd say, 'No, that won't do, it'll never hang right.'"

Davis was meticulous about his appearance:

"He always had at least two tailors on the go, and he would spend hours picking out cloth and being fitted, and everything had to be perfect. That's why he always looked so great. And of course everything had to match. He had fifty or sixty pairs of shoes and he had I don't know how many ties, a hundred and fifty or more, and he had a drawer full of poofs, you know, handkerchiefs. A lot of time was spent before he went out, and this was sometimes only a dinner with friends."

Fred and his children got along well. He had three with "Madame DeFarge," and two others from an earlier marriage, who now lived in New Zealand, Joy said. Father and children had developed some inside jokes when they were younger, "mostly to do with music and movies. He was a movie buff. He knew everybody who played every part, he liked to say, 'That's So-and-so.' They'd be very obscure people, but he was great that way.

"I learned more about movies, because I never noticed the secondary or third players, but he knew every one and he remembered their faces and what they had done in 1932."

He used to get "infuriated" with Elwy Yost, the host of "Saturday Night at the Movies" (on TVO):

"There would be Elizabeth Taylor, for example, in some movie, and she only walked in and walked out. And he'd say, 'You see, he's not going to tell them Elizabeth Taylor is in this movie.' And that was when she was thirteen. And there she is now, and it's important. And Elwy would never mention things like that, somebody's first movie. Elizabeth Taylor was in the first make of *Jane Eyre*. She was the little girl dying in the bed and, you see, Fred wanted him to tell people that, because it's important and interesting. But he (Yost) never did."

According to Joy, Fred enjoyed humour of two different kinds. He liked jokes, and traded them with certain friends or colleagues, but Joy didn't really like jokes, so he didn't tell them to her. He also had "a kind of humour that is sardonic, I guess, or satirical, and I would always be on the same wavelength with this kind of humour."

She recalled one true incident that she and Fred both found funny:

"He was good with fans. They'd walk up to him and they wanted him to do something like pose for a picture together. So we go on this flight, going to Barbados, and we were always in first class. And there was a couple of tourists who had been bumped up to first class because they were overbooked, they thought they were in heaven.

"So the guy came back and he was wearing a Tilley hat or Tilley pants, or something, and he came to Fred and said, 'Hi, Fred.' And Fred said, 'Hi.' And he said, 'Well, I'm just gonna change my Tilley hat or Tilley shirt before we get there. Before that,' he said, 'I wonder if we could get a picture.' So Fred said okay. He didn't particularly want to have his picture taken but he thought, well, okay. The guy's wife is there and they're sitting up ahead of us in the middle. The guy gets his camera and he leads Fred up the aisle, and Fred is smoothing his hair and thinking, you know, 'Am I okay?' So he gets all set and there's this space beside the wife, He said, 'This is my wife.' And Fred said, 'How do you do.' And Fred is going to sit down and the guy sits down and hands Fred the camera and says, 'Okay, we're ready.' And Fred took the picture and he came back and said, 'Did you see that?' 'I saw it.' I told him. 'I don't believe it.' And that's the kind of story Fred loved."

Joy Davis also talked about the last three years of "Front Page Challenge," starting with the moving of the show to Vancouver:

"Actually, he didn't mind going to Vancouver. Vancouver and Halifax were his two favourite places, other than Toronto. He always said if he had to make the choice of one place, he'd like Vancouver. He enjoyed the trip. That was one thing he never minded. He got so he was a little bored with the plane trip, because he'd done it for so long. And he didn't have any reason to escape. He used to be glad to get out of town, but since he and I were together he was happier here, he loved it here. But he did like Vancouver. So that one thing was in its favour.

"The thing that changed was the viewpoint of the people running (the show). First of all, they didn't have as much money to attract guests as they used to before, people from England or wherever. And then that producer (Cameron Bell) was not very much in favour of celebrities and the way you get big names is because they're pushing a book or a movie, so of course they're happy to go on. And they could have had all kinds of people, but that wasn't his personal idea of how to do it and I think that was a disappointment. Fred liked it when there were some big names and they should have, because that attracts people. When you think of the people they used to have, from Eleanor Roosevelt on down, I think that was a serious error."

She also disagreed with Bell's ideas about the panel:

"He thought there should be some younger faces on the show. Well, maybe. But where do you find young faces with that kind of experience? Who know how to conduct themselves. I think if they had better guests, I don't mean that you should just have ordinary people. You need the spice of people saying, 'Oh, do you know who's on…'"

She was aware, too, that Fred was unhappy about the show's being moved around from one time slot to another. "That made Fred really mad, because he knew the value of the time and the consistency, and everywhere he went people recognized him. He was one of the few Canadians you can say people recognized from Halifax to Vancouver. Just standing on the street, you know; he didn't have to be on a stage. They'd say, 'Are you still on? We can't find it ("Front Page Challenge"), we don't know where you are.'

"You can't depend on people being dedicated to *TV Guide*. A lot of people were not. What day, what time. That's not fair. So he was unhappy about that, yes. Fred felt very responsible for the show, because of the length of time he'd been on it."

She remembered the day Fred learned of the program's cancellation:

"They were waiting to hear, or something, because the show hadn't been renewed (at the end of the season) and they were waiting to hear one way or the other. And it was in the morning and I think it was Phyllis Platt who phoned. One hour before the news went public. One hour, no longer, because I remember, I was here and it was morning and he was doing whatever he was doing in his study and I was buzzing in and out of my study and I could tell from the phone call, I could hear, and I thought, 'Oh-oh, this is not so good.' And when he got off the phone, he said, 'They've cancelled.' And he sat down.

"But then somebody phoned him from somewhere, like a news source, either a radio station or somewhere, and asked him if he had been informed of anything. They said, 'Do you know what's going on?' And he said, 'No, I don't.' He did know, but he wasn't going to give them a scoop. He didn't know when she (Platt) intended to release it (the news of the show's cancellation) because she didn't tell him that. But we heard it on the radio very shortly after, I think it was an hour lead time that he had, but he wasn't going to break that, because that was not his way. He said to me, 'I'm not going to tell them anything. Why should I tell them. I don't owe them anything.' And he didn't.

"He expected it," she added. "They all expected it from the time they'd moved (the show) to Vancouver. But when it happened, they still felt it. And naturally, because it was so much a part of their lives. And they got along well, you know, at least in business, and we saw them socially a little bit, Pierre and Betty."

Joy Davis conceded that the cancellation "did put him down a bit... because he had other things (to do) but they weren't the same as being on national TV and he was well aware of the difference."

The "other things" she referred to concerned his long-time relationship with DuMaurier.

"He had other work coming up (for DuMaurier). That had probably gone on longer than 'Front Page Challenge,' I'm not sure... He was on a contract but he was almost like an employee to them, and they thought very highly of him."

When advertising tobacco on television was banned, "they had him as a kind of public relations kind of guy, doing things for sports and then 'Search for Stars.' And that was a very good thing, and they spent a lot of money and he loved ('Search for Stars')...he and Lorraine Thomson were on it at one time and two or three other people, and they went across country interviewing all kinds of people (young people)...They had quite a few that became really big stars."

She found it a bit amusing and a bit irritating that some people had "the wrong idea" about his connection to DuMaurier:

"First of all, he got into that when everybody thought smoking was all right. And then people have said to me, 'Well, of course, Fred had to smoke because he worked for DuMaurier.' I said, 'That is the worst nonsense.'

"First of all he started smoking when he was a teenage musician. And they smoked because it was cool. And then he was in the army, and when he was in London it was during the Blitz and everybody smoked because they were so nervous, and they got free cigarettes.

"He was, of course, a big smoker before he ever got connected with DuMaurier. And DuMaurier never ever cared if their employees smoked. I've been with all of the executives in every kind of situation, dinners and big affairs, small affairs, intimate dinners, and I know their executives very well, and no one ever said anything about anybody smoking.

"I wish he had stopped smoking," she said, "and I did try to help him stop, but people have to do it themselves. You have to decide yourself. He had cut down, too, but he hadn't stopped. If he had things might have been better for him, but they weren't."

Eventually, we talked about Fred's illness. He had melanoma for years. "He should never have been suntanned, his skin was just the wrong kind," said Joy. He had been treated for the condition many times, always successfully.

In 1996, however, about a month after his last melanoma treatment, he had "a swelling" that worried both of them.

"He had never been sick, you know," she said. "He never missed the show once in thirty-eight years."

Joy advised him to call their doctor, Dr. Moe Nedilski, who was a long-time friend. Moe did a needle biopsy, and then they had to wait about ten days for the result.

"He thought he was still going to do the DuMaurier thing (the Downtown Jazz Festival in Toronto) because he always went to the city hall and he always did the introduction, so he thought maybe everything was all right."

Until early June, Fred was "still going out because he didn't know there was anything wrong with him," said Joy.

I had seen Fred at the annual awards night held by the *Jazz Report* magazine on May 9. Fred was usually a presenter at these events. We sat at the same table, spent most of the evening together. He admitted to feeling disappointed about the cancellation of "Front Page Challenge," but he was in good spirits. He also told me about the melanoma, but dismissed it as a minor irritation.

But then it developed he had lung cancer. He talked to Dr. Nedilski again and they consulted other doctors to determine a course of treatment.

"We thought he would have some time, get some radiation." Joy said. "They never talked about chemo. I'm sure they had their reasons for that. And so he was thinking in terms of 'I have a limited time now,' but he didn't think it was just six weeks, and neither did I."

The doctor was more optimistic. He felt something could be done, said Joy. "So Fred was down, but he was certainly still thinking...that's why he wouldn't let me tell anybody that he was sick. He said, 'I think I'm still going to be able to go to the jazz festival. I'm okay, I'm going to be able to do it."

"That was in June," she remembered. "So then, about ten days after, he had a stroke. He really died of stroke, he didn't die of lung cancer. It never got that far.

"I'll tell you what they told me. They told me his arteries and veins were 'compromised' is the way they put it, in other words weak, I suppose, and that's why they couldn't stop the strokes. I got him in there (the hospital) within half an hour, into the emergency.

"I got Moe (Nedilski) on the phone, it was a Sunday night. And he said, 'I'll get somebody down there.' And he got the head of neurology at St. Michael's. So I took him down and got him in and he had...it was a minor stroke, mind you. He could talk and walk but his one arm was paralyzed... So we're still coasting along with this, but you see they couldn't stop the strokes. It happened again and again and again. Now each one was a little more deterioration, one more thing he couldn't do, one more thing gone, you know."

Even towards the end, Fred Davis kept his sense of humour, perhaps as a means of consoling his worried family. The two children from New Zealand flew over to see him.

She hadn't met the two children who lived in New Zealand, "but we talked on the phone, because they used to phone their father and he would phone them... So they arrived when Fred was very ill. They flew all that way to come and see him, and he was very touched. They had gone back before the funeral, but they were here the last two weeks of his life... They just couldn't stay because we didn't know how long he was gonna live."

Another daughter, Kate, also arrived to help.

"Kate is a nurse," said Joy. "She and I got along so well that she just moved in here. I didn't know what I was going to do, but she did move in and she helped me with Fred at the end."

Also helpful was Fred's son, Phil, who lives in Barrie, Ontario, and was a frequent visitor to the Davis condo. "He used to come and have dinner with Fred and me, and my family. He got along well with my children... And Phil spoke at the funeral... Pierre (Berton) also spoke at the funeral and he spoke at the memorial."

It was, of course, a trying time for her. "To tell you the truth, half the time I was in a daze. I couldn't believe it. It happened so quickly, you see, and I couldn't believe that he was actually dying... Part of me knew and part of me didn't."

Joy said Fred tried to make jokes "simply because he was trying to get through it. At that point, he thought he was still in the first stages and everybody was saying, 'You'll get the arm back,' and 'We've got treatments for that,' which they gave him, and actually they improved his arm and he was still able to talk, he didn't lose his speech and he could still walk, so the strokes were in the brain, and were affecting certain (neurological) connections, but they couldn't stop them. They didn't know why, it must be that the veins and arteries were so weak... Then, of course, he was in palliative care, at the end."

Difficult though his death was for her, Joy concedes that Fred would not have wanted to live on as an invalid.

"You see, if Fred couldn't play the piano or play the trumpet or drive his car, he would not have wanted to be limping around here, saying 'I can't do anything.' He would not have wanted that. And you know he never looked old.

"Thinking of it from his point of view, it was better that it happened so quickly, because he didn't have that awful business...he just wouldn't have known what to do..."

All things considered, Joy has coped with the situation.

"Fred left two cars," she said. "I sold the Jag. The other was a Cadillac in beautiful condition and I decided to keep it, and my daughter is my driver, and I keep the car up. She lives in Mississauga (Ontario), not too far. She's a great driver, she and her husband look after me. And I have friends in the building who help out.

"I feel very lucky. I was lucky to meet Fred when I did. We were very happy together and Fred left me without any financial worries whatsoever. I'm very comfortable and I'm going to keep this place the way he would want it. I'm not letting anything go. In fact, I'm doing over bathrooms and stuff. I'm not gonna let Fred down."

When I spoke with her again by phone, some months after our meeting at the Davis condo, we chatted for a bit and then I asked her how she was.

"I still miss Fred," Joy said.

chapter 21

AFTERMATH AND
AFTER THOUGHTS

Even now, several years after the demise of "Front Page Challenge," the program's record of achievements, especially in luring to the show an almost endless parade of distinguished or, at least, famous, people as challengers remains impressive:

Among them were world leaders such as Indira Gandhi, Lord Clement Attlee, Golda Meir, Harold Wilson, Menachem Begin, Andreas Papandreou and Edward Heath.

Besides numerous Canadian provincial premiers, the program also corralled former prime ministers Louis St. Laurent, Lester B. Pearson, Pierre Elliott Trudeau, John Diefenbaker, Joe Clark and John Turner. (Only Brian Mulroney declined.)

There were famous explorers from Jacques Cousteau to Sir Edmund Hillary to Thor Heyerdahl, and astronauts Buzz Aldrin, Roberta Bondar, Scott Carpenter and Marc Garneau.

And there were famous flyers, too, including air ace Captain Eddie Rickenbacker, who flew in the First World War, and Francis Gary Powers, of the U-2 incident.

The theatre world yielded Dame Edith Evans, director Tyrone Guthrie, Douglas Campbell, Irene Worth, Christopher Plummer, Theodore Bikel,

Joel Grey, David Merrick, Frances Hyland, Donald Sutherland and Peter Ustinov.

Among the famed historians presented were William L. Shirer, Barbara Tuchman and Arthur Schlesinger, Jr.

Such Hollywood icons as Mary Pickford, Bette Davis, Jack Lemmon, Errol Flynn, Douglas Fairbanks, Jr., Vincent Price, Joan Fontaine and Boris Karloff turned up, as did film directors Frank Capra, Otto Preminger, Stanley Kramer and Norman Jewison.

There were tycoons, too, from E. P. Taylor and Roy Thomson to Charles Bronfman and Max Ward.

Religious leaders from Emmett Cardinal Carter to Dr. Martin Luther King and the Rt. Rev. H. R. Hunt all appeared on the program.

Broadcasting yielded David Frost, Lorne Greene, Max Ferguson, Walter Cronkite, Bill Moyers, Ed Sullivan, Knowlton Nash and Wayne and Shuster.

The sports arena provided Jack Dempsey, Jackie Robinson, Elaine Tanner, Joe Louis, Gordie Howe, Mickey Mantle, Joe Namath, Roger Bannister, Bob Feller, Ron Turcotte, Maurice Richard and many more.

There were such famous barristers as Louis Nizer and Melvin Belli, plus the distinguished jurist William O. Douglas and Judge Sarah Hughes, who swore in Lyndon Johnson.

The world of music was represented by the likes of Duke Ellington, Marian Anderson, Harry Belafonte, Teresa Stratas, Ella Fitzgerald, Maureen Forrester, Tony Bennett, Anne Murray, Burton Cummings, Sir Rudolf Bing and Artie Shaw.

Dance offered up Dame Margot Fonteyn, Celia Franca, Karen Kain and Erik Bruhn, plus Ray Bolger and Ann Miller.

Military men on the program included Lt. Gen. E. L. M. Burns, Maj. Gen. Frederic Worthington, Maj. Gen. Jean Allard and the U.S. commander in Vietnam, Gen. William Westmoreland.

The program also presented such diverse writers as Morley Callaghan, Mordecai Richler, Malcolm Muggeridge, Dr. Benjamin Spock, Hugh Garner, Brendan Behan, Frederick Forsyth and James Clavell.

Then there were various challengers who defy categorization but nevertheless added some lustre to the program, among them the Baroness Von

Trapp of Austria, renowned photographer Yousuf Karsh, Edgar Bergen, "Ma" Murray and such irrepressible types as Groucho Marx and Jerry Colonna.

And there was the woman who was the first "big name" guest ever to appear on "Front Page Challenge," Eleanor Roosevelt.

Given the fact that the program began in 1957 and ended in 1995, it should come as no surprise that a good many of these distinguished challengers are now dead. Their contributions to "Front Page Challenge," however, remain indelibly in the memories of those millions of Canadians who saw them on the show.

The program's other notable achievment was its role in making genuine Canadian stars of its on-camera people—Fred Davis, Gordon Sinclair, Pierre Berton, Toby Robins, Betty Kennedy, Jack Webster and Allan Fotheringham.

And what of that smaller group of people who, over the years, worked, either in front of or behind the cameras, to make "Front Page Challenge" a Canadian institution?

To begin at the end, the last producer, Cameron Bell, was a contract producer (as opposed to staff), so when the program was not renewed, neither was his contract. He later was hired by Ivan Fecan, the same man who had hired him to produce "Front Page Challenge," as a consultant for a new Vancouver television station being set up by Baton Broadcasting.

Fecan himself left CBC for Baton in 1993, not long after he had engineered the shift of the program to Vancouver and hired Cameron Bell to give it "some edge."

As of this writing, Helen Slinger is still working for the CBC in Vancouver.

Sadly, the death toll among the production people on "Front Page Challenge" has been inescapable.

Of the seven men who produced the program over its thirty-eight-year life, six are still alive.

Drew Crossan, producer of the show from 1962 to 1964, died in 1987.

Two of the program's seven writers between 1957 and the show's demise in 1995 have died. They were Gary Lautens and Ross McLean.

Paul Kligman, who did the program warm-ups for longer than two decades, died in 1985.

Bunny Cowan, the program's announcer from its inception, died in 1991.

Lucio Agostini, FPC's music director and arranger, died in 1996 at the age of 83.

As to the stars of the show, Gordon Sinclair was the first to die, in 1984. Toby Robins died two years later.

Fred Davis died in July 1996, a few months after Agostini. Jack Webster died in March 1999.

And even though the program had begun its long and mostly happy life in 1957, all those deaths occurred between 1984 and 1999.

Considering the small number of people involved in doing the show, that's a much higher mortality rate than that of the thousands of challengers who appeared on-camera. But like most of those challengers, the survivors among the people concerned with one or another aspect of the show's production have mostly good memories of their experiences.

And so do millions of Canadian viewers.

index